WHEN LUCK RUNS OUT

DEBUNKS THE MYTHS ABOUT COMPULSIVE GAMBLING

- Compulsive gamblers are *not* typically uneducated, low-income people. Instead, they're lawyers, accountants, bankers, and stockbrokers!

- Today, two out of ten compulsive gamblers are women. However, by the year 2000, women are predicted to number five out of ten.

- The attempted suicide rate among compulsive gamblers is 100 times the national average.

- The attempted suicide rate among wives of compulsive gamblers is 50 times the national average.

- Unlike alcoholism or drug addiction, compulsive gambling is difficult for those outside the family to detect, even in its advanced stage.

■   ■   ■   ■   ■

"One of the first efforts to present a comprehensive picture of the phenomenon. . . . The reader wanting facts about compulsive gambling will find them."
—<u>Library Journal</u>

"An illuminating primer for understanding what has long been a misunderstood subject."
—<u>Reno Gazette-Journal</u>

About the Authors

Robert Custer, M.D., is recognized as one of the world's leading authorities on compulsive gambling and its treatment. He established the world's first treatment program for compulsive gamblers and is presently a practicing psychiatrist and Chief of the Treatment Services Division of the Mental Health and Behavioral Science Center of the Veterans' Administration in Washington, D.C.

Harry Milt is the author of numerous highly acclaimed books on mental health subjects, including *Your Phobia: Understanding Your Fears Through Contextual Therapy.* He served for 15 years as Director of Public Information at the National Association for Mental Health.

WHEN LUCK RUNS OUT

HELP FOR COMPULSIVE GAMBLERS AND THEIR FAMILIES

Robert Custer, M.D. and Harry Milt

WARNER BOOKS

A Warner Communications Company

This Warner Books Edition is published by
arrangement with Facts on File Inc., Subsidiary of
Commerce Clearinghouse, 460 Park Avenue South, New
York, N.Y. 10016

Warner Books, Inc.
666 Fifth Avenue
New York, N.Y. 10103

 A Warner Communications Company

Printed in the United States of America

First Warner Books Printing: August, 1986

10 9 8 7 6 5 4 3 2 1

Contents

PROLOGUE

Ruth and Adam

THE POLICE CAME SHORTLY AFTER MIDNIGHT AND RANG
and knocked and woke her up. Looking down from her
bedroom window she saw the patrol car at the sidewalk, its
lights flashing, and felt a surge of panic.

When she came to the door, there were two of them
standing there. One asked: "Are you Mrs. Ruth Kohler?"
and when she answered, "Yes," he said, "We have a
warrant for your husband's arrest . . . Adam Kohler."

"He doesn't live here. We were separated nine months
ago."

"We understand that he's been staying here."

"He was for a few days, but not for the past week."

"How come he's been staying here if you're separated?
Are you living together again?"

She wanted to protest their intrusion into her private
life, their arrogance. But there wasn't enough energy left for
that. She had had enough resentment, enough quarreling,
enough confrontation and screaming, enough agitation and
hatred to last her for the rest of her life and to leave some
over for eternity. Now all she wanted was to be left alone, to

not feel anything, to stay numb inside herself, to get through each day quietly, without incident, without hearing the telephone ring, without the stab of fear everytime it did ring, without the insults and threats at the other end, without having to discuss the past with anybody. But here were the police asking questions, and the questions had to be answered.

"No, we are not living together again."

"Then why is he coming here?"

"He isn't coming here; I told you it's been a week."

"What about before then?"

"He came here about 10 days ago... it was late at night. He said he had no place to sleep. He looked sick. I couldn't turn him away. So I told him he could sleep on the couch, but he would have to leave in the morning."

"Then what happened after that?"

"In the morning I gave him money to get a room at the Y and to get himself something to eat. I gave him enough for a week. Two days later he came back. He didn't go the Y. He gambled the money and lost it. He's a compulsive gambler."

She waited for a change of expression on their faces, some indication that these words—compulsive gambler— had some meaning for them, that they would understand now what she had lived through, that they would know that the person they were hunting was the victim of an obsession, that he could not help what he did. She hoped they might show a little sympathy. But nothing. Not a sign of acknowledgment. Not a flicker of compassion. The phrase "compulsive gambler" meant absolutely nothing to them. Or, if it did, they didn't care. Or perhaps this was the way the police had to do their work, without any show of feeling.

"I told him he could stay just that night and no longer. He would have to leave in the morning. If he came back, I would have to call the police... you... and have him put out."

"How long did he stay?"

"He was gone the next morning. He left before we got up."

"Where is he now?"

"I don't know."

"Do you think he'll come back here?"

"I hope to God not."

"Do you know any other place where he might go?"

She was about to blurt out, "Sure, you can try him at Atlantic City or Las Vegas or the track. I can even give you the names of his bookies," but she held back and said only that she had no idea where they could find him.

One of them wrote something on a slip of paper and handed it to her. "If he comes here, you call this number." She handed him back the paper and told him she didn't need it, that this wasn't the first time she had had to respond to police inquiries about her husband and that she knew the number. She assumed they were new on the force; otherwise they would have known it had been going on for years.

The following morning her cousin Elizabeth phoned her at work. She wanted to be sure nobody was listening in on the conversation and then asked whether the police had been over to Ruth's house looking for Adam. Ruth said they had been there the night before, but how did Elizabeth know? Elizabeth explained that she had learned about it from her boyfriend, who worked in the District Attorney's office. He had come across the legal documents. Ruth asked what was in them.

"Adam embezzled $34,000," Elizabeth replied. "He took it from Blank and Blank, that big law firm where he worked. That was three months ago, but they held off pressing charges, thinking he might find some way to make it good. But he didn't contact them and they couldn't locate him, so they swore out a warrant."

At first the facts did not register. Ruth had been through so much that she thought nothing else could possibly surprise her. But then she heard Elizabeth saying it again. Adam had embezzled—stolen—$34,000. She thanked Elizabeth for calling, inquired about her uncle and aunt and then hung up, stunned.

There had been other incidents in the past, shattering when they had occurred. But now, in comparison, they seemed trivial, almost innocent. When he had first begun to gamble heavily, years earlier, Adam had written checks to

himself from his firm's contingency account—checks for
$100, $300, $1,000.

She had learned about it from one of his friends but
would not believe it, even after she had confronted Adam
and he had admitted it. "You are stealing, Adam," she had
screamed, "and it doesn't even bother you? It doesn't even
bother your conscience? What in God's name is happening
to you? You're the man who used to run back to return the
money when somebody gave you too much change...."

But he had just stood there, surly and belligerent. It
wasn't stealing, he insisted. He was just borrowing the
money. "I just use it to bet and when I win I put it back. I
can do it without their knowing about it."

When she pressed him further, he just turned away and
went wherever it was he went to gamble—the track, a card
game, his bookmakers.

She thought back, still with undiminished amazement,
to the way he had been able to get the money to cover up
the thefts and to pay his debts to the bookmakers, amounting
at times to the thousands. He would run to the track with
$200 and come back with $3,000. He would run out to get
another loan from a finance company or a bank. He would
write a check on an exhausted account and then cover it
with an equally worthless check from another bank. He
would run to his mother, his brother, his aunt and move
them with tearful entreaties, tell them that if they didn't help
him he would be caught and have to go to jail, or that the
bookmakers had Mafia connections and that he would be
killed if he didn't pay what he owed. Then he would take
that money, pay back part of what he owed and use the rest
to gamble some more.

This would go on month after month after month . . . the
frenetic running to bet, to borrow to cover losses, to steal,
to bet, to borrow and cover thefts and bad checks, to bet, to
wheedle and beg money to cover debts to bookmakers, to
bet. . . .

Only once had he been arrested, early in his gambling
career, and that had been for passing a worthless check. But
the sum was small and the judge had suspended sentence so
he could make restitution. But they all knew that after that,

if ever he were caught again for a similar crime, he would certainly have to go to jail. And now, it seemed, that time had come.

Her head began to throb with another headache and the pain blotted out any further reflections about Adam and his problems, for the while, at least.

Later that week a Mr. Michael Collins called, an officer in the firm from which Adam had embezzled the money. His tone was surly, impatient. Did Ruth know that Adam had embezzled $34,000 from the firm, and did she know that he had done this to someone who had risked his own standing in the firm to help him?

Ruth tried to interrupt him, to tell him that she and Adam were separated, that she no longer had anything to do with him, but Mr. Collins would not stop.

"I did it for Adam's mother. I've known them since I was a kid. She came to me crying, begging me to hire him. She said he was down and out, desperate, that he needed a job, any kind of a job."

He paused for a second to speak to someone in his office and when he resumed, Ruth felt obliged to ask, "Didn't she tell you about his gambling? Didn't she warn you?"

Mr. Collins laughed. "Oh yes, she warned me, but I thought I was smart enough to handle it. I put him on as administrative assistant where he couldn't put his hands on any money or have contact with any of the accounts."

Ruth knew what he was going to say next.

"But I was a damned fool. He was smarter than I. He found a way to ingratiate himself with one of our junior partners and learned how to get into the trust fund accounts. He forged a half dozen checks amounting to $34,000 and covered up his tracks. By the time our accounting department found out, he was gone, vanished, disappeared."

"But what," Ruth asked, "do you want of me, Mr. Collins? What do you expect me to do?"

"I am looking to get that money back. If I can get even half of it for now, I think I can stop the trustees from pressing the case. Otherwise, the police are going to catch up with your husband and he is going to get sent up for a good long time.''

Wearily, Ruth explained, as she had to the police, that she and Adam were separated. But even if she did want to get involved, she said, there were just no resources left anywhere. She and the children were barely getting along on her meager earnings as a secretary. He had used the $22,000 they had together put into savings. The house she lived in was carrying a second and third mortgage to which he had forged her signature. He had cashed in their bonds. She was happy just to be earning enough to support herself and the children, to keep the utilities from being turned off as they had been many times when Adam was still living there.

''What about the other side of the family?''

''His side? You can go there if you want to, but you're not going to find anything either. He took $30,000 from his mother and left her nothing but her Social Security and a little pension check. His brothers cosigned his loan for $25,000 and they lost that when he defaulted. Do you think they're going to help him? His aunt died and left all her money to a son. He detests Adam and wouldn't lift a finger to help him. Adam has been nothing but heartache and misery to all of us, to both sides of the family. And now, Mr. Collins, I've got to go. I cannot stand this any longer.''

She was weeping when she finished, and Mr. Collins apologized for having troubled her. He said that if she, personally, ever needed any money or a job, to call on him and he would help.

After that, the days and weeks went by uneventfully and she was able to slip back into her neutral, insulated state of being. But this was not to last.

About a month after the call from Mr. Collins, she awoke suddenly in the middle of the night not knowing what had awakened her. She listened but heard nothing. Then she heard it . . . a sound coming from the side entrance downstairs, a door that opened onto the porch. Someone was twisting the doorknob trying to get in. Her heart racing, she started to reach for the telephone on the night table to call the police. Then she hesitated. It might be Adam, and if it was he, the police would come and arrest him. But if she didn't call the police, she would have Adam on her hands again. . . .

Then she heard her name being called in an insistent whisper. Slipping on her bathrobe and slippers, she came quietly down the stairs and made her way through the hall to the door. She turned on a small night-light in the hallway, parted the curtains and peered out. She could barely make out his features, but there was no question; it was Adam. She unlocked the door, let him in, led the way to the kitchen and turned on the light.

What she saw made her gasp. The man standing in the kitchen doorway was Adam, but an Adam so changed that if she had passed him on the street she would not have recognized him. Although he was only 37, he looked at least 50. His face was unshaven, gray and lined, his cheeks sunken. His suit, a cheap wash-and-wear model, was stained and unpressed and hung baggily on a slumping frame that had once been erect and athletic. One hand, held away from his body, apparently in pain, was wrapped in a soiled and tattered bandage. In the other hand he held a paper bag with what appeared to be a sweater stuffed in the top.

His eyes caught hers staring at the bag and he looked away, embarrassed. "That's my clothes," he said. "I've been sleeping in cars." Then he shuffled over to a chair, sat down, laid his head on the table, and began to weep.

Ruth walked over and put a hand on his shoulder, then pulled it away. She stood there a few seconds and put it back again and kept it there, until he had stopped sobbing. What was it she was feeling? A mother's solace for a suffering child? A woman's love for a man who had for so many years held her in his embrace? The compassion of one vulnerable human being for another in despair? She did not know.

She cooked some eggs and boiled water for coffee. While he was eating, she went into the living room, sat down in an easy chair, leaned her head back, closed her eyes and rested.

Again, as she sat there, the same insistent questions came back to plague her and send her off on a search into memory, a search that never produced any answers, only bewilderment, confusion, resignation.

How had it happened? Why? What had gone on inside this man to bring about this unimaginable change, a change that had come about so slowly and surreptitiously that she had had no warning that something sinister was happening, that her husband was being transformed?

They had met in their senior year in college and had fallen instantly in love. It was an intense and romantic affair, known quickly to the entire senior class. "The princess and the Knave of Hearts" one poetic classmate had called them; she was pretty, slight, blond, blue-eyed and he was tall, dark-haired, dashingly handsome, dramatic.

They were married the day of their graduation and sped off on a two-week honeymoon. On their return they went to live with her parents so they would have a chance to set up their own home without rushing and so that he would have a chance to become established in the job he had landed in the sales office of an industrial equipment firm.

Those were days filled with happiness, she recalled, full and exciting days ... finding and furnishing an apartment, finding their way quickly into a circle of friends, entertaining, going to the movies, playing tennis, making love joyfully and passionately, celebrating his salary increases, putting money aside for the home they were going to buy and for the children they were going to have.

One day he came home with a surprise. He had enrolled in an evening course and was going to become an accountant. Later he might even start his own accounting firm.

Nothing Adam did surprised Ruth. She was used to his taking on something new, on impulse, and making a success of it.

One year passed, two years, three. They were now living in their own home. They had one little girl, two years old, and Ruth was pregnant with another child. Adam was working as an accountant with a large firm, preparing to obtain his certification and set up his own company. His income from his job and private accounts was in excess of $40,000.

It was a Sunday afternoon in the fall of that third year. Adam was in the den, sprawled out in front of the television set, watching a football game, a can of beer in his hand, his eyes glued to the screen. Ruth had just finished setting the table and putting on the salad. The roast was done and warming. To make sure of her timing, she peered into the den to the television. The indicator showed 55 seconds to play with the clock running. This meant the game should be over in a minute or two and that Adam would be ready to have dinner. Ruth put the rolls in to heat. Trisha was upstairs playing and she would have to go up and get her as soon as the game was over. The muffled sound of the sportscaster's voice was still coming from the den, so she waited.

Suddenly there was a nerve-shattering scream from the den, "Pass, you bastard, pass. . . . Oh, my God, they've lost the ball!" and then the sound of crashing glass. When she got there, Adam was standing in the corner of the room, banging his fists on the wall. One large pane of the window was almost entirely gone. Outside, on the driveway, amid the jagged fragments of window glass, lay the broken remains of an antique porcelain clock, an heirloom her grandmother had given them as a wedding gift. She looked back to the TV screen and saw a victorious team loping off the field, some players shown in close-up, grinning, making the "Number One" sign.

Before she had a chance to question him, Adam brushed past her, strode upstairs to their bedroom and slammed the door shut. She had never seen him so agitated before, about anything. She knew by then that he gambled and bet heavily, but never before had he reacted to a loss so violently. Frightened, she waited a while, went upstairs, knocked and told him dinner was ready. A few minutes later he came down silent, sullen and grim. Ruth made several attempts at conversation during the meal but got nothing more out of him than a two- or three-word reply.

She tried to remember. When had it begun? How long had it taken to reach this point? When was it he had become preoccupied with watching football games on television? When had it become a sacrosanct happening that nobody dared disturb without being subjected to an abusive, intemperate scolding? When was it they had started to quarrel about his gambling, and then about other things that had nothing to do with gambling, things about which they had never quarreled before? When was it he had started to react with explosions of elation after some games and spells of dejection, lasting for days, after others?

When was it she had finally realized that his excitement or depression had nothing to do with football, that it had to do with money—money being lost . . . money being won . . . not just $10 or $20 bets but bets running into the hundreds, even thousands . . . not just on the game he was watching but on four or five others . . . not only on football but also on baseball, basketball, hockey . . . a burning obsession to gamble fanned into a fury by winning, fanned into a fury by losing, burning into his soul and brain, burning out the tenderness and love and caring, anesthetizing his sensitivity and sentiment, deadening his interest and concern for his wife, his children, his home.

She had read about such drastic personality changes in fiction and had wondered whether such transformations actually did occur or whether they were only the creations of an author's imagination. And then she had seen it happening to Adam, as though he was the hapless character in a horror tale that some writer was creating.

There were times, when the losses were continuous and heavy, the creditors pressing, the bookmakers threatening, the sources of money exhausted, when he thought he was dying and she had to rush him to the hospital—anxiety attacks that peaked and faded. Other times, when the tensions and pressures became unbearable he would escape into sleep, sleeping 12 and 14 hours at a time, getting up for a few hours and then going back to sleep again.

He was becoming a living dead man, a zombie, a shell, an automaton moving about mechanically, going through the motions of living. There was no making contact with him in this state. You could talk to him and he would not know you were there. You could serve him dinner and he would eat what was put before him without interest, without comment. You could tell him his child was sick, his father dying, their mortgage being foreclosed, the electricity being turned off, and there would be no reaction. You could scream, cajole, sympathize, threaten, try anything to shake him out of this stupor, this sitting in front of the television vacant-eyed, immobile, muttering to himself, but nothing could penetrate the enclosure into which he had retreated.

And yet there were times, she recalled, when he would change back overnight, as though a switch had been turned on to pour the current of life into him again. The light would go in his eyes and the gentle, laughing, caring person would return. The children would sense the change immediately, run to him and cling to him, their fright gone. And then just as suddenly, as though another switch had been turned, the light would go out of his eyes, the withdrawn, agitated, depressed state would return and the children would flee from him again.

Friends had asked her, after the marriage was over, how she could have continued to live in that hell for so long without fleeing, without going out of her mind. Why had it taken her so long to free herself of this life of torture and misery? And she had remained quiet, pretending she did not know the answer, not wanting to relive the pain. How could they know what it meant to be caught in a maelstrom, whirled about and pinned down by powerful, paralyzing forces, unable to generate enough counterforce to move even an inch, let alone to break out of its control? The cities and the traumas had followed one another with such rapidity that there was no time even to think about life on the outside, or life the way it could or should be. It took everything she had in emotional strength just to cope with each episode and get over it, to survive just for that day.

And when there was respite from the turmoil for a day or two or for a week, the relief and the peace were so precious she didn't want to do anything to disturb them. She would begin again to hope that this might continue, that there would be no return to the agony, that this time her pleas had taken hold and that something inside him had changed. But then, inevitably, it would start again, and so it would go on: the plunge into hell, then the relief and the hope; the plunge into hell, then the relief and the hope.

There were indeed times, she recalled, when the unendurable stretches had lasted so long without relief that she knew that in order to survive she would have to take the children and flee. But where? His parents? Her parents? For a week or two perhaps, but after that, what? How was she going to make a life for herself and the children? Where would the money come from? Who would hire her when she had been away from work so long? And how would she be able to stand the loneliness? How would she ever be able to muster up the strength and initiative to make a new home and start a new life? It was at those times, when it was impossible to stay and just as impossible to go, that she had contemplated suicide . . . but then what would happen to the children?

How had this all come about and why? What had happened to this man? What was it that made him change? . . . She put her hands to her temples and squeezed, trying to shut off this train of thought, the painful memories, the insistent questions to which she could not find the answers.

The sound of dishes penetrated her revery and precipitated her back into the present and reality, and with that an even more disturbing question. What was she going to do about the man there in the kitchen?

When she came back in, he had finished putting the dishes in the sink and was sitting waiting for her.

"Go lie down and get some sleep," she told him. "In the morning we'll take care of your hand, and then we'll talk about what to do next. It's too late to talk about it now, and we're both too tired to think clearly."

He shook his head.

"What, Adam? Why are you shaking your head? What are you saying?"

"I can't run any longer, Ruth. I don't have the strength."

She knew then that he had come to a decision, but waited for him to say it.

"I'm going to give myself up. There's no place I can hide . . . nothing else I can do anymore."

He paused, his eyes closed.

"Except maybe to kill myself, and I've even been getting ready to do that, but I know when the time comes I won't have the courage or willpower to go through with it."

The tears began to come again. "Whatever happens to me now is just going to have to happen."

He said he would call his mother in the morning and ask if she would come with him, to be there when he surrendered. He did not have the courage to do it alone. Hesitantly, he asked Ruth if she would come with him, too, and she told him she would.

"What about the children?" he asked. "What should we tell the children?"

For a second she found herself thinking about some explanation she could devise, something that would shield the children from the truth. But then she realized she was falling back into the old pattern, an insidious practice of lying to shield, to cover up, to deceive, that had prevailed during the years of his gambling. He had lied to her, to their relatives, to the loan companies, to the bookmakers. She had lied to protect him when angry creditors called. Even the children had learned to lie, to say, "Daddy isn't home."

"We'll tell them the truth, Adam. And now let's get some sleep. It's terribly late and I'm going up to bed."

Two days later—they had waited so he could get some new clothing and have his hand properly taken care of—Adam, his mother and Ruth appeared at the police station for his surrender.

What had been until then just a gray concrete building they hadn't even noticed on their way to the store or to work, a place where other people were taken when they were arrested, had become for them now a grim and imminent reality, the entryway, for Adam, to what could be months or even years in a prison, separated from the rest of the world.

The two women waited while Adam was booked and taken inside to be fingerprinted. When he reappeared some 15 minutes later, obviously frightened and dazed, a policeman clutching him by the arm, Adam's mother began to weep and Ruth turned aside to hide her tears.

Several days later, Adam appeared for arraignment, and his mother and Ruth were there with him. An attorney Adam's brother had retained was there, too. When it came Adam's turn, he pleaded guilty to four counts of forgery and

four counts of embezzlement. On his attorney's plea, Adam
was released on his own recognizance and the date was set
for sentencing three weeks later.

On the day of the sentencing, Adam, his attorney, his
mother and Ruth met in front of the courthouse. It was still
early, but when they entered the courtroom, it was already
half-filled with small clusters of people, conversing among
themselves in low voices. The attorney led his little group to
some empty seats toward the front. They waited as case
after case was called and then they heard the clerk call,
"The State against Kohler." The attorney led Adam to a
position in front of the bench.

The judge continued leafing through a sheaf of papers,
pausing from time to time to write something. Two or three
times he looked up at Adam and seemed to be studying him.
He then called the attorney closer to the bench and the two
conversed for three or four minutes. Adam waited, twisting
his handkerchief nervously, trying to hide his agitation and
fright behind a forced smile.

When he had finished conversing with the attorney, the
judge motioned Adam to come closer and began to speak to
him in a voice barely audible to anyone except Adam and his
attorney.

Mr. Kohler, in attempting to reach a decision on what your
sentence should be, I have tried to take into account all
the pertinent facts that could have a bearing on that
decision.

First, there is your court record, which, you must know,
weighs very heavily against you and imposes a mandate on
what my course should be. Three years ago, you stood
before another justice in this court and heard sentence
pronounced on you for cashing a check drawn on a bank in
which you had no account. You are now before this court
to be sentenced for much more serious crimes, four counts
of forgery and four counts of embezzlement.

Your attorney has submitted a motion for leniency,
explaining that you are suffering from an addiction called
compulsive gambling, that you had lost control of your
habit, as they say of alcoholics, and that therefore you

should not be held fully responsible for your offenses. To that explanation, I must give some consideration, because I could not otherwise understand how a man who had by virtue of his abundant energy and talent achieved such fine success in his chosen field, and who had for so many years been a loyal and devoted husband and father, to which many have testified, could have wreaked so much disaster and destruction on those who loved, trusted and befriended him, and most of all upon himself.

But then, I must deal with the question of leniency and in that regard, I ask myself, what would it achieve. Once before you were shown leniency, and on your solemn promise not to gamble again your sentence was suspended. For four months you kept your promise, but then it began again—the frantic chase after heaven knows what illusion, what fantasy, trying your luck at gambling over and over again in spite of the fact that this so-called luck had betrayed you repeatedly, had never led anywhere except to disaster and desperation. I don't know how you have been able to forestall a reckoning for so long a time. I will never understand it. What deceit it must have taken, what gullibility and misplaced trust from your wife, your relatives, your employers.

But now the chase has come to an end for this cycle, at least, for I am going to sentence you to a term in prison and I believe you will not have much to gamble with there. I wonder what will happen after you have served this sentence. Will disuse extinguish the compulsion? Will you be cured of it after you come out? For your sake and for the sake of everyone else involved with you, I most sincerely hope that it will. But I am afraid, terribly afraid, that despite the promises you might make to me, to your wife, to your children, to yourself, even to God, it will not be long after you have served your sentence that you will find a way, once more, to work yourself into the trust of some other kind and innocent people, and with the money you may be able to earn, beg, borrow or steal you will once more be swept into the whirlwind of compulsive gambling. But over that I have no control. There may be a way that you can be cured of your addiction, but that is something you yourself will have to deal with after you have served your sentence.

Knowing that you are a compulsive gambler has helped me to understand what has happened to you and the circumstances under which you committed the crimes of which you have been convicted. It also moves me to sentence you to a lesser term than I might otherwise have given you, but beyond that I cannot go. I therefore sentence you to a term of three years imprisonment to be served in the state penitentiary.

Adam blanched when he heard the sentence, but said nothing. He looked over his shoulder once at his mother and Ruth and then was led away.

The prison to which he was remanded was a minimum-security institution, and Adam was permitted to leave the prison grounds during the day to work in the office of a state institution for the mentally ill.

Ruth had expected that once Adam was out of the way, removed from her by his imprisonment, she could begin to enjoy life again, freely, and devote herself to making a new life for herself and the children. But as much as she wished it, it did not happen. She woke up each morning with a yearning; she felt irritable, fretful, anxious, depressed. When a friend suggested that it was possible that she had begun to miss Adam, she hooted and shrieked in derision. Miss him? Miss the torture and turmoil, the anguish and the agony? Anyone who thought that must be insane!

Most of us do not truly understand ourselves or recognize our innermost feelings; nor do we fathom the attachments and interdependence that bind us to one other in intimate relationships. One may feel hatred toward a spouse for the cruel things he or she may do, yet continue to feel a deep tie, which will reemerge when the immediate conflict dies down. In fact, this need for one another may actually intensify in the course of a deteriorating marriage. Paradoxically, the couple may find themselves needing each other more intensely at the very time that their conflicts and antagonism are pulling them further apart. In their togetherness, they shield each other from loneliness; as they separate, the loneliness reasserts itself and propels them back toward each other. Once they are together again, comfortable and no longer lonely, their conflicts reassert themselves, driving them away from each other again; then the cycle repeats itself over and over. This is why both partners often feel depression in the aftermath of divorce. The loneliness and the need for one another that surge to the surface after the physical separation are likely to continue unless or until a new partner has been found to whom the emotional attachment can be transferred.

And so it was with Ruth, who was being separated, physically, from Adam. Yet she was unaware that that was what was happening, and she could not understand why it was that she wanted to visit Adam frequently on the grounds of the hospital where he worked. She thought it was because of the children. She did not want them to lose contact with their father. She did not feel it fair to deprive him of contact with them. . . . This was the explanation she gave herself.

As the months went by, and memories of the past began to fade, she found herself mellowing toward Adam, even beginning to like him again, to enjoy being with him. Despite the repressiveness of his confinement, he managed, somehow, to regain his buoyancy and spirit and to show his loving and tender side. Anyone observing them sitting on a bench on the hospital grounds, chatting animatedly, smiling and laughing, holding hands, would have thought they were witnessing a romance between a couple that had just fallen in love. And they might have wondered about the boy and girl tossing a Frisbee back and forth, nearby.

When Adam had served 18 months of his sentence he was released from prison on parole, and he and Ruth were reunited. Adam quickly found a job as a salesclerk in a department store and once more became the husband and father Ruth and the children had known before the troubles began. There was no mention of gambling in their conversation, and now when Adam watched the football games on television it was without very much excitement. Nor were there any visits to the track or time away from home that was not readily accounted for. It appeared that his imprisonment and his separation from the milieu of gambling and gamblers had done its job, curing him of his compulsion.

After a few months had passed, their relatives on both sides felt it was time to forget the past and to draw Adam into their midst again. There was a large family gathering, and while all the others carefully avoided discussion of the past, Adam insisted that the residual issues had to be dealt with. One by one he took aside each of the family members he had injured, asked their forgiveness and assured them that he would, in time, return to them every penny they had lost because of him. His gambling was a thing of the past and now all he needed was another chance so he could win back their faith and respect. He promised he would continue to work hard without complaint as a department-store sales-clerk, meanwhile keeping an eye open for advancement, there or in some other situation.

The opportunity came more quickly than he had expected. It came, in fact, at that very family gathering. His two brothers, joint owners of a small chain of retail clothing store, came forward with an offer. They were going to open a new store in another part of the state; if Adam wanted, he could have the job of manager. It would mean, of course, that he and his family would have to move to the new location, but this might be all to the good, since it would give them a chance to get away from the scene of their troubles and start again in a place where nobody knew anything about Adam's past. Adam accepted with tears of gratitude.

Several weeks later they moved into their new home, a house they had been able to buy with a down payment advanced by Ruth's father. Adam was thrilled with the new situation. It was the kind of challenge he loved—to take a new venture from its beginnings and build it into a successful enterprise. For weeks he and Ruth sat up nights devising strategies to make the merchandise appealing, to attract new customers, to stimulate sales.

Each morning, Adam left for the store eagerly, expecting that this day or the next or the next after that the flow of customers would begin, and that the store would begin showing a profit. Realistically, he knew he should not be expecting this so soon, that it would have to take much longer. But he could not control his impatience, his restlessness, his intolerance of this delay, and soon his frustration and annoyance began to reflect themselves in irritability and impatience at home, with Ruth and with the children. For her part, Ruth was patient about the store and about her husband. "This, too, shall pass," she said to herself, consoling herself with the anticipation that business at the store would improve soon, and with that her husband's emotional state.

One evening during this period, Adam came rushing home, bursting with excitement. Ruth's heart sank. "He's borrowed money," she thought, "and he's gambled with it and won." Adam saw the expression on her face and laughed. He assured her that it was not what she feared.

Then he explained. One of his cronies, a real estate broker, had learned that a large real estate organization was planning to develop an industrial park in a section a few miles north of the city. No one else knew about it yet. This would be an opportunity to get in on the ground floor. The broker himself had quietly been buying up small parcels. There was a six-acre parcel Adam could buy for $20,000 with only a $5,000 down payment. It could go up to $35,000, $40,000 or more once the news got out.

Adam wanted to know whether Ruth would agree to taking out a $5,000 loan to finance the purchase.

Again Ruth's viscera rang a five-alarm warning. This was speculation, playing with money, gambling, looking for "the big hit." But then, she reflected, it might not be. Under other circumstances, it would be the kind of proposition she would have regarded as a very good one, one to which she would have given her support without reservation. Furthermore, things had been going well since Adam's return and there had not been the slightest indication of a reawakening of his interest in gambling. She decided, then, that it would be best to hold her suspicions in reserve and examine the proposal's practical aspects. She told Adam she thought it sounded like a good opportunity, but that she would need a little time to consider it.

Adam's mood changed in an instant. Black anger

replaced his genial smile and Ruth was afraid he might strike her. "God damn it," he screamed. "What's to think about? If we wait, someone else is going to grab it and we lose a chance to make a real killing."

With effort Ruth controlled herself, but insisted she still wanted to review the idea. He would positively have her answer in 24 hours.

The following day she found out from the real estate broker where the property was located. She also learned it was owned by a young man who had inherited it and who wanted to be rid of it for ready cash. It had been on the market a year and had evoked no interest at all.

Ruth drove out to look at the property. It fronted on a secondary road half a mile from the state highway. Like all the land around it, it was covered with scrub growth and there was not a sign of business or habitation anywhere in the vicinity. She could understand now why nobody had been interested. But if the rumor about the industrial park were true, it could quickly become very valuable. Even if that were not true, it might be worth buying. The city was spreading out in that direction and its value was bound to increase in the long run.

Adam hugged her when she told him she thought they ought to buy it. They drove together to the bank to make the loan and then to the real estate office to complete the transaction. They agreed that this done, they would put the matter out of their minds and wait for developments, if any, to happen. And happen they did. Within a month, real estate speculators had moved into the field and were snatching up every piece of land they could in the vicinity of the proposed industrial park. Adam himself was approached and offered $30,000 if he would sell right away. Adam refused the offer and decided to hold out. In another month, the bidding was up to $40,000 and still Adam refused to sell. If the speculators were ready to give him $40,000, he reasoned, the agents for the industrial park developers would give him more. He was not going to be panicked into selling, and he was right. Two months later he was approached directly by the agents and was offered $65,000. Adam accepted the offer.

The deal was concluded and with the $45,000 balance in their account, Adam said he wanted to celebrate in a special way. He wanted them all to fly back to their hometown and spend a few days with their relatives. While they were there he would go to the offices of Blank and Blank and there present Mr. Collins, personally, with $34,000 in repayment of the money he had embezzled.

The thought of a personal meeting between Adam and the officer of the company from whom he had stolen this money made Ruth shudder. She herself would regard such an encounter as a devastatingly humiliating experience. But then, she reflected, perhaps Adam needed this. Perhaps this was his way of relieving his guilt through personal absolution. But here, again, she found that she did not truly understand her husband.

"I want to show him," said Adam, "that I'm no small-time piker. I want to show him that I'm a man of substance, that I can peel off 34 thousand-dollar bills and say, 'Here it is, old man. This is the debt I owe you, and I always pay my debts.'"

Ruth could not believe what she was hearing. "A man of substance? Repayment of a debt? Good Lord, he doesn't even realize any longer that he committed a theft, a crime, that he went to jail for it, that this is something about which he should be everlastingly humble and ashamed. And here he is, actually boastful and proud."

She felt sick, but gave no indication of it and agreed to the visit back home.

Several days after their return from this trip, Adam said he had another trip to make. He had made a contract with a real estate developer in New York and had to fly there to work out the details of a deal that was being put together. They stood to make a very handsome profit, he said, if the deal went through.

Adam left on Friday, saying he would be home on Sunday. Sunday, Ruth drove to the airport to meet him. She could tell the instant she saw him, from the smile on his face and his gait, that something important had happened. It was clear he wanted to get home before talking about it, so they passed the time chatting about New York, the children, other things.

When they had put the car away and unlocked the door to the house, he took her by the hand, led her to a chair in the living room and sat her down. Out of one pocket he pulled a little velvet box, opened it and showed her a diamond ring—a beautiful stone set in platinum—worth at least $15,000. From another pocket he took out a roll of bills, which he counted out slowly, and totaled at $38,000.

The "real estate business trip" to New York had been a junket to Las Vegas. He was sure, he said, that she wouldn't mind, because look at what he had come home with.

Ruth looked at the flushed, handsome, joyous face, the boyish grin, the eyes sparkling with excitement, victory, power, and she thought back to another scene and another man two years ago—or was it a hundred: the stooped, shrunken figure standing in the kitchen doorway; the unshaven, pallid, sunken face of an old man; the vacant eyes; the injured hand and the soiled, tattered bandage; the shopping bag stuffed with soiled shirts and underwear and a sweater; the composite picture of despair and defeat.

And now she saw the horrible scenario being played out all over again—a man consumed by the compulsion to gamble; the winning then the losing, borrowing, pawning, begging, cheating, stealing, lying; the loss of their possessions; the harassment from the banks and finance companies; the threats from the bookmakers; the shame of having to come to relatives for help; the desperate struggle to keep herself and the children alive; the deterioration, once more, of this man into a helpless, weak, immoral zombie whipped on by his obsession until he was destroyed.

Ruth knew that, so far as she was concerned, this was the end. She would never again allow him to put her through what she had had to endure before. She knew that if she was going to save herself and the children she would have to act quickly, before she was caught up again in his downward spiral.

She had no idea what she was going to do, right then, but she did know that she was going to leave him, and that she would need money to support herself and the children until she could find work. Pretending to share his excitement and pleasure, she slipped the ring on her finger. Then she asked Adam to give her the money so she could put it in the bank.

Still grinning, Adam counted out the bills, separated them into two piles, shoved one pile of $19,000 toward Ruth and put the other in his pocket. Then he went to the liquor cabinet, brought out a bottle of wine, poured out two glasses, handed one ceremoniously to Ruth and said: "Let's drink to a new, prosperous and happy life." Ruth sipped from the glass, turning her face so he wouldn't see her revulsion.

The following morning, she drove to a bank in the next town, opened an account in her own name, and deposited the $19,000. Then she drove home and threw herself into her housework, unable to summon up enough initiative to decide what move to make next. For now, she could only go quietly about the daily routine and wait to see what would happen next.

She didn't have long to wait. The very next day Adam's assistant called from the store saying Adam had not showed up for work that morning. He wanted to know if there was anything wrong. Ruth told him she was sure her husband had some business to take care of and would undoubtedly be at the store a little later. When the telephone rang again that afternoon, she knew it was the assistant to tell her that Adam had not come in yet. She suggested that he lock up the store at the regular hour if Adam had not come back by then.

When dinnertime came, Adam had not returned home so Ruth and the children ate without him. It was about 11 o'clock when he came home. The exuberance and brightness were gone from his face and eyes. Instead, there was silence, sullenness and irritability. Ruth didn't have to ask or guess. She knew. The transformation was all too familiar. She had seen it a thousand times before: the euphoria, excitement, cockiness and superiority after a string of wins; and then the deflation, depression and sullenness when he tried to extend his winning streak and lost.

She didn't bother to ask where he had been and what had happened. What was the point?

The following morning, there was something in Adam's manner that told her he had done some reflecting during the night and that he was going to make an effort to regain control of himself. In fact, for the next two weeks or so, he went to work regularly, stayed at the store all day and came home for dinner on time. Ruth prayed for a miracle.

But for this compulsive gambler there were no miracles. When the store assistant telephoned a few days later, she knew she had been foolish for even dreaming the situation could change. That evening, Adam came home late again, sullen and dispirited.

The night was a sleepless one for both of them. Adam tossed and turned, got out of bed and went back again half a dozen times. Ruth lay as still as she could so he would not know she was awake. Disturbing thoughts kept racing through her head. Had he lost all his Los Vegas winnings already? How soon would it be before he came to ask her for the bankbook? What would he do when he found out she had not deposited the $19,000 in their joint account? Would she be able to stand up against his rage and refuse to give him any of that money? Would he then start taking the receipts from the store?

As soon as Adam left the house the next morning, Ruth called his older brother, David, and told him what was happening. David took the next plane out and was waiting with Ruth when Adam came home at midnight. When Adam saw his brother, he lunged at Ruth, screaming, and tried to strike her. David caught him and pulled him down into a chair. Pale and shaking with fright, Ruth drew back into a corner. When Adam's fury had subsided, David released his hold on him and tried to calm him.

"No one is accusing you of anything, Adam. Ruth is worried about you and she's worried about herself and the children. Why don't you and I go down to the store tomorrow and we'll check it over and see how things are going? then I plan to hang around for a few days—I'd like to stay here with you and Ruth."

Things went quietly for the next several days. The two

brothers went to the store together in the morning, stayed there all day and came home together. Evenings were remarkably normal. The adults sat around, watched television, played scrabble and chatted.

Sunday morning, as Ruth later recalled, Adam did appear to be behaving peculiarly, "sort of forced and mechanical, as though trying to put on an impression of being happy," but she had ignored this as just another aspect of his behavior. She didn't give it a second thought, either, when Adam said he needed to run out to the shopping mall to buy himself some shoes. Sunday was the only day he had to take care of his personal needs and there was nothing out of the way about a shopping trip to the mall.

But when three o'clock came and Adam had not returned, Ruth began to be concerned. His car may have broken down, she thought; but then he would have telephoned. He may have met a friend and lost track of time. A secret affair with a girl? Ruth grinned to herself at the thought. Adam was attractive and she had noticed how women looked at him, but that wasn't Adam's style. Then what? She decided to put aside her concern and wait. Surely he would be coming in the door any minute.

When five o'clock came and he still had not returned, Ruth called several of their friends; none of them had seen him. At seven, David called the local police, the state police and the hospitals. But none of them had any report of a person answering to Adam's name or description.

There was only one realistic possibility left . . . but where would he have gotten the money? Ruth ran to look for the bankbook in the place where she had hidden it. It was gone. Adam had searched for it and found it. But how could he have drawn any money without her? And then she knew what had happened; it was not the first time. But there was no way they could find out until the banks opened the following morning.

They stayed up late that night, hoping the telephone would ring and that there would be some news of Adam, or that Adam himself might call or come home. But the telephone did not ring and at midnight they went to sleep. They were up early the following morning, and when it was time, they drove to the bank and spoke to one of the officers.

A call to the bookkeeping department showed there had been a $15,000 withdrawal from Ruth's account the previous Friday. Next a clerk searched for the withdrawal slip and when it was located, it showed the signature "Ruth Kohler," a forgery. Then the officer called the teller whose initials appeared on the withdrawal slip, and when they had all moved back to a private office, he asked her to explain what had happened.

The teller said that Mr. Kohler had come in shortly after noon the previous Friday with the bankbook and the withdrawal slip signed by Mrs. Kohler. He had explained that Mrs. Kohler was sick and could not come herself to the bank to make the withdrawal. The thought that something might be wrong with the transaction, that the signature might have been a forgery, had never entered her head. Why should it have? She knew Mr. Kohler personally. He was such a nice gentleman. Who would ever dream that he would do something like this? The officer assured her she had nothing to worry about personally, that she could not be expected to detect the deceit.

The officer told Ruth he was sorry that this had happened, and he instructed her on the procedure to follow to recover the money from the bank. Meanwhile, he said, the bank would initiate legal action to obtain a warrant for Adam's arrest. Ruth flinched when she heard this, but said nothing. Again Adam had become a hunted man, and what would become of him this time?

Days went by and then weeks. Ruth expected every day to get a phone call from Adam telling her he was in desperate straits or that he had been arrested, and that he wanted her to help. But no calls came. Then one day her cousin Elizabeth telephoned and said that she and her boyfriend had been to Las Vegas and had seen Adam there, in one of the hotel casinos, betting heavily and winning. In the course of the next several days, they had seen him again at the casinos and had learned that he was traveling under an assumed name. He looked very well, Elizabeth said, was dressing expensively, was driving a Jaguar.

Several weeks later, a friend called Ruth and said that she, too, had seen Adam in Las Vegas, but now he was losing, and losing heavily. She had seen him lose $30,000 in one hour at the blackjack table one evening, and when she had come down the following morning and passed through the casino on her way to breakfast, she had seen Adam still playing, pale, disheveled, unshaven, grim.

Then the reports from Las Vegas stopped coming and once more he seemed to have vanished into nowhere. Again Ruth waited for the telephone call from Adam asking her to wire him money. She even found herself waking up and listening, expecting he might come back in the middle of the night as he had the other time he was being hunted.

Five months after Adam's disappearance, the telephone call finally did come, but it wasn't Adam on the line.

"Is this Mrs. Adam Kohler?"

"Yes, it is. Who is this calling?"

"This is Officer Hendricks of the Los Angeles police."

"Yes, what is it?"

"There's a man we picked up four days ago; we found him lying in an alley. His wrists were cut and he was unconscious. Tried to commit suicide. We got him to the hospital and they got him around with transfusions. He had no identification on him but he says his name is Adam Kohler. He gave us your name and telephone number and said you're his wife. Are you?"

"Yes, I am."

"He's going to be able to leave in two days. He wants to know, will you come out and get him?"

CHAPTER ONE

Compulsive Gambling— What Is It?

COMPULSIVE GAMBLING IS AN ADDICTIVE ILLNESS IN WHICH THE subject is driven by an overwhelming uncontrollable impulse to gamble. The impulse progresses in intensity and urgency, consuming more and more of the individual's time, energy and emotional and material resources. Ultimately, it invades, undermines and often destroys everything that is meaningful in his life.

Gambling is universal. It goes on everywhere, in every part of the world, and has been going on, probably, since the dawn of civilization. Recorded accounts tell of gambling in ancient Greece, China, Egypt, Persia and Rome, thousands of years ago. In most countries of the world today, gambling is carried on openly, extensively and even, in some countries, as a national pastime.

About 10 years ago, a national survey disclosed that 6 out of every 10 Americans aged 18 and over indulge in some sort of gambling, including anything from putting a few dollars a week on the lottery to spending every waking hour of every day gambling. Since that time there has been an immense growth in legalized gambling, and if a survey were taken today, and if it were to include also those between 16 and 18 years of age, the results would undoubtedly show that three out of every four Americans gamble.

Why do people gamble? Obviously, to win. Is there a person alive who has not thought, at one time or another, how nice it would be to win $100, $1,000, $25,000, $1,000,000, just by the lucky spin of the wheel, fall of the card, bounce of the ball or roll of the dice? Who has not, at one time or another, dreamed that fortune might touch his life, changing it all, relieving him of practical concerns and worries, making him suddenly wealthy with all the power to require or do anything he ever wanted? It is a dream pursued by tens of millions in the lotteries, the sweepstakes, the casinos as well as in speculative investments in the stock market. And for those whose dreams have to do not with wealth and power but just with being able to make ends meet, winning may mean being able to buy a coat, a television set, a bicycle for a child, even just having more food on the table.

But the financial gain is only one aspect of winning. For some who gamble, winning money has importance beyond the things it can buy. For them the important thing is the envy, respect, admiration, adulation that winning the money can command. What a thrill to be able to flash a roll of bills or just to be able to say, "I won five big ones" and to bask in the glory.

Winning may reinforce the feeling some gamblers have that they're "really smart," that they're a cut above the others, that they've "got something special going." You can hear them do this kind of boasting to a relative or close friend: "I don't just go ahead and bet like the others. I've got it worked out scientifically. I figure the odds. I study the horse's bloodlines, the trainers, the jockeys, the past performances. I don't bet on a football team because I like the quarterback's looks. I know the team backwards and forwards. I know all their weak spots and strong spots, the way they stack up against the others, their long-range records, etc., etc." And without a doubt many of them manage, for a time at least, to come out ahead of the game.

In addition to the chance of winning, gambling also offers for many the opportunity to socialize. For these people, the bingo game in the basement of the church or card game at the country club once or twice a week is a major social activity. The crowd at the OTB office shares a feeling of fraternity. Racetrack denizens say that the minute they get inside the track grounds they feel as though they've "come home." The Friday-night poker game has for millions of Americans become a traditional social function. Even the tens of thousands of transients who mill about the gambling casinos nightly enjoy a sense of camaraderie and belonging, a feeling of being comfortable and safe.

For tens of millions who gamble, the activity is a pastime, a diversion, an entertainment. Gambling does for them what the movies, the theater, television, fishing, golf or tennis do for others. It gives them a chance to relax, to get away from the tensions and stress of daily living, to enjoy a bit of a glow in pleasant, stimulating surroundings.

And then there is the excitement—evidenced in the racing pulse, tingling nerves, clenched fists and sweating palms that so many experience and enjoy—an excitement that renews itself with every move, every roll, every draw, every spin, every play, every game, every race. Everybody, or almost everybody, craves excitement. Some find it in the leap of a thousand-pound marlin after it takes the bait. Others find it in the incredible verve, grace and beauty of Baryshnikov and Makarova in a *Swan Lake* pas de deux. Others experience it in seeing a young rookie pitch a no-hitter his first game in the major leagues. And still others find it in gambling.

DIFFERENT TYPES OF GAMBLERS

Obviously, not all gamblers are alike. They differ from each other in what they get out of gambling, how big a part gambling plays in their lives, how much of their time and money they put into gambling, whether they gamble mainly for entertainment or for the money they can win, how it affects their work and their family life, whether they do it as a diversion or for a living, whether it remains a pastime or becomes a full-time obsession.

There are approximately 100,000,000 gamblers in the United States, and these can be broken down into six distinct groups: the professional gambler, the antisocial-personality gambler, the casual social gambler, the serious social gambler, the "relief-and-escape" gambler and the compulsive gambler.

The first two we are going to discuss only briefly, because they represent only a very small proportion of the entirety.

The professional gambler is one who makes his living by gambling. He makes a very serious study of his particular game or games and then goes about the business of trying to win as much as he can, either in card games with other high-stakes gamblers or in playing against the house at the casino. He sits there calmly and patiently, waits for the "edge" and then bets.

"Antisocial personality" is the psychiatric term for criminal type. This is a person whose life career is getting money by illegal means. Some specialize in theft and robbery, others in pimping or pushing drugs, still others in crooked gambling—or any combination of these or other activities. Those who are involved in crooked gambling ply their trade with marked cards or loaded dice, or specialize in fixing horse races or dog races. They may also engage in legitimate gambling and steal in order to obtain money for this purpose.

Because the compulsive gambler, in the later stages of his illness, is likely to steal or cheat others in order to obtain money for gambling, he is often confused with the antisocial personality whose criminal activities bring him into the gambling scene. In order to avoid this confusion, the distinction needs to be made sharply at the outset. The antisocial personality, who may get involved in gambling, does not have and likely never has had any ethics or concern about doing harm to others. His whole lifestyle has to do with getting money by illegal means. Not so the compulsive gambler. The compulsive gambler is a person who has lived all his life by society's rules and values. It is only when he is driven by the compulsion to gamble and the need to obtain money either to gamble or to pay his gambling debts that he may depart from his lifelong adherence to ethical behavior.

The antisocial personality is typically a rootless person, one who has never lived for a long time in any one place or held a job for more than a few months at a time. If he has a family, he is alienated from them. His social ties are limited and shallow. The compulsive gambler, on the other hand, is in most cases a family man or family woman, with close ties to members of the extended family, with a good work history, with roots in a particular community, with an active and rewarding social life until the advent of the illness.

The Casual Social Gambler

The casual social gambler is the person who gets together with friends or relatives, perhaps once a month or so, to play a game of poker for small stakes, or goes to the track a few times a year, betting $5 or $10 on a race, or takes a trip to Las Vegas or Atlantic City two or three times a year as much for the sociability, the entertainment and the razzle-dazzle as for the thrill of gambling in a professional setting and the chance of winning a few hundred dollars.

For the casual social gambler, gambling is distraction, entertainment, relaxation—a chance to get away for a little pleasure. But this is not his only diversion. He may also go to the movies or theater, take his family on outings, go to football or baseball or hockey games, have friends over for a party or dinner, read, play the piano, go bowling, play golf or whatever suits his personal preference and lifestyle. Gambling fills a need in his life. But it is not one that other activities could not satisfy just as well. If you were to take gambling out of his life, he could easily fill the gap with other pursuits.

(Before going any further, we need to point out that

when we say "he" we really mean "he or she." If we had to say "he or she" every time, however, it would make for awkward writing and reading. Therefore, from now on, every time we say "he" it should be understood to refer to both sexes, except where one or the other is designated specifically.)

The Serious Social Gambler

The serious social gambler is one who plays not just occasionally but regularly, at one or more types of gambling, and who does so with great absorption and intensity. For him, as for the casual gambler, gambling is a source of relaxation, entertainment, pleasure and excitement. But it is not just an incidental source; it is a major source. There are other things he likes to do in his leisure time, but they take second place to gambling. His preoccupation with gambling as recreation may be likened to that of the "tennis nut" or other devotee of a particular source of recreation.

Winning is, of course, important to him, for the money as well as for his ego. But he is prepared to lose, expecting or at least hoping that in the long run he will come out ahead. It is the excitement, the "action," the involvement that keeps him coming back no matter whether he wins or loses. Naturally, the anticipation of winning is an important part of the excitement.

There are "gambling widows," too—as there are "golf widows" or "tennis widows" or "football widows"—wives who stay home alone or with the children while the husbands take off evenings and/or weekends for the particular recreational activity to which they are wedded. But it does not go beyond that. Serious social gamblers are generally attentive to their families, spending time with them and being involved in their problems and their pleasures; if they are not, it is not because of their preoccupation with gambling.

A Weekly Pilgrimage to Atlantic City

Alonso B. is a serious social gambler. He owns a card and gift shop and lives in Pennsylvania, about 150 miles from Atlantic City. Every Saturday afternoon, like clockwork, he and his wife get into their car and take off for the casinos at Atlantic City. Mr. B. is the serious player. His wife comes along mainly to be with him, but may make an occasional wager or play the slot machines. Mr. B. plays blackjack and roulette almost exclusively. Occasionally, when his winnings are good, he will try the baccarat table. He allows himself $100 to play each time he goes and is generally able to win enough to enable him to keep playing until the early morning hours. Frequently he comes away with a few hundred dollars in winnings, sometimes with a few thousand, often with nothing at all. When he feels he has had enough, he and his wife go to their room in the casino hotel and go to bed. The following day they spend a few hours poking around the shops and then they head for home.

During the week, Mr. B. plays the lottery every day, allowing himself $10 a day for the instant lottery tickets and $5 for the weekly six-number ticket. His winnings from this source are meager, but this does not stop him from playing the lottery week in and week out.

While these gambling activities sustain him throughout the year, he gets a special charge out of betting on the big sporting events: the Kentucky Derby, the World Series and the Superbowl.

A Devoted Player at the Track

Loretta C. is another serious social gambler. She and her husband go to the track four or five times a week, every week, including the holiday season. They arrive there early, have a drink at the bar, then dinner, and then spend the rest of the evening betting and watching the races. Mrs. C. is the one who does all the betting. Mr. C. does not bet at all. Mrs. C. bets on every race, allowing herself $20 on each race or on combination bets such as daily doubles or exactas. If she wins in the early races, she may add another $20 or so on some of the subsequent races, but she will never put back all her winnings. Her income is derived from two small apartment buildings she owns. Each month she puts aside a set amount from this income for gambling. She will never draw on money that has been set aside for other purposes or that she had put into bonds or other investments. She is harshly critical of people who "gamble when they can't afford it." "I myself will only gamble," she says, "with money that I can afford to spend. Other people go to the Islands or buy themselves jewelry and fur coats. My enjoyment is going to the track."

Morris R., Businessman

Morris R., a businessman, is a serious social gambler. He plays poker regularly two evenings a week, and occasionally on Sunday. The players are all friends, except for an occasional newcomer brought in by one of the regulars. The games are played either at the homes of the regulars, in turn, or at the club to which they all belong. The evening games start at about nine and last, generally, until three or four in the morning, or even later. While sandwiches, beer, wine and whiskey are there in abundance, the players do not regard the games as a social get-together, a chance to eat, drink and converse. They take their playing very seriously, and are impatient with distractions. The stakes start at $1 with a $55 limit on raises. In an average game, a player could come out losing $250 or winning $1,000 or more. The players are all well-to-do-businessmen, doctors, dentists, lawyers and accountants, and sums of this kind are well within their means.

When Mr. R. and his wife go out of the United States on vacation, they generally choose a place where there is a casino, or where one can be reached within an hour or two by automobile. However, on vacation, gambling moves into the background. Instead, they seek out entertainment both of them can enjoy together.

A half dozen times a year, or more, three or four members of the group take off for a trip to Las Vegas where they engage in some heavy betting. They prefer blackjack, craps and baccarat. They come prepared to lose as much as $5,000 each, and on occasion one or more of them goes away with winnings of $15,000 or $20,000. They will play back only part of their winnings; they do not continue to play until they have lost it all.

* * *

While these three illustrations of serious social gambling represent different gambling interests and styles, and are drawn from different socio-economic strata, they have many things in common. The gambling is taken seriously and is done with concentration and intensity. It is a principal form of entertainment. And the gambling is controlled. The money that is allotted for and spent on gambling is well within the individual's means. Only some of the winnings are played back; these players do not keep playing until all their winnings are lost. Gambling does not intrude into the rest of the individual's life, does not preempt other important concerns, does not create problems for the individual in his family life or in his business.

The "Relief-and-Escape" Gambler

Many serious gamblers say that gambling does much more for them than provide recreation, sociability and excitement. They say they use it as a way to find relief from anxiety, tension, worry, depression. Typical is the way this gambler describes it: "When I feel that way, when I am out of sorts and feeling upset, I go someplace where I can gamble, and it doesn't matter too much what kind of gambling it is. It could be at the track or a card game or a casino or just OTB. It could even be placing a bet with a bookie, but the minute I get there and get into it, the minute the action starts, that miserable feeling disappears and I start feeling good again."

Others say that gambling gives them relief when they're feeling bored, drifting about aimlessly not knowing what to do with themselves, frustrated about their lack of progress in their studies, their work or their romantic endeavors. "Gambling seems to wash all that away, makes you feel good, even gives you a high, a glow."

Gambling also seems to serve some players in altering, at least for the time being, their perceptions of themselves. One gambler puts it this way:

I can be feeling pretty low about myself, thinking that I haven't ever amounted to anything and never will. I feel other people don't like me and don't think very much of me. Then, when I start gambling, all that changes. All of a sudden, I feel important, I feel I'm in control of my life. I can imagine people looking at me and saying to themselves, "...now there's an important guy. He really amounts to something. He's a wheel." And that feeling keeps on juicing me up so long as I'm gambling. It's better when I'm winning, Then that really makes me feel like I'm 10 feet tall. But, even when I'm losing, I still feel that way, because I'm in there doing something. I'm deciding, betting, making things happen, and that gives me a sense of power.

Gambling serves some people as a primary escape when they are confronted with life's difficulties or crises. It could be a quarrel with a spouse, the loss of a job, a failing grade on an exam, discipline problems with a son or daughter, financial difficulties, a serious illness in the family, the death of a loved one, rejection by a girlfriend or boyfriend, separation from a spouse or a divorce. But it doesn't always have to be a misfortune that stirs up the need to escape by gambling. There are people who react to good fortune that way, too: a promotion, the birth of a child, a child going off to college or getting married, the purchase of a new car or a home. Apparently, good fortune brings with it new responsibilities and anxieties that the individual is unable to handle, and so the "happy event" produces the same kinds of internal stresses as are precipitated by an unhappy event.

People who escape from problem situations by indulging in gambling say, in thinking back, that they knew it wasn't going to solve the problem. But what they were looking for right there and then was relief and escape, not solutions. One gambler explained: "When you're suffering with a splitting headache or an agonizing toothache, what do you think of? Long-term medical, psychiatric or dental treatment? No. All you want, desperately, is to get rid of that pain right away, this minute. You look for the simplest, quickest way to get relief, and if that's what gambling does for you when you're facing a tough, painful problem, naturally, you just plunge into gambling.''

Notice here the remarkable similarity between the mood-altering and perception-altering results produced by gambling and those produced by drinking. In fact, you could take everything we have written under the heading "The 'Relief-and-Escape' Gambler" and substitute the word "drinker" for "gambler" and the word "drinking" for "gambling" and you would not have to change another word. The effects of both are practically identical.

Alcohol is a psychic anesthetizer—it provides relief from psychic distress, including feelings of anxiety, depression, anger, loneliness, emptiness, boredom, worry, hopelessness. So does gambling. Alcohol is a euphoriant. It produces feelings of well-being, pleasure, excitement. It produces a "glow" and a "high." So does gambling.

Alcohol alters the drinker's perception of himself and of the world around him. A person may have a low opinion of himself, think he is unattractive and unlikable, dull and boring, incompetent and unimportant, an outcast and a failure. But after he has had a few drinks, all that is likely to change. Under the influence of the alcohol he sees himself as attractive, witty, charming, desirable, important, successful and powerful. Or he may be someone who thinks of life as a hazardous and painful experience, the world as full of risks and crises, people as deceitful and untrustworthy. After he has had a few drinks, these negative perceptions change. The world is seen as a safe place, free of insurmountable problems, a place where one can raise a family with relative ease and pleasure. People are no longer to be held at arm's length because you can't trust them. On the contrary, they are now friendly, likable and generous. Gamblers say that the same sort of tranformation takes place as soon as they "get away from it all" and make their escape into gambling.

Of course one doesn't have to be a relief-and-escape drinker or gambler to seek this kind of respite when feeling out of sorts or when facing a wearying and difficult problem. We all do this from time to time. But, having gotten temporary relief, the majority of us get back to the real-life problem and try to work it out in a realistic way.

Not everybody can do this, however. Not everybody has the capacity to pull himself together and say, "All right, now that I feel a little better, now that I've collected myself, I'm going to get back in there and face the issue, the suffering, the pain, the problem, and see what I can do about it.'' They may lack the emotional resources to be able to do this. They may find that it is much easier and more pleasant to escape from reality than to deal with it. People with this sort of personality will return to drinking or gambling, or both, every time they're feeling unhappy or every time they've got a tough problem to deal with. After a while—several months, a year, two years, differing from case to case—relief and escape become a way of life, and that person becomes a relief-and-escape drinker or a relief-and-escape gambler, or both. These conditions can coexist in a person, operating simultaneously or substituting for one another at different times.

For Mrs. T. It Started Late in Life

Mrs. Elsa T. is a relief-and-escape gambler. No one who had known her as a girl, or during the first 20 years of her marriage, would ever have dreamed that this would happen to her. In fact, there was hardly any gambling at all in her life during that time. She and her husband would play an occasional game of cards with friends, go to the track now and then, put a few dollars on the lottery every once in a while. They were what we call casual social gamblers.

Mrs. T. cannot recall exactly when it was that her gambling took a more serious turn. It seems to have started at the time that her youngest daughter, Cathy, became pregnant at the age of 16, had the baby and gave it up for adoption. For this family, steeped in strict religious and moral tradition, this was a shattering blow. One day during that painful period, a friend invited Mrs. T. to go to the track with her. She did, and found she enjoyed the experience more than she ever had before. ''It took my mind off that terrible thing with Cathy,'' she recalls, ''and it took me out of myself.'' Within a few months, trips to the track two or three afternoons a week had become routine.

About a year later, the family had another shock. Cathy's older brother John was caught with some friends selling small quantities of marijuana. The judge, under pressure from the community to make an example of the boys, sentenced them to a year in jail, suspending all but 30 days of the sentence. The news was all over the front pages and Mrs. T. quarantined herself in her home to avoid neighbors, tradesmen and friends. "I must also have become depressed," Mrs. T. recalls, "because I could not muster up enough energy to get out of bed until 10 or 11 in the morning, and then I just sat around and wept." When she finally could mobilize herself to get out, the first place she went to was the track, and from then on the twice-a-week routine went to four or five times a week. In addition, Mrs. T. sought out places where she could play cards at least two evenings a week.

Two years later, the oldest daughter was married, leaving just Mrs. T. and her husband. A year later, her husband suffered a stroke and died. She was now totally alone, except for a few distant relatives and some friends. The friends tried to get her involved in social activities, but lacking the emotional energy and initiative, she refused. She felt life had been unfair to her, had dealt her too many blows, an attitude conducive to depression. Her only recourse, then, to fill her days and nights and to escape from a state of melancholy, was to gamble.

Today, Mrs. T. gambles practically every day and night . . . at the track, at OTB parlors, at illegal gambling clubs, at bingo games, at home by phone calls to bookmakers.

Mrs. T. is consummately dependent on gambling for relief from psychic distress and escape from life's problems. But her condition gets neither better nor worse. While she is quite well-to-do and able to bet large sums of money, she holds her betting within reasonable bounds except for an occasional "splurge." While she spends practically all her days and nights gambling, she does not plunge, lose large sums, and then "chase" to recover her losses by throwing good money after bad. Nor does she bet heedlessly in pursuit of a fortune. In other words, her condition is not progressive. It remains at a fairly steady level, gambling giving her what she seeks most, a state of near-oblivion.

An Explosive Relief-and-Escape Gambler

Mr. Anthony D. is another relief-and-escape gambler,

but his style is different from that of Mrs. T. She is what one might call a "quiet gambler"; he is an "explosive" one.

Mr. D., now 54, has been gambling from the time he was 15. Gambling was part of the way of life in his home. Weekends, his family would regularly assemble a group of friends and play poker, pinochle or gin rummy, sometimes until dawn. Anthony remembers being awakened by the shouting, cursing and laughter coming from the card players. From the quarrels between his parents, he knew that large sums of money were being lost. When Anthony was old enough to earn some money from odd jobs, he began to play poker with friends for modest stakes. After he graduated from high school and went to work in his father's trucking business, he began to bet in crap games and at the racetrack for much higher stakes.

It was a lot of fun, but it wasn't just that. It gave me a chance to let off steam, to work out some of the gripes I had inside me. My parents were always quarreling and my father was always yelling at us kids, even beating us. He was a bastard, a tyrant. He had no interest in us, no feelings for us; nothing we ever did meant anything to him. Gambling was my escape, my outlet, my kicks. That's where I could be important, a "big shot." I could be feeling nasty, rotten, mean, but the minute I started playing that would be all gone, like magic. I needed it the way I needed a drink sometimes. It gave me a lift; both of them did, drinking and gambling.

By the time he was 21 and married, Anthony was a confirmed relief-and-escape gambler. Gambling had become a major thing in his life: the horses, poker, private crap games, illegal gambling clubs, trips to Las Vegas, trips to Caribbean gambling spots. His family remained important to him, but more out of a traditional sense of duty than out of love. Although he was very successful in business—he had taken over the trucking firm after his father's death—he never felt that he had really succeeded in life.

I had more money than most of our friends. I drove around in a Cadillac. I spent money like it was water. I wore expensive, imported silk suits. But as much as I had, and as much as I tried to convince myself that I was really something, that I had made it, there was something inside of me that continued to put me down and made me feel just the way my father had made me feel—a nothing and a nobody. Maybe you can explain it. I sure can't. To have all that and to be that successful and still feel that you don't amount to anything. But I can tell you this . . . that feeling wasn't there when I was gambling. It was like taking some kind of a magic drink and all that would go away. You can say that the only time I really felt good, the only time I wasn't eating at myself, was when I was gambling.

Sometimes, when he bet large sums of money and lost, he was forced to draw money out of the company's funds, a practice that violated his own strict business code. This would happen after disastrous gambling trips to the Caribbean, and it happened once, also, when he gambled and lost $15,000 he had set aside for his daughter's wedding.

Yet, with all, Anthony was able to cut down on his gambling, even to stop it for months when confronted by a family crisis. "You could say I was hooked on it," Anthony observed, "because I needed it so bad. But you could say I wasn't hooked because I could quit when things got real tough," as when his youngest daughter was stricken with rheumatoid arthritis or when he himself lost more than $100,000 in a questionable business venture engineered by a cousin.

Despite his dependence on gambling, Anthony never lost control, nor was his dependence progressive. The intense level it had reached early in his adult life remained stable, with minor fluctuations, over a span of some 30 years. Gambling played a very important role in his life, but it never progressed to the point where it was a serious detriment to his family or his business, or caused him to sweep aside all other interests and considerations or gamble away everything he owned.

The Compulsive Gambler

Every day we give up pleasures of one kind or another because they conflict with our obligations, with our concerns for health or safety or with our code of ethics.

We would just love to stay in bed that extra hour in the morning when we are dying for some more sleep. But we can't. We have to get up to go to work; or we have to get our husbands off to work and the children off to school.

We would just love to have that doughnut, piece of pie, scoop of ice cream, extra helping of potatoes and gravy. But we say, "No, I won't." We are concerned about being overweight and what that might do to our appearance and our health.

That sweater, record album, TV set, fishing rod, antique cabinet look awfully tempting, and we would just love to go into the store and buy them. But then we remember there are other more pressing priorities—bills to pay, saving for the children's education, replacing the rickety old clothes dryer.

The new secretary in the office or the handsome golf pro stir up all sorts of exciting fantasies, and we may even go so far as to flirt a little. But then we say to ourselves: "That's enough. That's where it stops. I'm married. I don't want to be unfaithful. It's against my principles. Further, even if I were willing to bend the rules, there's a chance I might get caught, and that would wreck my marriage."

By and large, most of us are able, throughout our lives, to keep pretty well within the limits we have set for ourselves and that society has set for us. We may, from time to time, yield to an urge or craving and step outside the limits, but the evasions are generally transitory and after the episode is past we fall back into our responsible pattern of living. The desire for safety, the need to conform, the weight of duty and our need to adhere to a code of ethics prevail over the impulses for gratification and pleasure.

There are occasions, however, where a person is subject to urges so powerful that he is unable to control them, no matter how much he might want to and no matter how hard he tries. The impulses arise from powerful psychic forces and overwhelm every conscious effort to keep them in check. Concern about the consequences, no matter how disastrous, is brushed aside, and the victim dashes into whatever it is that the impulse is tempting him to do.

This is the essence of compulsion . . . the inability to deny or control an impulse for gratification, no matter how disastrous the consequences, together with the need to relieve an unbearable tension by plunging into action.

The compulsive eater gorges himself though he knows this will make him unattractive and increase his risk of sickness and death. The compulsive smoker keeps on smoking, though this will shorten his life span and expose him to serious risk of heart disease and cancer. The man driven by sick sexual impulses to molest children will commit the offense repeatedly even though he knows he will be jailed if caught, or even after he has already served a jail sentence for the crime. The compulsive drinker keeps on drinking though this may cost him his health, his job, his family, even his life. Kleptomaniacs keep on stealing—generally items they neither need nor want—even though they know they will be disgraced and go to jail if they are caught.

The compulsive gambler keeps on gambling though this may strip him of everything he owns, cause unimaginable suffering for his family, plunge him into abysmal debt, drive him to lie, cheat and steal, ruin his health, bring about his imprisonment and even compel him to suicide.

The casual social gambler can stop gambling when he wants to, so can the serious social gambler, so can the relief-and-escape gambler, although for him it may be more difficult. The compulsive gambler *cannot stop*, no matter how much he may want to, no matter how hard he tries, even though he may think he can. He has lost control. The impulse to gamble is so insistent, so overpowering, so consuming that he is unable to resist it and he must continue to gamble.

For the casual social gambler, gambling is just an incidental pastime, one among many others. For the serious social gambler, gambling is a major source of entertainment and diversion. There may be others, but gambling is the most important. For the relief-and-escape gambler, gambling is more than a pastime. It is a major activity in his life, of equal importance with and sometimes of greater importance than the devotion to family or business. However, the rest of life does go on, its integrity basically unimpaired; and even though gambling may cause neglect of family or business, it does not seriously invade these areas and undermine them.

For the compulsive gambler, however, gambling is not only the most important thing in his life, it is *the only thing*. The course of this disorder is progressive. It may start as a casual social interest and remain at that level for years. Then, at some point, the casual interest becomes a serious one, consuming more of the gambler's time, interest and money. Again, it may remain at that level for several years, or it may move quickly to the next level, where gambling has become one of the most important things in the gambler's life. After that it moves on to the compulsive stage where all control is lost and the gambling invades every aspect of life—family, job, social standing, ethical values, physical and psychological health—undermining and destroying them and leaving nothing but ruins.

The disorder may therefore be defined as follows:

Compulsive gambling is a disorder in which the individual is driven by an overpowering and uncontrollable impulse to gamble. The impulse persists and progresses in intensity and urgency, consuming more and more of the individual's time, energy, material goods and emotional resources until, ultimately, it invades, undermines and often destroys everything that is meaningful in his life.

For anyone who has not himself or herself been subject to an uncontrollable impulse, the inability of the compulsive gambler to withstand the craving to gamble may be difficult to understand. Wives of compulsive gamblers are apt to say: "How can that be? There's nothing really wrong with him except that he doesn't want to try. If he would only use his willpower he could stop this terrible thing. He has good strong willpower about other things. He's a hard worker, never even allows himself to take a day off when he's sick.

If he makes up his mind to paint the house or fix the plumbing, he'll do it even if it takes up all his spare time. That takes willpower, doesn't it? So if he's got willpower for that sort of thing, why doesn't he have the willpower to stop gambling?''

The answer to that can be found in the personal experience of every one of us. We all have a ''weakness'' about one thing or another, a weakness we give in to even though we may be absolutely firm and resolute about everything else. It may be a weakness for rich desserts, for smoking, drinking, expensive clothes, ''goofing off,'' sex, cheating on taxes—things that we know are wrong or bad for us or may get us into trouble but that we do anyhow, because the impulse is so strong. If we can think of how hard it is for us to resist that particular weakness or impulse, and then multiply that a thousand times, we can begin to understand what a compulsive gambler goes through when he is driven by the impulse to gamble.

COMPULSIVE GAMBLING AS AN ILLNESS

There was a time, perhaps as recently as 30 years ago, when the term ''illness'' or ''disease'' was automatically taken to mean something physically wrong with a person. Psychiatrists, psychologists and others who insisted that a person could become incapacitated by a psychological illness arising from psychological causes were widely regarded with skepticism or subjected to outright derision.

Today, however, this negative attitude no longer prevails. In fact, it has become commonplace for people to accept the fact that we are subject to such psychological illnesses as depression, anxiety states and phobias, and that these can arise from psychological stresses that the patient has undergone in the past or is undergoing in the present. In explaining depression, for example, we say that this illness is likely to develop when a susceptible person experiences a traumatic loss, disappointment or rejection and a feeling of helplessness to do anything about the situation.

Typical is the depression a man or woman may develop after a separation or a divorce, or that a parent may develop after the loss of a child. Similarly, depression may occur after a person has lost his job, retired from a job or suffered a severe financial setback. All involve a traumatic loss and a feeling of helplessness and hopelessness.

In such cases the individual has developed a psychological illness—depression—from psychological causes. This conception of illness meets with total acceptance today. We no longer regard people suffering from depression or other psychological illness as "different" or "strange." We accept, without even a second thought, that that person is sick, that he has an illness, that he is in need of treatment.

Compulsive gambling—or "pathological gambling," as it is called in professional terms—is an illness, a psychological illness. While not enough research has been done as yet to be able to determine the precise causes, there is agreement on this, at least . . . that it is a psychological illness with psychological causes, and that it is possible to treat it and to bring about recovery.

The World Health Organization publishes a directory of all known diseases subject to medical and psychiatric treatment. It is known as the *International Classification of Diseases*. A new edition is published approximately every 10 years, bringing the list up to date and adding diseases not previously included. The 1968 edition did not include pathological gambling. The 1979 edition—the ninth—did.

The American Psychiatric Association publishes a directory of all known psychiatric diseases subject to psychiatric treatment. It is known as the *Diagnostic and Statistical Manual*. The second edition, published in 1968, did not include pathological gambling. The third edition, published in 1980, does.

In other words, pathological gambling has now been recognized as an illness by the professions authorized to make this sort of judgment. The fact that this did not happen earlier is not surprising and cannot be blamed on the medical profession. The helping professions become aware of an illness only when people with that condition come to them seeking help. Until about five years ago or so, very few compulsive gamblers had done so, and there are still very few of them seeking help today.

Why? Because it is characteristic of the compulsive gambler that he does not even recognize that he has a problem, let alone an illness. One can see this demonstrated dramatically at virtually every meeting of Gamblers Anonymous, an organization for compulsive gamblers.

At a typical meeting, newcomers are asked to answer a standard list of 20 questions concerning their gambling activities and the way the gambling has affected their lives. From long experience, the organization has determined that anyone who answers seven or more of these questions in the affirmative is likely to be a compulsive gambler. Yet in meeting after meeting, there will be at least one newcomer, who, after having answered as many as 15 or 20 questions in the affirmative, will answer "no" to the question, "Do you think you are a compulsive gambler?" Typically, the compulsive gambler sees his problem as having to do with a need for money and a loss of luck or skill in gambling. He does not recognize the compulsive nature of his gambling. He still thinks he can stop gambling whenever he wants to.

This process, common among compulsive drinkers as well as compulsive gamblers, is called "denial." It does not mean that the individual knows he is sick but refuses to acknowledge it to others. It means that he actually does not recognize that he has a compulsion over which he has lost control.

What is remarkable and virtually unbelievable is to hear a man who is recovering from a violent two- or three-day siege of delirium tremens (DTs) insist that he is not an alcoholic, that he can control his drinking, that he can stop drinking whenever he wants to. Yet this is typical. Equally remarkable and difficult to believe is the experience of hearing a man, who has embezzled a large sum of money and lost it gambling, whose wife has left him because he has gambled away everything the family has ever owned, who has been sleeping in flophouses, insist that he does not have an illness, that he is not a compulsive gambler, that he can stop any time he wants to.

Very often compulsive gamblers will come to professional attention when they seek help for a physical ailment or because of depression or an anxiety attack. It is only in the course of the interview that the physician or psychiatrist learns that the patient is suffering from the illness of pathological, or compulsive, gambling.

COMPULSIVE GAMBLING AS AN ADDICTION

A recent professional publication on addictive disorders opens with this sentence: "This book is concerned with the various addictive disorders: alcoholism, drug abuse, and compulsive gambling."

Compulsive gambling an addiction? Aren't addictions caused by addictive drugs? How can you have an addiction without a drug?

The answer, simply, is this: Addictive drugs are addictive not because of some peculiar physiological or chemical change they produce in the body. They are addictive because they produce instant, intense pleasure and/or because they produce instant relief from painful mental and emotional states the individual may be living through. If that person happens to be one who lacks either the ability or the opportunity to derive pleasure and relief from other sources, he will want to go back to using the drug in order to obtain these instant and satisfying effects, and he will do so over and over again. After that goes on for a prolonged period, a *psychological* change occurs within that individual, as a result of which he begins to crave the drug for the pleasure and relief that it produces. If he cannot obtain the drug, he becomes unhappy and distressed and sets himself on a course to obtain the drug and use it in order to allay the craving and to relieve the distressed feeling. When that begins to happen, when the person feels he must have the drug and will do anything to get it, we say that he has lost control, that he has become addicted.

For a long time, psychopharmacologists—scientists who study the effects of drugs on the body and the mind—believed that the craving for the drug was caused by some mysterious change in the body's tissues produced by the drug itself. Today, they no longer hold this view. They say that this mysterious change—whatever it may be—is psychological, not physical, that it has to do with an intensification of the need for instant pleasure and relief and a paralysis of the psychological controls a person normally exercises over his pleasure-seeking and pain-avoidance behavior.

Here is a quotation on this very point from a statement by the World Health Organization (WHO) Commission on Drug Dependency. (The term "drug dependency" is used as a synonym for "addiction.")

Individuals may become dependent upon a wide variety of chemical substances. . . . All of these drugs have one effect in common: they are capable of creating in certain individuals a particular state of mind that is termed "*psychic dependence*." In this situation, there is a feeling of satisfaction and a psychic drive that requires periodic administration of the drug to produce the pleasure or avoid discomfort. Indeed this mental state is the most powerful factor involved in chronic intoxication with psychotropic drugs and it may be the only factor involved, even in the most intense craving and perpetuation of a compulsive abuse.

What about the withdrawal symptoms people get when they abruptly stop taking the drug they have been using, and to which they have become addicted? Doesn't the presence of withdrawal symptoms prove that the addiction is physical? Here is what the WHO commission has to say on that subject:

Psychic dependence can and does develop, especially with stimulant type drugs (e.g., cocaine or the amphetamines), without any evidence of physical dependence and therefore without any abstinence (withdrawal) syndrome developing after drug withdrawal. Physical dependence (the withdrawal symptoms which occur when the use of the drug is stopped abruptly) is an inevitable result of the pharmacological action of some drugs with sufficient amount and time of administration.

In other words, withdrawal symptoms have nothing to do with addiction. For one thing, any number of chemicals, never even regarded as having anything to do with addiction, can produce withdrawal symptoms if administered long enough and then withdrawn. Second, there are no withdrawal symptoms when a person stops taking cocaine or other stimulant drugs such as the amphetamines. Third, when withdrawal symptoms do occur after a user stops taking heroin or other narcotic drugs, they are simply the body's reaction to the withdrawal of a drug that has been depressing the functions of the central nervous system. It is similar to the rebound reaction that occurs when you press down on a powerful spring and then suddenly let go. The spring does not return to its normal condition quietly, slowly and gently. The rebound is immediate and violent. That is the nature of the withdrawal reaction. Once a drug user has experienced the discomfort and often the horror of the withdrawal reaction, he will do anything he can to get a fix before this reaction sets in. It is this frantic, desperate need to get hold of and ingest some more of the drug to avoid the withdrawal reaction that has been interpreted, incorrectly, as evidence that the addiction to drugs is physical, and that withdrawal symptoms are indicative of physical addiction.

In short, all addiction is psychological, even addictions to alcohol and other drugs. Consequently we can accept that compulsive gambling is an addiction, even though no substance is involved.

Addiction to a drug develops after a person has used that substance over and over again to obtain instant pleasure and/or relief and escape, ultimately developing a craving for that drug and loss of control over that craving. The very same mechanism operates with respect to gambling. Addiction to gambling (compulsive gambling) develops after a person resorts to gambling over and over and over again to obtain instant pleasure and/or relief and escape, ultimately developing a craving for that activity and loss of control over that craving.

Why and how the loss of control occurs, we do not know. We do not yet understand the mechanism by which the individual's control over his pleasure-seeking and pain-avoiding impulses is paralyzed. Nor do we understand why this happens to some people and not to others. There are people who drink heavily and regularly year after year after year for pleasure, escape and relief, yet never become alcoholics. And, by the same token, there are people who gamble heavily and regularly year after year after year for pleasure, escape and relief, and yet do not become compulsive gamblers. The entire subject of impulsiveness and loss of control over impulses has as yet been only superficially explored. It still remains very much a matter of hypothesis and conjecture. Beyond that, research on compulsive gambling itself cannot even be said to be in its infancy. The scientific literature would yield no more than a hundred papers on this subject, as compared, for example, with hundreds of thousands of research papers on alcohol abuse and alcoholism.

Having established that compulsive gambling is both an illness and an addiction, we can revise our definition to include these facts and make the definition complete.

Compulsive gambling is an addictive illness in which the subject is driven by an overwhelming, uncontrollable impulse to gamble. The impulse persists and progresses in intensity and urgency, consuming more and more of the individual's time, energy and emotional and material resources. Ultimately, it invades, undermines and often destroys everything that is meaningful in a person's life.

HOW MANY COMPULSIVE GAMBLERS ARE THERE?

The only available source of national statistics on compulsive gambling is *Gambling in America,* the report of The Commission on the Review of the National Policy Toward Gambling, an agency established by Congress in 1970.

According to that report, issued in 1976, there were then an estimated 1,100,000 compulsive gamblers in this country and another 3,300,000 potential compulsive gamblers. Even at that time the National Council on Compulsive Gambling and Gamblers Anonymous said those figures were much too low. They estimated that there were at least some 6,000,000 actual compulsive gamblers in this country.

Since then there has been a great expansion in legal gambling throughout the country, and with it, an inevitable increase in the number of compulsive gamblers.

In its 1976 report, the Commission on the Review of the National Policy Toward Gambling pointed out the direct relationship between gambling availability and the incidence of compulsive gambling:

> Legalization of gambling increases public exposure to more types of gambling, reduces negative attitudes toward the other (illegal) types of gambling and encourages wider participation. . . . Survey findings also indicate that the widespread availability of legal gambling causes an increase in the incidence of compulsive gambling. . . . These data are consistent with the hypothesis that widespread availability of gambling in its legal forms leads those classified as potential compulsive gamblers to actualize their potential compulsion.

These findings do not come as a surprise. The same kind of relationship has been found to exist with respect to alcoholism, another kind of compulsive behavior. Numerous studies have found that when alcoholic drinks become more easily available, whether because prices are reduced or the legal purchasing age is lowered, this is invariably followed by a rise in the rate of problem drinking and alcoholism, as well as in the social, economic, psychological, medical and legal problems associated with those conditions.

HOW OTHERS VIEW THE COMPULSIVE GAMBLER

Although millions of Americans have had experience with compulsive gamblers and compulsive gambling, few know the problem by name, and even among those who know about it there are few who understand it, especially the victims themselves.

Most people who know the compulsive gambler personally, who have experienced suffering at his hands, who have witnessed the suffering to which he has subjected his family, who have seen the gambler manipulate and mulct trusting relatives, friends, employers, business associates and others, regard him as a con man, as a person without conscience, decency or honor, as a wrong-doer who needs to be punished. This attitude is pervasive not only among the public at large but also among health and welfare professionals, among police and lawyers and judges, among people in the lending institutions.

Few understand that what they are seeing is a desperately sick person in the late stage of his illness. Few know that in the great majority of cases the wretched person they see before them was once a decent, energetic, honest worker, a creative entrepreneur, a good provider, a participant in charitable organizations and activities, a loving and concerned parent and marital partner; and that the positive values and standards that once guided this person's life have been abandoned under the inexorable pressure of the compulsion to gamble and to obtain money for gambling by whatever means it might take.

There are not many who recognize that compulsive gambling is an addiction or who know that the compulsive gambler can be treated and restored to a useful life, no matter how much he has injured himself, his family and society.

As a result, compulsive gamblers are almost universally regarded with prejudice, treated the way one would a malefactor.

A Court Martial for Sergeant McC.

Sergeant Robert McC., stationed with the U.S. Army in Germany, had had an excellent service record, without blemish, and was regarded by his officers as an exceptionally reliable person and a credit to the corps. It was discovered one day that he had taken $3,500 from the army relief fund and that he had used the money to gamble and had lost it.

At his court martial, his attorney explained the circumstances under which the money had been taken and that the man was a compulsive gambler. The attorney also informed the court that a relative had sent a check for $3,500 to make up for the money that had been taken. Sergeant McC. was found guilty and given a dishonorable discharge. Aside from the blemish on his record, the dishonorable discharge cost him a great deal more. It deprived him of all veterans' benefits, including the right to be treated at a Veterans Administration hospital. Ironically, this denied him, among other things, the chance to be treated for his compulsive gambling, since, at that time, virtually the only places a person could get treatment for compulsive gambling were a number of VA hospitals where treatment programs had been established.

But that was not the end to his trouble. Sergeant McC., a widower, was engaged to be married to an army nurse he had met on the base. After the court martial and dishonorable discharge, his fiancée broke the engagement. When he returned to his hometown in Oklahoma and tried to find work, the sergeant found that the news of his dishonorable discharge had traveled ahead of him and that no one would give him a job. After six months of joblessness, he went into a severe depression and had to be admitted to a mental hospital, where he remained as a patient for three months. On his release, unable to find work, he had to seek welfare help and move into a furnished room, where he is now living, alone, without family or friends.

A Town Without Mercy

Alfred M. was the manager of a branch store of an auto-supply chain in a small town in West Virginia. Several years ago, he took out a $15,000 loan from the local bank, ostensibly to expand his attic into two extra rooms and a bathroom. Since he had grown up in the town and was known to most of the bank's officers, he had no difficulty in obtaining the loan with a two-year repayment arrangement. For the first six months, payments were made on time. But then they suddenly stopped. The bank investigated and learned that Mr. M. was not using the money to finish his attic, but had in fact gambled and lost it. The bank called in the loan and demanded immediate payment. Since, obviously, Mr. M. was unable to comply, the bank took him to court, won a judgment for the full balance and court costs, and subsequent to that, a writ of attachment.

It is customary for cases involving nonpayment of loans or other monetary obligations to be handled quietly and routinely, without as much as a line in the newspapers. But in this case, the judge took it upon himself to subject Mr. M. to a merciless tongue-lashing, calling him "dishonest, untrustworthy, a disgrace to his family, a blight on the good name of the community, a dishonorable man who would deceive a bank in order to satisfy a shameful lust for gambling."

The morning following the trial, the local newspaper carried the story on the front page, including verbatim excerpts from the judge's diatribe. A day later, Mr. M.'s employer gave him two weeks notice and forbade him to come back to the store. Mr. M. next had to resign as a deacon of his church and as a president of his fraternal organization. The M.'s were compelled to sell their home in order to satisfy the judgment. Their 15-year-old daughter refused to go back to school because of the disgrace and had to move in with an aunt in another state in order to continue her schooling.

When interviewed some time later, the bank's loan officer admitted that had not Mr. M.'s gambling been an issue, the bank undoubtedly would have given him an extension on his loan and the opportunity to repay it as soon as he could. Had that happened, the case would never have come to court, and had the case not come to court the ensuing chain of events would never have occurred.

Even in the Civil Service

Herman W., a sociologist, entered the employ of the federal government in Washington, D.C. at the age of 22 and by the time he was 29 had risen to a responsible position heading a research bureau in one of the departments. Counting heavily in his rapid rise were his responsibility, inventiveness, leadership and his willingness to work evenings and weekends when a project was pressing.

Shortly after his promotion to bureau chief, colleagues noticed a change in Mr. W.'s manner of dress. Generally conservative, in the Brooks Brothers style, he began to sport very expensive Italian suits, Swiss shoes, elegant shirts. He no longer drove a VW; now it was an expensive sports car. His associates assumed that he or his wife had inherited a fortune, which was not the case. The fact was that Mr. W was gambling and winning heavily.

About six months after this change, another dramatic one occurred. Customarily friendly, jovial and outgoing, Mr. W. suddenly became preoccupied, withdrawn and sullen. This his colleagues attributed to personal problems, which he did indeed have—problems arising out of heavy gambling losses. One thing that did not suffer, however, was his performance at work. This he maintained at his customary superior level.

One day during this period, his supervisor called him in and informed him that the personnel section of the department had discovered that Mr. W. had passed a bad check for $1,000. Mr. W. admitted this had happened, but said it had been a mistake and that the matter had been rectified, which, in fact, it had. The supervisor then confronted Mr. W. with the fact that he had been overheard, during working hours, placing bets over the telephone, also that during the previous months he had frequently been away from his desk for hours without any explanation—apparently to gamble. Mr. W. admitted that he had taken time away from his work to gamble; he insisted, however, and justly, that this had not interfered with his efficiency or productivity. The supervisor listened to the explanation and gave no indication that disciplinary action was contemplated.

A month later Mr. W. was called in and told he was being dismissed for inefficiency and poor performance. When he protested that there had, in fact, been no decline in his performance, the supervisor remained silent. In tears, Mr. W. said he knew he was being dismissed because of his gambling and promised he would seek treatment and would

become a member of Gamblers Anonymous. The plea fell
on deaf ears.

This man could have fought the dismissal through the
civil service and in all likelihood would have won his case,
but he was afraid of the notoriety for himself and his family
should the facts about his gambling come out in the open.

Mrs. W. was devastated when she heard about the
dismissal and the gambling. Nevertheless, she remained
supportive and said she would help him get treatment. With
their friends, however, it was another story. The news of his
dismissal, and the reason for it, got around quickly. One
after another, the friends fell away, giving one excuse or
another for turning down invitations to have dinner, play
tennis or go on outings.

With the civil service dismissal on his record, Mr. W.
could not find employment as a sociologist or research
investigator in a government agency or a university. He is
now employed as a marketing analyst by a small consulting
firm in Chicago owned by his brother-in-law. Slowly the
W.'s are recovering from the trauma of their social ostracism
and are venturing out, timidly, to make friends in their new
surroundings.

History Repeats Itself

To anyone who is acquainted with the history of public
attitudes on alcoholism, the contents of the past several
pages must have produced a sense of déjà vu. In fact, the
historical parallels are nothing short of remarkable. We
quote from the pages of the *Understanding Alcoholism,*
published by Scribners in 1968.

The typical concept of the alcoholic was symbolized by the
figure of the red-nosed, skid-row bum, derelict, homeless,
irredeemable—an object of scorn and derision. In religious thinking this stock character was regarded as a
sinner; in social and economic thinking as useless, hopeless and without character. As recently as the 1930's a
majority of American citizens held the belief that respectable people do not become alcoholics.

During the early 1940's people became aware of the

existence of an informal organization whose members, former alcoholics from various social strata, openly admitted their condition and worked together to remain sober and help others to do so. . . . The organization had no name until 1939 when a book recounting the experiences of some hundred members was published. Its title, *Alcoholics Anonymous*, was adopted as the name of the movement. This organization attracted widespread attention during the 1940's not only in the United States but in Canada and abroad.

Also during the 1940's articles by medical and science writers dealing with the idea that alcoholism is a disease began to appear in magazines and newspapers. The subject was occasionally discussed on radio programs. Social workers, public health nurses and members of the clergy who attended the Summer School of Alcohol Studies at Yale University brought the new concept back to their communities. After 1945 local committees on alcoholism, comprised of private citizens and business leaders as well as professional people came into being in an increasing number of American cities and towns and in many cases operated informational centers where people could discuss problems of alcoholism. These committees were affiliates of a voluntary organization, the National Committee for Education on Alcoholism (later the National Council on Alcoholism).

But the stigma attached to alcoholism died hard in the public mind. In 1948 when J.W. Riley of Rutgers University in a nationwide survey questioned a representative sample of men and women on their opinions on alcoholism, only 20 percent of those questioned regarded an alcoholic as a sick person. . . . Furthermore, 50 percent of those interviewed thought that alcoholics did not require treatment but could stop drinking if they wanted to.

Ten years later, Elmo Roper and Associates conducted another nationwide survey. . . . To the question "If you knew someone who habitually drank so much that it affected his job and his relations with people, would you say he is morally weak or would you say he is sick?" the distribution of answers was: morally weak, 35 percent; sick, 58 percent; no opinion, 7 percent. . . .

Over the years, the conception of alcoholism as a disease became the central point of community activities related to the problem of alcohol . . . until now in America one may speak of a majority acceptance of the illness conception of alcoholism. . . . In 1956, the American Medical Association formally accepted the concept of alcoholism as a disease, a move which marked a tremendous step toward national public acceptance of the idea.

In most respects, public attitudes about compulsive gambling may be said to be similar today to those about alcoholism 40 years ago. The public is largely unaware of the problem, and where compulsive gamblers are encountered, they are, for the most part, regarded with prejudice and hostility, viewed as moral weaklings and social outcasts. Newspapers, magazines and the broadcast media are just beginning to carry articles and programs on the subject. Organizations such as Gamblers Anonymous and the National Council on Compulsive Gambling are just starting to attract public attention. In only one major respect may the compulsive gamblers' cause today be ahead of the alcoholics' cause 40 years ago—the medical and psychiatric professions have quickly recognized pathological or compulsive gambling as a disease.

What effect this will have on public attitudes and whether it will stimulate the development of treatment services for compulsive gambling remains to be seen. But while public attitudes are changing and while treatment programs are being contemplated and planned, there are other, much more pressing needs.

The millions of compulsive gamblers, their families and friends need a reliable and authentic source of information, understanding and guidance so they can learn how to deal with this disorder and how to help themselves and each other. Parents who detect a tendency toward compulsive gambling in a child need information on ways to forestall it. Members of the press—newspapers, magazines and the broadcast media—need a source of scientifically based information so they can interpret this subject for the public and become a vehicle for education.

This book has been written to fulfill these needs. In its pages readers will find answers to their questions to the extent that medicine, psychiatry and wide-ranging experience with compulsive gamblers themselves is able to supply them.

CHAPTER TWO

The Compulsive Gamblers—
Who Are They?

WHO ARE THE COMPULSIVE GAMBLERS? WHAT SORT OF
people are they? What part of society do they come from?
Are they young? Old? Male? Female?

We can answer these questions; but only up to a point.
Most of the information that is available comes from the
study of compulsive gamblers who are under treatment and
others who attend meetings of Gamblers Anonymous,
supplemented by interviews with their friends and relatives.
We cannot say whether the things that have been learned
from these sources would apply to the population of compulsive gamblers as a whole. We won't know until there is
enough research to answer this question. But we can tell
you what we do know from the sources we have.

WHO ARE THEY?

There are some compulsive gamblers—fully addicted—
as young as 16 and, there are some as old as 70 who are still
in the grip of the obsession. But not many are to be found at
these extremes. The majority are between 20 and 50, and
the average is somewhere between 35 and 40. Since these

data represent the gambler in the late stages of addiction or already on the way to recovery, we would estimate that the average age for compulsive gamblers at all stages of addiction—early, middle and late—would be several years younger than 35.

Not all compulsive gamblers are men, but the men greatly outnumber the women. Some estimate the ratio at 5 to 1; other estimates go as high as 20 to 1. We think that 5 to 1 is about right; that is, for every female compulsive gambler, there are about 5 male compulsive gamblers.

Most compulsive gamblers have had at least a high school education; many have graduated from college, and quite a number have graduate degrees. A substantial number are businessmen and professionals, and among these there appears to be a disproportionately large number of bankers, brokers, attorneys and accountants.

Most compulsive gamblers are married and still living with their spouses. Others who are not are for the most part widowed or divorced. There are very few never-married people among them, except for some in the 16–25 age range. The majority have a background of traditional family life and history of steady, consistent achievement in school and work. Hardly any have had a problem with the law prior to the onset of their compulsive-gambling illness.

For reasons still unknown, Jews, who constitute only 3 percent of the U.S. population, constitute about 30 percent of compulsive gamblers.

Compulsive gamblers are to be found in all walks of life—working class, lower middle class, middle class and upper class. The majority, however, appear to be concentrated in the lower middle class and middle class.

THE "TYPICAL COMPULSIVE GAMBLER"

What does the "typical" compulsive gambler look like?

This question needs to be answered carefully. The compulsive gambler in the late stages of his addiction is drastically different from the compulsive gambler who is just beginning to succumb to gambling, and even more different from the compulsive gambler in the preaddictive stage. The process is one of metamorphosis.

In the metamorphosis of the compulsive gambler, what you see in the person's youth has only the slightest resemblance to what you will see when he has become fully addicted. Many of the characteristics are already there in youth, but not all are visible at the time. Most are still only potential, and it will take time and the right conditions to spark them into generation. Then they will emerge a few at a time in a stage-by-stage development, until the recognizable image of the fully addicted gambler takes form. The progression then continues until the final stages of desperation and defeat are reached.

Here is a picture of the compulsive gambler in the last stage of his metamorphosis, at the stage when he can no longer cope and is in desperate need of help. He is a man in his late thirties or early forties, without any financial resources, in debt between $10,000 to $100,000 (or more) to relatives, friends, banks, credit institutions and loan sharks. He is behind in his payment of his auto loan and house mortgage, or the car has already been repossessed and the house has already been sold. He is behind in his payments on utilities, or these may already have been turned off. He has no life, health or hospital insurance. His family's basic needs are being taken care of by relatives or welfare. He has lost his job because of absence, irresponsibility or theft, or, if he is a businessman, he has lost his business because he has bankrupted it or because of legal action taken by creditors.

His wife is threatening to divorce him. She complains about family deprivations, calls from creditors, his silence, withdrawal and violent mood swings. He is having discipline problems with the children. He is away from home frequently without explanation. Friends and relatives are alienated because of his unpaid debts to them and because they no longer like him or trust him. He is being threatened with or already undergoing legal action because of unpaid loans, IRS demands, forgery or theft.

He is sleeping poorly, eating irregularly, is indifferent to his physical needs and appearance and entirely unconcerned about survival. All he can think about is where he can get more money to gamble.

Even though he has come for help, either voluntarily or under pressure from his relatives, he has no insight into his problem. He does not recognize that he is sick, an addict. He knows he is in deep trouble, at the end of his rope in every respect, miserable and depressed, thinking about committing suicide, but he does not connect any of this with addictive gambling. His problem has nothing to do with gambling, he insists. He can stop anytime he wants to. What he needs is to help to get back on his feet, so he can gamble some more, recoup his losses, pay his debts and get himself straightened out.

Full of self-pity, he sees himself as a victim. He is entirely insensitive to the injury he has caused others and even expects sympathy from the very people he has harmed. Fortune has dealt him a terrible blow, he believes, unable to recognize that it is he who has done this to himself.

Dependent as he is on the help of a therapist, he is skeptical about how much good it is going to do him. His skepticism and mistrust extend to his fellow patients, whom he treats with disdain and whom he tries to manipulate to serve his own needs.

The composite is one of bewilderment, pessimism, intense anxiety, dejection—a desperate person at the point of going under, reaching out for something to cling to, but not knowing what that something should be and pushing away the hand that is stretched out to save him.

There you have the picture of the compulsive gambler in the last stages of his addiction. But what sort of person was he before that, when he was still young, when he was taking on responsibilities as an adult, before gambling started to be a problem?

Let us find out by tracking the metamorphosis of a typical compulsive gambler, from the first stage to the last.

The Metamorphosis of Louis H.

Louis was eight when his mother had to go to the hospital for a checkup that disclosed an incurable cancer. For two months she remained in the hospital and then was sent home to await her death. In the months that followed, the boy saw his mother transformed into a frightening, cadaverous stranger whose eyes stared out at him from a death mask, livid with pain and fear.

Three years later his father also died, and Louis went to live with a wealthy aunt, with whom his family had had little to do because of the difference in their economic and social standing. The home into which Louis moved was an elegant residence situated in an exclusive suburb of Minneapolis. Louis was given his own room and was well taken care of, materially. But the family never did open up to him to make him one of their own. The uncle spent little time at home and had little interest in his nephew. The aunt, a young matron with social aspirations and preoccupied with her golf and club activities, remained unresponsive to Louis's yearnings for the warmth and love of a mother. His three cousins became his friends but managed, subtly, to maintain the social barrier between them.

The uncle and aunt belonged to a circle of well-to-do business people and professionals who entertained each other, frequently, at their homes and at their country club. The conversation at these gatherings, Louis recalled, had mostly to do with money and possessions: a killing in the stock market, villas in France and yachts in the Aegean, the terribly high cost of sending a son to Yale Medical School and a daughter to Harvard Law School and the like. He heard them evaluating others in terms of their financial worth and saw them turn away from one of their group who had suffered a disastrous reverse in business and could no longer keep up with them socially. Money was everything. It was luxury, elegance, prestige, power.

Sunday afternoons, the group would gather at the country club for poker. Louis remembered sneaking away from his cousins, with whom he had been swimming or playing tennis, and coming to sit and watch the adults play cards. It was an intensely fascinating scene for him—the stylishly dressed men and women, the laughter and camaraderie, the champagne and trays of hors d'oeuvres, the clinking of glasses and the clicking of the chips, the amazing sums of money that were wagered and won and lost. He would come away from these games in a trance and dream dreams of his own . . . of wealth, luxury, power.

When Louis entered high school, two of his cousins were already there, members of an elite clique. A live wire and good sport, amiable, easygoing and attractive, Louis had no problem being accepted into this circle. Yet, as time went by, he found himself drifting away to another set of friends, students from less affluent families, interested more in baseball, "hanging out" and beer-drinking than in academic pursuits, tennis and posh parties. Louis was drawn to them also because of their interest in gambling, and much of their time together was spent playing poker, shooting craps and betting on the outcome of their sportscard wagers.

In his junior year, Louis took a weekend job caddying, which separated him even further from his cousins. In his senior year he became romantically involved with a young married woman at the country club, and when word of this affair got out, the alienation between Louis and his aunt's family was complete. The family couldn't wait for the school year to end so that Louis would be off on his own and out of the household. Louis could not wait to be free of the encumbrance of a family that had never accepted him and that held him under continual restraint.

But what was to become of Louis? What did he want to do with his life? His uncle offered to support him through college with a major in business administration, a career Louis himself had thought he might like. Or Louis could go to work—in another city, and preferably in another state—with financial support from his uncle until he could establish himself.

Louis had no difficulty in making the choice. The idea of four to six more years of schooling, confined within a college campus, bound to books, studying and exams, gave him nightmares. He was desperate for independence. Definitely, he was going to go to work.

Again the family conferred. Go to work? Fine. But where? And again Louis had the answer waiting. New York. He had been to New York in his sophomore year, on a vacation visit with the family, and had fallen in love with the city . . . the excitement, the hustle and bustle, the glitter of the theater district and the after-theater nightlife, lunching at the 21 Club, dining at The Pavillon. He wanted to work and live in New York.

Someone else might have had to struggle for months finding a respectable job in New York and getting settled. But in Louis's case it was simple. His uncle made one telephone call and Louis had a job in the office of a dress manufacturer in the garment district. Then the uncle made another telephone call and Louis had a studio apartment, rent guaranteed for six months, in a fashionable section on the upper East Side.

His aunt and uncle wondered why Louis was so ready to accept a job in an office where he would be confined to eight hours daily of humdrum administrative responsibilities. But Louis knew what he was doing. This was just going to be a stepping stone to something bigger and better. But exactly to what he did not know.

He was quickly drawn to the sales end of the business. He was allowed to attend meetings where the salesmen reported on their activities in the field: the lines that were selling the best, the amount of pressure from competitive lines, the likes and dislikes and personal foibles of particular buyers, the handsome commissions earned by the enterprising members of the sales force.

The impact was tremendous. Injections of adrenalin could not have pumped him up more. He asked to be allowed to accompany one of the salesmen on a trip so he could get the feel of what it was really like, so he could apply the things he would learn to the creation of new sales ideas. The sales manager listened to him tolerantly but unsympathetically, and told him he would get his chance when he was a little older and had been there a little longer. Louis agreed that was a reasonable decision and said he would be happy to wait. For the next two years, Louis applied himself to his office tasks, staying on for an hour or two after the rest of the office force had gone home, making an occasional suggestion for improvement in administrative procedures, ingratiating himself with his coworkers and superiors.

One of the owner's sons took a liking to Louis and

introduced him into his own circle of friends. Life outside of working hours became a round of parties, dances, skiing trips, visits to racetracks and card games, and casual love affairs with models, between-jobs actresses and airline stewardesses. Although he was not quite 20, Louis told his friends he was 24, a deceit he was able to carry off because of his mature appearance and the speed with which he acquired experience. Quickly, he became a favorite of the group and then one of its leaders. People liked him. He was outgoing. He was concerned and considerate. He was lively. He had a good sense of humor. He was free with his money. He was adventurous, constantly coming up with new and exciting ideas for the group's entertainment.

But, for all that, he never lost sight of his goal and the promise the sales manager had made him, and after he had been at the firm two years, he was sent out in the company of an older salesman to learn the ropes, and then by himself, to get some experience on his own.

The turn of events at that juncture, was, as Louis recalled it, "astounding." Never having expected to do any selling except in order to learn more about the business, Louis found that selling, of and by itself, was immensely exciting. He loved the personal interaction with the buyers and the challenge to his knowledge and skill, to his ability to persuade and win over an indifferent, skeptical or even hostile buyer. Equally astounding was the speed and alacrity with which he was able to make sales and the quantities of goods he sold. By the end of his first year of selling, he was already pushing hard at the heels of veteran salesmen who had been in the business for decades.

As upsetting as this was to these salesmen, their resentment was mixed with admiration, since Louis was able, through his own enterprise and studying the trade and business newspapers, to search out and develop opportunities to bring the firm's lines into markets they had never entered before.

The next nine years, as Louis recalled it, "went by like a flash." During that period, his fortunes skyrocketed, taking him from salesman to sales manager, from sales manager to general manager and finally to a full partnership at the age of 30.

Each move to the next higher level was made decisively and with confidence. Nowhere along the line of his climb had he encountered any major obstacles or problems, and he took it for granted he never would. Things seemed to fall right for him at every turn, and he accepted this as part of his natural destiny. So, when his firm found itself in the midst of an exploding market in the sports lines they were manufacturing, Louis felt that his good fortune, too, had been preordained for him. In the next two years, the firm's earnings climbed above the $4 million mark and Louis was able to put aside and invest close to three-quarters of a million dollars.

Then came the next move, a big one. Louis decided this was the time to go into business for himself. He had already established an enviable reputation in the business as an entrepreneur, and he knew he would not have any difficulty establishing his own firm as a leader in the industry.

Before his partners were even aware of what was happening, Louis had rented loft and office space, bought the machinery and other equipment, hired the designers, machine operators, cutters, salesmen and office staff. Then he made the jump, taking with him several of the lines he himself had created and several of the firm's major accounts. "I had no qualms about doing this," he recalled. "That's business. I owed them nothing. They owed me nothing. Everything I did was on the up-and-up. Sentiment is fine, but it's got no place in business. If my partners had had the opportunity, they'd have done the same thing to me."

It was not long after that that Louis made another big jump—from bachelorhood into marriage. It was a step he had not contemplated before. But there he was, in love with one of his models, and after a brief engagement they were married.

Two weeks aboard a chartered yacht, cruising in the Caribbean, stopping off for a night's dining and dancing and entertainment at one island and then another, dropping in at a casino for a few hours of gambling, made an idyllic, rapturous honeymoon for Louis and his bride, Lisa. The amount he won or lost at the casinos meant little to him, he recalled. "Five, ten, fifteen thousand. It was nothing. What I loved was the excitement, the glamor, the royal treatment we got. It was just another part of my boyhood dream coming true. A beautiful bride, an exotic setting, money to spend without limit, respect and admiration from everybody. . . ."

The next four years brought more good fortune to Louis—the birth of a son and a daughter, the purchase of a luxurious home in a New York suburb and a condominium in Palm Beach for the winter months. There were vacation trips to France, Greece, Israel and the Caribbean, and in many of these places Louis and Lisa were accompanied, at Louis's invitation and expense, by several of Lisa's relatives. Whenever, on their travels, there was a casino nearby, Louis would spend an occasional night gambling, staking Lisa's relatives to gambling money when they cared to come along. Although he loved to travel, Louis was always happy when a trip was over and he could return to his home and to his children to whom he was deeply devoted.

The dress business continued to flourish, and Louis, seeing a good opportunity to invest in Florida's booming real estate market, put more than $2 million into the construction of a condominium outside Fort Lauderdale, meanwhile watching his holdings appreciate handsomely in a rising stock market.

"What could have been more beautiful, what more could a man have wanted," Louis reminisced. "I had everything. A wife and children whom I adored, wealth, two beautiful homes, a thriving business, extensive investments. . . ."

The fifth year after he went into business, signs began to appear that the economy was headed for a decline. Business began to slow down and the stock market began to fall. While he was able to liquidate some of his less certain Wall Street holdings, there was nothing he could do about his Florida real estate investment. There he was locked in with no way to move. He realized, too late, that he had gone into condominium building in a market that was already glutted. He could not sell the individual units, nor could he sell the building. There just were no buyers, and in a few months his $2 million investment was wiped out.

Louis could not understand. Fortune had never failed him before. What was happening now? What had gone wrong? Had he lost his touch? Was his life going to turn around now and start to go downhill? It was then, he recalled, that his heavy gambling began. "I know I was shaken, frightened, but I can't say that I deliberately went out to gamble in order to get some reassurance or to get away from the pressure. But there must have been some connection, because that was when I really got into gambling."

Trips to Las Vegas and to casinos in the Caribbean became almost a weekly event. He began to bet heavily on football and hockey games, something he had never done before. Saturday afternoons he would be at the track.

And then something happened that I would have sworn would never happen. I began losing interest in Lisa, and I didn't have any time for the kids. Before, they were the biggest things in my life. Now my gambling was crowding them out.

We could have 50 people out on the terrace on a Sunday afternoon, at one of our big parties. Do you know where I would be? Upstairs in my room watching the football game, or listening on the radio for the results of other games or for the race results. Lisa's sister was giving a big party over at her home for their parents' twenty-fifth anniversary. I didn't go. I told her to tell them I was sick. I had to go to the track.

When Lisa would get upset about this, I wasn't even apologetic. I got nasty with her, and then we started quarreling not only about that but about everything. The children began to annoy me. I yelled at them and scolded them. I could feel I was losing them, but that didn't bother me.

And thus "the good years" ended and "the terrible years" began. What, specifically, went on in the next few

years, Louis could not recall. They were just a blur in his
memory, and every effort to dredge up the particulars
produced little more than vague recollections, snippets of
information, isolated incidents.

I can't remember when I started to lose control, to gamble
recklessly, to lose, to plunge. There was this one time in
Las Vegas. After an hour at the crap table, I was ahead
$100,000. I said to myself that now I was just going to bet
$10,000 a day. If I won the same way, each day, I would
come out with a fortune. But after I bet the first $10,000
and lost, I couldn't walk away from the table, so I bet the
next day's $10,000 and I lost that. Then I bet the following
day's $10,000 and I lost that, too, and another $20,000
besides. Then I won back $35,000 and quit for the night,
but the next night and the next I was back, and by the end
of the four-day junket I had lost the $100,000 and another
$25,000 besides.

But why, why when he had $100,000 didn't he quit?
Why did he have to continue playing? Why couldn't he just
pack it in and walk away?

Because, no matter how much I had, it was never enough.
Winning was the important thing. I had to keep on playing
so I could keep on winning. And the winning had to be
big. It had to be in the hundreds of thousands, in the
millions, a fortune, if possible.

Did he have anything special in mind that he wanted to
do with his "fortune?"

No, I just had to keep on gambling for more. There was
the action and the excitement that kept me juiced up, but
winning was the most important thing. Even when I started
to lose heavily, I convinced myself it was only an accident,
a fluke. I knew I couldn't lose. I was convinced my luck
would turn that night or the next after 'that, and that I
would be on top again. But I guess you know it didn't
happen that way. I lost control. I became reckless. I

plunged foolishly when I should have known better, when the odds were against me.

And once that started it was hell. I couldn't stop and say, "Quit. You've had enough. Pack it in. You've got your business, your investments, your property, your family." And that's when I lost concern for everything outside of gambling. I had to keep on gambling so I could recoup. The thought that I wouldn't have enough money with which to gamble the next day was horrible. I guess it is like a junkie in terror about not having enough money for the next day's fix.

It had taken me more than 10 years to build up a prosperous business and a luxurious lifestyle with all sorts of property and holdings. It took me less than a year to lose it all. It was a desperate time. One night during that year, I came home after losing $150,000 at Las Vegas. When I came upstairs, there was Lisa on the bedroom floor, half-conscious, the kids were in there crying. The housekeeper had gone home, and the kids didn't know what to do. Do you know what I was thinking? I was wishing Lisa would die so I could collect the $500,000 insurance.

Mustering the few fragments of sanity he still retained, Louis managed to get Lisa to the hospital after phoning his family doctor to meet them there.

When the doctor had finished examining Lisa, he came out to tell Louis that his wife was four months pregnant, that she was suffering from a rare internal disorder, that she was likely to lose the baby and that if the baby did survive to full term, the pregnancy could result in her death.

"I barely heard what he was saying. It didn't register with me. I was impatient about how long all this was taking. I wanted to get out to check with my bookie about some big games I had bet on."

When Lisa came home from the hospital two days later, the housekeeper let her in. Louis was at the track. Five months later, Lisa was taken to the hospital for delivery, her life hanging in the balance. Lisa's mother, father and sister were there. Louis was at the track. When Lisa came home,

10 days later, with the baby, Louis was at the track. All of Lisa's jewelry, worth more than $50,000, was gone. Louis had taken it and sold it.

The descent to disaster was precipitous. In the following three months Louis had bankrupted his business, had sold his Palm Beach condominium and had lost the $250,000 in proceeds from the sale, as well as $100,000 he had borrowed from banks.

Desperate, he flew to Florida where an uncle was living in retirement, hoping to get some money there.

My uncle refused to give me any money, told me that I was a horror, a monster, a disgrace. We had a terrible argument, and I was so out of my mind that I almost hit him—that old, sick man. In the middle of the argument, he grabbed his chest and started screaming. He was having a heart attack. I got him into the bed and called for an ambulance. Before the ambulance got there, he was dead. I checked his pulse, and I saw he had stopped breathing. His eyes were staring up at me so I pulled down his eyelids. Then I went through his wallet and pants pockets to see if he had any money.

SOME BASIC TRAITS

As we review the early years of Louis's metamorphosis, we can pick out certain basic personality traits that compulsive gamblers have in common in the years before they become addicted.

Friendly sociable, generous. Compulsive gamblers are friendly, sociable people. They love to go out in groups, adore parties and other social gatherings, join clubs and teams and committees, make friends wherever they go.

They present the typical picture of the extrovert: outgoing, cheerful, enthusiastic; spirited, with a good sense of humor; willing to go along with whatever other members of the group suggest, but ready to come up with their own suggestions when the group needs leadership and ideas.

They are extremely generous—sometimes to a fault.

They love to do things for other people, to help out when others need help. They share their possessions readily, and if they have more than they need they bestow their bounty freely on others.

Superior intelligence. Most compulsive gamblers have superior intelligence. This would account, in part, for the fact that so many are successful businessmen or professionals. But whether or not they go to college or move on to a business or profession, people refer to them as "clever," "sharp" or "shrewd." Put them to the task of working out a practical problem or throw them into a brand-new situation, and you'll see how quickly they come up with an answer, a solution, a way out. It has less to do with abstract reasoning than it does with "figuring out the angles," "getting the point," "seeing the pitfalls and the advantages." They seem, also, to have an uncanny ability to know what is going on in another person's mind, to anticipate what he is going to do and to plan their next move accordingly.

Already manifest in youth, this talent is put to use in working out deals and arrangements for material and social advantages. These youngsters manage, somehow, to devise strategies that will win them the friendship of adults and gain them access to places and activities from which other teenagers are excluded. While still in school they are scheming up money-making enterprises; later, in business, they are the innovative entrepreneurs.

Energetic, hardworking. Nature seems to have endowed these people with superabundant energy and limitless capacity for work and for physical and emotional endurance. Already evident in childhood, these traits persist through adolescence, are there when the addiction begins and seem to grow even stronger as the gambling addict whirls through the incredibly taxing course along which his addiction drives him. This energy wanes only in the very late stages of addiction.

As you listen to compulsive gamblers, either in a therapy session or in a group meeting, telling about their experiences in childhood, youth and early adult life, you get the impression that there isn't a single compulsive gambler who did not work evenings or weekends while attending high school or full-time while attending college, or who did not hold two jobs at a time in the course of his working life.

Here are some excerpts from comments recorded in the course of a single evening.

I worked at a warehouse after school every year that I attended high school. Weekends I caddied at the country club. My schoolwork did not suffer.

I was holding down two regular jobs. When I got through at the post office at 4:30, I'd rest a half hour, grab a bite and then go on to the aluminum plant to work on the assembly line from six to midnight.

My parents couldn't afford to send me to law school so I had to support myself and pay tuition. I went to law school days, on a regular program, and worked full-time as a copy editor on a newspaper in the evening.

When I was in the army and we were stationed in the States, I would moonlight at night off the base as a bartender. My CO knew it, but he liked me and he let me do it. I was able to send home money to my wife to save so I could go into business when I got out.

I taught economics in high school, a regular full-time job, then I would teach four nights a week at a junior college.

My practice consisted of real estate closings, and I operated without any partners. I kept six secretaries going at one time. They handled the papers and I supervised; I was also present at all the closings. My day started at four in the morning and I worked 14 hours a day.

Crave stimulation, excitement, change. No one can spend much time with a compulsive gambler without becoming aware of his restlessness and hyperactivity, his inability to settle down to a quiet task or pursuit requiring time and patience, the ease with which he is bored, his need to be constantly on the move, his need for change, stimulation and excitement.

Like the other traits we have discussed, this one doesn't emerge suddenly in adult life; it is already present in early childhood. Parents recall about these children that they would play with one toy, drop it, go on to another, become restless, ask to be picked up and held, wiggle around and ask to be let down, ask to go outside to play, come back a few minutes later and ask for something else. Parents recall getting complaints from teachers that these children created an atmosphere of tension and unrest in the classroom, talking in silent periods, unable to concentrate on reading or other quiet activities, happy only during recess when they were let out to play on the playground or when they were engaged in a game involving physical activity.

As teenagers they would be the first ones up in the morning, the first ones out of the house on their way to school, seldom waiting for brothers and sisters, taking their own independent course. You could never know what time they would be home from school. Efforts to regularize their behavior, to get them to settle down and conform were fruitless.

They would tend to become bored with the friends with whom they had been brought up and to seek out friends in other neighborhoods, older than themselves and engaged in more exciting, grown-up pursuits. While their peers were still riding bicycles, they were already riding motorcycles, or even driving their friends' cars, risking being caught driving without a license. They were experimenting with sex, alcohol, drugs and gambling long before their age peers, working and earning money to finance these activities.

Love challenge, risk, adventure. The essence of gambling is risk. For many people that is the reason *not* to gamble; they would rather hold on to what they've got or put it into something safe. For the person who becomes a compulsive gambler it is the other way around. It is the risk that attracts him—pitting himself against the odds, against chance, against the operators of the game—as well as the prize that awaits him if he should win: 10, 20, 100, 1,000 times the money he invested.

Risk, challenge, adventure—that is what these people thrive on long before they go into serious gambling. They are dating and making sexual conquests while others are still going through their first timid approaches. The opposite sex may be a little frightening to them at first, but that makes it even more exciting. Sports draw them like a magnet, not only because of the competition but also because of the challenge to their strength, skill and agility, and because of the stimulation and excitement in competitive situations. They love to put themselves on the line in win-lose situations. They are the daring ones, the innovators, the risk-takers in business and the professions.

A man tells about his brother, a surgeon, who became a compulsive gambler:

David was a top internist, a super diagnostician. He had a fantastic practice when he was only 32. Then he dumped it, gave it all up. It was too routine. He was bored with poking people and reading lab-test results. So he packed it in and started all over again, went into—you guessed it—heart surgery. Why? Here's what he said: "It's a challenge. Cutting into arteries and the heart is always a risky business. You're always dealing with life and death. I think of death as my personal enemy. I pit my skill, training, faith again death, and every time I save a patient's life, it's a personal victory against death."

Another man, a compulsive gambler himself and now the owner of a mortgage-finance company, tells how he had amassed a fortune in trading commodities, one of the riskiest and most speculative types of investment. And another tells about his plunge into high-tech industry, becoming a multimillionaire overnight, before being wiped out by his subsequent plunge into another high-risk business—gambling.

Whatever the occupation or the endeavor, the theme is always the same: the need for excitement and stimulation,

the response to challenge and risk—long before there are
any hints that gambling is going to be a problem.

Assertive, persuasive, confident.   In group situations where
joint action is required, you will generally find two kinds of
people—those who hold back and wait for others to make
the proposals and take the lead, and those who automatically take the initiative in proposing a course of action and then
assume the leadership in seeing the proposal through. The
compulsive gambler will be found in the latter group—
assertive, persuasive, with leadership qualities. His ideas
come quickly and he formulates them well; once he puts
them forward, he is generally able to persuade others that
this is the course they should follow. When it is time to
undertake the action, you will find him in the lead, the
others following behind. Others may hesitate to come forward for fear they will meet with disapproval. Not so the
compulsive gambler. He knows he's right, he knows he has
the answer, and so comes forward boldly. He fits into this
role naturally and confidently and enjoys the ego boost it
gives him.

Competitive.   To compete, to be on top, to win—there is
the key to the compulsive gambler's personality. Other
people may be satisfied to take their share of the honor, or
to gain some modicum of recognition or just to enjoy the
exhilaration, the fun and the sport of the game or the
enterprise. But not the compulsive gambler. For him the
important thing is winning, being better than anybody else,
being "Number One." As we listen to the testimony of
compulsive gamblers we realize that this drive is already
present in childhood and that it is exhibited thereafter in
every area of life.

I was already doing it when I was a little kid. I played
checkers with the other kids, my brother, my father. The
kids and my brother were easy. I could beat them all the
time. But beating my father—that was hard work, but I could
do it. That was one of the biggest pleasures of my child-

hood. I can even feel the excitement in my belly, right now, 30 years later.

I was wound up like a spring. I had to get into everything where there was a chance to complete—track, swimming, baseball. Part of it was just the excitement of competing, of matching myself up against the others and giving everything I had to beat them. But winning, that was the thing, to hear the crowd yell my name, hear the applause and the cheering. It was like drinking champagne.

I loved the girls, loved to date them and to take them to bed. I was a good-looking young fellow, and I spent a lot of money on them, so I could have whichever one I wanted. But I wouldn't be satisfied with that. I had to go after the ones who were already going out with somebody else. It was making a conquest, showing how good I was, showing I was better than the other guy.

Making money was very important. I loved to get the nice things of life for myself and my family—fancy cars, a big house, a fancy place at the lake, trips abroad. But having more luxurious, more expensive, more unusual things than my friends and neighbors—that was even more important. I had to be better than they, and in my crowd, money and possessions were what counted.

It didn't just stop with me. I carried it over to my kids. My three boys were all playing Little League baseball by the time they were seven. They had to. I made them. It was like a ritual. Every Saturday or whenever they got together for Little League ball, our family was out there, the whole clan, playing or rooting on the sidelines. And the kids knew they had to be the best or they would hear from the old man when they got home.

THE COMPOSITE PICTURE

Putting these traits together, here is the picture we get

of the compulsive gambler's personality in the years when he is growing up and carrying on life's normal pursuits.

He is a friendly, sociable fellow, cheerful and enthusiastic, generous and full of good will. He is clever, energetic, hardworking and he generally does successfully whatever he undertakes. In social, organizational and business situations, he is confident, assertive, persuasive; he moves spontaneously and naturally into the role of leadership. Restless, hyperactive and easily bored, he is in constant need of stimulation, excitement, change. Bland, predictable situations with an assured outcome don't interest him. He thrives on challenge, adventure, risk. The key to his personality is competitiveness. He needs to contend, to win, to be better than everybody else, to be Number One.

This, you have to admit, is quite an impressive personality portrait. If you were to remove this composite picture from its context, present it to a group of people randomly selected and ask them what sort of person this describes, they would probably say it describes the sort of person you would expect to find on leadership lists, on lists of the most successful. And they would be absolutely right. These are indeed the ingredients for success in our society.

If that is the case, why then do these people wind up instead as desperate, broken addicts?

It often happens that the image an individual projects is not his true personality; it may be a mask that hides an entirely different sort of person. It is only after you have had a chance to observe that person at close range and for a fairly long time that you may begin to see clues to what is hidden underneath. And so it is with the compulsive gambler. What the outsider sees is only part of the picture. Those who live with him at close range see another side of him. And there are certain aspects of the personality of the compulsive gambler that neither his intimates nor the compulsive gambler himself are able to see, certain traits, motives, drives, insecurities that are hidden from consciousness.

Take, for example, the traits of friendliness and generosity. We said earlier that compulsive gamblers are friendly, sociable people, cheerful, outgoing and enthusiastic.

But we learn from friends and relatives that this demeanor is not consistent, nor is it very stable. Even in his preaddiction years, they say, he was at times sullen, moody, irritable and withdrawn, and his dark moods were as intense as his bright ones. Also, one could never tell when the sunshine would give way to thunderclouds. A friend of a compulsive gambler gives this description:

You can be out with the gang or the family and everyone is having a good time, laughing, talking. And then somebody may say something or do something. Or it could be nothing at all—and boom! Good-bye, Dr. Jekyll. Hello, Mr. Hyde. The change takes place in a flash. He'll stop talking, stop smiling, clam up, walk away. And he'll stay that way the rest of the evening, moody, sulking. You try to cheer him up, get him out of it, but he won't talk. The next day he might be himself again, or he might not. Days might go by without his showing up or your hearing from him, and then there he is back again, the same nice guy you always knew.

Also, according to friends and relatives, there is a quality to the compulsive gambler's friendship that makes you wonder how deep it really goes. For all his geniality and amiability, they say, you can never really get to know him intimately. There is some part of himself he keeps private; he does not like to share his innermost thoughts and feelings with you and does not want you to share yours with him.

Furthermore—and this insight comes primarily from psychiatric study—hidden beneath the display of friendliness and sociability you will find a lonely, insecure person, one who feels that no one likes him, wants him or accepts him. To appease his loneliness he surrounds himself with people. To appease the feeling that he is not liked or wanted he goes out of his way to acquire as many friends as he can. One strategy he employs to achieve this is to portray himself as an outgoing, witty, charming person. Another is to be generous without restraint. When he treats the crowd to ice-cream sodas or beer, when he picks up the dinner tab at every opportunity, when he buys luxurious gifts for friends or relatives or pays their way on vacations, he is in effect saying, "Look how nice I am to you. In return I want you to be my friend, stay close to me, be loyal to me above others, like and admire me."

He does not understand the true meaning of affection. He does not realize that people like you, genuinely, not because you are witty, smart, appealing, generous or important—but rather because you are a decent person, caring, kind, attentive, because you have a genuine interest in them and not exclusively in yourself.

In other words, for all of his aggressive display, the prospective compulsive gambler is at bottom a shaky, insecure person. He uses the show of strength to cover up a feeling of weakness. In psychiatry we call this the law of compensation, and we see it demonstrated in all sorts of situations. A man goes into bodybuilding because he sees himself as puny and is afraid others may see him that way, too. Similarly, a soldier performs feats of heroism because he thinks he is, basically, a coward; he wants to prove he is not. Likewise, a person becomes a "health nut" because he has an irrational fear of sickness and death.

REEXAMINING THE "COMPETITIVENESS" TRAIT

The law of compensation applies also to the compulsive gambler's competitiveness.

Some people like to compete, for a prize, recognition, for a job or a position in an organization, for money or material gains. They are ambitious. They want to get ahead. They have to compete to do this, and this is something they enjoy.

The prospective compulsive gambler does not only *like* to compete, *he needs to compete*. That way, when he wins and comes out on top, he is able to say to himself, and to everyone else, "Look how important I am."

The reason he must prove he is important is that basically he feels unimportant and powerless. To feel unimportant means to feel inadequate, inferior, insignificant compared with others and to believe that others look down on you as a "nobody." To feel powerless means to feel you don't have the internal strength to control your own life, to make your own decisions, and that others can push and pull you around. It means also that you feel overwhelmed by life's problems and difficulties, that they are too much for you, and you cannot see how you are going to manage to cope with them.

Because that is the way he feels about himself, the compulsive gambler will go to every extreme in order to prove he is the opposite—important, masterful, strong. He becomes a workaholic, not necessarily because he loves work but because hard work means extra money and extra money means he can buy and display the things that society admires and values most: wealth, possessions, luxury, symbols of prestige. He strives to rise to the top in sports, work, his profession, politics, social standing, because then he can say to the world, "Look at me; I am important."

THE COMPOSITE PORTRAIT REVISED

Having reassessed a number of basic traits that characterize the compulsive gambler in the years prior to his addiction, we need to revise the composite portrait set forth earlier.

We can still say that he is, in general, a friendly, sociable, generous fellow, but we need to qualify that by adding that this demeanor is not consistent. He isn't always that way. He can be sullen, irritable and withdrawn. And he is given to sharp mood swings, from cheerful to sullen and back. His sociability and friendliness hide a feeling that he is not liked or approved, a fear that he will be rejected. His generosity is a way to win friends and keep them beholden to him.

Assertive though he may be, with powers of persuasion and leadership, this may very well be a facade covering an insecure, shaky ego.

No doubt he is devoted to hard work and long hours, but this commitment is motivated by a desperate need to acquire the material symbols of success and the recognition they will bring him. This, and his competitive drive, are fired by a need to erase an impoverished self-image—that of a person who is unimportant and powerless to deal with life's problems.

In sum, we see a lonely, insecure person with a shaky ego and low self-esteem, striving frenetically to

* overcome his loneliness;
* avoid rejection;
* acquire the possessions and position that will win him recognition and approval;
* demonstrate strength and power to prove to himself that he is not helpless.

What is so tragic about this is that in his relentless drive to prove himself, the compulsive gambler can become totally insensitive to the feelings and needs of others and change from a normally kind and considerate person into one who is arrogant, ruthless and cruel. Even more tragic is the fact that no matter how influential, important and powerful such a person becomes, no matter how much he is admired and acclaimed, it will never be enough for him. Applause, recognition and admiration may anesthetize for a while the gnawing feeling that he is inadequate, unimportant, helpless. But when the flush of conquest wears off and the attention of his admirers turns to someone or something else, his anguish reasserts itself full force and triggers, once again, the unending competitive drive to win acclaim.

Anxiety, Depression, Omnipotence

Three other traits need to be added to complete the personality portrait of the prospective compulsive gambler: the tendency to be overanxious, the tendency to be depressed and the feeling of omnipotence.

The tendency to be overanxious. Anxiety is a sense of apprehension that something terrible is going to happen. It can be a normal response: If a person knows there's a cutback coming in his plant, he becomes anxious; he may be one of those laid off. If a child comes down with a life-threatening contagious disease, neighboring parents become anxious; they're afraid their child will catch it, too. It is not normal, however, for a person to be beset with anxiety most of the time about such things as losing one's job, not measuring up, being rejected, contracting a fatal illness. This is abnormal, irrational.

At the time they come for treatment, compulsive gamblers show an extraordinary level of irrational anxiety. One would expect them to be anxious, with justification, about the terrible fix they are in. But, strangely enough, their anxiety does not have to do with the fact that they are terribly in debt, that the police may be after them, that their families have disowned them, that they have lost everything they ever owned. Somehow they manage to push those woes out of their minds. Instead, they are anxious, to a morbid degree, about being seriously ill and dying.

Although this may appear to be strange, it is, with a closer look, quite understandable. We learn from friends and relatives of compulsive gamblers that in the years when the gamblers were growing up, they were apt to be unusually anxious about such things as their appearance, their abilities, their standing with friends and their health. The anxiety was seldom expressed frankly, because that would have betrayed weakness and fear. It showed itself, instead, in silences, moodiness, fretfulness and irritability, and it was only through insistent questioning or through close observation that one could discover the anxiety that was at the bottom of this behavior. Also, it has been possible to dig up some case records of compulsive gamblers who had been treated in childhood or adolescence for an emotional problem, and several of these records show that excessive anxiety was one of the symptoms for which the patient was treated. The compulsive gambler's abnormal anxiety about death and dying, manifested during treatment, is, we believe, an intensified expression of the excessive anxiety he has carried all his life.

The tendency to become depressed. Complaints about being depressed also come up frequently in the course of treatment, and as you question the compulsive gambler further you learn that there had been a close connection between his gambling and his depression throughout his gambling career. You get that from such comments as these: "When I wasn't gambling, I felt lousy, depressed." "The most depressing thing that could happen was not to be able to get money to gamble." "I used to feel low, depressed a lot of the time, and the only thing that would get me out of it would be to go someplace and gamble." "Some people take anti-depressant pills. Some people drink when they're depressed. When I got depressed, I gambled."

The connection between gambling and depression is stressed in one of the few pieces of research on the subject of compulsive gambling. Here is an excerpt from the research report: "Gambling did seem to act as an antidepressant activity for many subjects who reported periods when their overall mood was very depressed except when they were gambling. Gambling was the only activity capable of energizing them and altering their mood."

Again, resorting to the records of friends and relatives and to case records of earlier psychiatric treatment, we learn that the tendency to be depressed was, along with anxiety, a basic part of the personality structure of the compulsive gambler in his youth and early adult life, even before his gambling had become addictive; this depression was manifested in sullenness, moodiness and withdrawal.

When we look further, in the next chapter, into the causes of compulsive gambling, we will see that the need to find relief from anxiety and depression can be a potent force that pushes some people into a gambling addiction.

Omnipotence: The "I Can't Lose" Feeling. A favorite children's story is about Aladdin and the Wonderful Lamp. That story, you will remember, has to do with a little boy who finds a magic lamp and discovers that when he rubs it a genie appears to do his bidding, bringing him untold riches and power. To the mind of a little child who has not yet learned to distinguish between reality and fantasy, everything that happens in that story is real. The child believes that the events of the story are true and that something like that could happen to him, too; he, too, might someday find a magic lamp or some other magic device that would make all his wishes come true.

But children grow up and recognize fairy stories for what they are, colorful creations of the imagination, and they give up the notion that it is possible for people to alter their lives by magic. But perhaps not entirely. Even as adults, most of us do hold on to the notion that some mysterious force we call luck or fortune can work for us at times and make things come out the way we want them to. But most of us regard this only as a fanciful notion not worthy of serious belief.

As you talk to the compulsive gambler, however, you get the impression that for him this sort of thinking is more than a fanciful notion, that he actually does believe that some mysterious force, some secret power he has, has been operating to make things come out right for him in school, in work, in love and in business, and that it is now working for him in gambling, directing him to pick the "right" horse or team or number, causing the dice or cards to fall the way he wants them to. It is a feeling of invincibility, of omnipotence, a feeling that he simply cannot lose.

This attitude can work as a powerful incentive to pursue a venture and to make it work. On the other hand, it can lead to a disregard of reality and induce a person to pursue unrealistic, unattainable goals and dreams.

CHAPTER THREE

The Roots of Compulsive Gambling

SEVERAL THEORIES HAVE BEEN PROPOSED TO EXPLAIN why people become compulsive gamblers.

One of the earliest of these, offered by Sigmund Freud, father of psychoanalysis, relates compulsive gambling to compulsive masturbation. Freud believed that even in infancy the child derives sexual satisfaction from the stimulation of various regions of the body, the so-called erogenous zones, including the lips, the mouth, the anal region and the genitals themselves. Whether children actually get sexual satisfaction, as we know it, from stimulation of these erogenous zones we will probably never know, since infants themselves cannot tell us and adult memory does not go back that far. However, we do know that children play with their genitals and that, from all appearances, they do derive pleasure from doing so—at least that they cry and put up a fuss when a parent attempts to interfere with this play.

At any rate, Freud theorized that little children get the same sort of pleasure from this masturbatory behavior that adolescents and adults do from mature forms of masturbation. The compulsive drive to gamble, Freud believed, is a transformation of the child's compulsive drive to masturbate. He saw several similarities in the two acts—the rising tension, the excitement and pleasure, the frenetic drivenness and the use of the hands. Freud also believed that the compulsion to gamble is an outlet for the unconscious guilt the individual felt in early childhood because of his desire to replace his father as his mother's mate and lover.

Another psychoanalyst, Wilhelm Stekel, offered the hypothesis that gambling is a form of childhood play. He saw the compulsive gambler as an adult who is frightened of adult responsibility, thinks he is incapable of dealing with it and flees from it by regressing into the equivalent of childhood fantasy and play—gambling.

Ernest Simmel, also of the psychoanalytic school, described the compulsive gambler as a person who feels himself to be deprived, a person who feels that he has been denied parental love and attention and the other good things of life. This feeling of deprivation is manifested in an impatient hunger for pleasure and gratification. According to this view, the pleasurable excitement of gambling and the anticipation of being showered with money and luxuries dull the edge of the hunger and offer the promise to satisfy it entirely. However, like all neurotic yearnings, this hunger can never be satisfied or placated. No matter what the tormented individual does to appease them, they continue to reassert themselves and to demand gratification. And so, according to this hypothesis, it does not matter how much the compulsive gambler gambles, nor how much or how often he wins; the neurotic hunger for gratification, affection, pleasure persists and compels him to continue to gamble, and never allows him to stop.

A theory that has won great favor among the followers of the psychoanalytic school is the one offered by Edmund Bergler. Many interpret Bergler's theory in a rather simplistic fashion, namely, that the compulsive gambler is a person with an unconscious wish to lose, a masochist who enjoys being punished. Although this interpretation represents the essence of Bergler's theory, there is more to it than that.

According to Bergler all children are endowed with a primitive feeling of omnipotence. The infant thinks he is the center of the universe and that when things happen in his surroundings it is he who is making them happen. His every whimper brings the reassuring response of the mother, the breast, a bottle, a caress. Every gurgle and coo bring demonstrations of affection and pleasure from his parents and other adults. However, this blissful state, in which he commands the world, does not last. There comes a time when the mother stops responding to every whimper and gurgle. She starts imposing limits indicating that "You can't have the breast or the bottle every time you make a sound. . . . You can't keep on demanding attention. . . . You can't keep on wetting and soiling. You've got to learn to control yourself." His response to these restraints, this end of his omnipotence, is angry screaming fits, which in turn bring scolding and more restraints, which arouse even greater resentment and rage.

As a result, the theory goes, the child grows to hate his mother and wants to see her destroyed. But then he becomes frightened of these wishes, feels guilty and expects to be punished; in fact, he *wants* to be punished so he can be relieved of his guilt. When the compulsive gambler gambles, so the theory holds, he is experiencing the exultation of rebellion against the parents, the people who turned away from him, took away their love, robbed him of his omnipotence. When he gambles and loses he is experiencing the pain of punishment for his transgression against his parents. He needs, and relishes, this pain, because it is the only thing that brings him relief from his guilt. Therefore, he gambles not to win, but to lose, so he can be relieved of his unconscious guilt. Also, to extend this theory just a bit further, the infant believes that if he suffers enough, he will win back the blissful state that first existed between himself and his parents, before he was "expelled from Paradise." So the compulsive gambler, reenacting the drama of infancy, wants to continue to lose and to suffer, and in that way regain his place in "Paradise," the unconditional, ever-flowing love of his mother and father of infancy.

We relate these theories—in simplified form to be

sure—so the reader may know and evaluate them. We do not propose to analyze them or to support or refute them. Instead, we want to offer our own.

OUR OWN EXPLANATION

Our explanation of compulsive gambling and its causes has to do with three basic emotional needs of every human being—the need for

- affection and approval—to be wanted and liked;
- recognition—to be regarded as a person of worth;
- confidence in one's ability to deal effectively with life's problems and to garner its rewards.

When these needs are fulfilled, a person can be happy, creative, effective. He can truly give of himself to others through love, concern, emotional support and mutual interdependence.

If these needs are not fulfilled, or only scantily or inconsistently, a person will struggle to attain them, devising every strategy of which he is capable, strategies that may carry him to heights of achievement, positions of importance, fame and acclaim—or to a life of fantasy, escape and illusion.

Bert J.

The arrest of Bert J. for embezzling funds from the bank where he held the post of executive vice president sent shock waves through his town in Minnesota. People wouldn't believe it even when they read it in the local newspapers. "A model citizen." "A pillar of our church." "One of the most respected and admired leaders of this community." "It's a mistake; they're going to find out it was somebody else who did it."

But it wasn't anybody else. Bert had confessed. In fact, he had surrendered voluntarily. The bank examiners admitted that it might have been months before he was detected, so cleverly had he covered up his malfeasance.

The shock was justified. Bert J.—36 at the time—had

been everything his neighbors in this Plains town had said: a pillar of society, an admired leader, a sober, conservative man whose "wildest" social activities consisted of golf, dances and dinners at the club or an innocent bit of cutting up at Rotary conventions. He, his wife, their two girls and one boy were a family people pointed to when they needed a model of good, decent, happy family life.

Dishonesty, and especially something as serious as larceny, was so alien to the image people had of Bert J. as to be inconceivable. And gambling—the reason for his embezzlement of bank funds—was even more improbable. It was just too wild, too far out.

When the story did come out in all its details and it became known that Bert had been gambling recklessly for more than four years, and that he had stolen from the bank to pay gambling debts and to gamble more, there were some who shook their heads knowingly and allowed that they "had suspected something all along." But they were just making it up. Bert had kept his gambling a secret—up to five or six months before the arrest and exposure—even from his wife, inventing stories about bank meetings, out-of-town conferences, sessions with bank auditors to explain his evenings and weekends away from home. All his bets were placed through a discreet bookmaker handling an exclusive clientele. He did his out-of-town gambling at Reno, instead of Las Vegas, and at out-of-the-way casinos not likely to be frequented by friends and acquaintances.

Bert suffered terribly when all this happened. He couldn't face his wife; he didn't know how to explain it to her. And the bewilderment and fright of his children were more than he could bear. He was relieved, in fact—at least for the time—when he was sent to prison, where he would be removed from contact with anybody he knew.

It was his father who caused him the greatest hurt, refusing to come to see Bert or even to telephone or write to him. He could see his father, a minister, gray-haired and tall, stern and solemn, shaking his head sadly, as if to say, "No, I never did expect you to measure up—but not this, not this!"

That was the way it had always been, from Bert's

childhood on. A stern, demanding father, letting his children know that he not only expected them to be scrupulously virtuous, but also superior in intellect and scholastic achievement.

Like all other teenagers in his group, Bert would engage in the sexual exploration and play normal to that age and culture, but after each exciting contact, he would suffer the guilt of having done "something wrong" and the fear that his father would find out.

As a youth, Bert suffered also because of his height. At the age of 17 he had attained his full growth of five feet five inches, several inches below the average height of his group and a full foot shorter than his father. Fearful that the girls in his group would reject him, he satisfied his sexual hungers by secret visits to a prostitute, unattractive and much older than he, coming away from each encounter full of shame and self-loathing.

In high school, Bert stood in the top 10 percent of his class, his marks running in the high eighties to low nineties. But that was never enough. His father would praise him for doing well, but never let him think that it was good enough, that he should be contented with what he had accomplished. The boy was left with the feeling that he had let his father down and that no matter how hard he tried or how much he achieved, he could never fulfill his father's perfectionist expectations. Bert's most painful memory—one that never left him, that kept on plaguing him, even as he sat in his prison cell—was that of an incident that had occurred the day of his graduation from high school. On their return from the commencement exercises, his father had asked Bert to wait downstairs while he went upstairs to get something. A few minutes later the father came down, holding in his hand his own Phi Beta Kappa key. "Here," he said to Bert. "Take it. And when you go away to college and are elected to Phi Beta Kappa, you can wear this key as a family tradition."

Bert tried, oh, how he did try, to live up to his father's expectations, studying when his classmates were goofing off, taking extra courses for honors credits. And he did well, but always just short of those expectations. Often he would fume, internally, cursing his father for the burden he had imposed on himself, that now it was he who was setting expectations for himself that he would never be able to meet.

Majoring in economics, he dreamed of becoming an international financier, attending meetings of world bankers in Geneva, Paris and other foreign capitals. When his path led no further than back to his hometown in Minnesota and to an officership in a small midwestern bank instead of to the rarified atmosphere of international banking, he was disappointed, frustrated, bitter and depressed.

People in his town looked up to him, admired him, envied him, saw him as a model of success. But this was not the way Bert saw himself. His own private perception of himself—one he shared with no one—was that of an inconsequential person of few achievements, unfulfilled, unrecognized, a failure. This feeling ate at him constantly, pervading his thoughts during the day, invading his dreams at night.

Others might have sought relief from this unremitting mental torture in drinking or debauchery. Bert might have, too, except that the few times he had experimented with drinking it had failed to give him the "high," the relaxation and relief that most of his friends had experienced. Alcohol just did not do anything for him. But gambling did. This he found out shortly after his graduation from college, when he and some friends took a vacation in the south of France and drove to Monte Carlo.

This was not international banking, to be sure, but it was international glamor . . . the fabled casino . . . the gaming rooms extravagantly decorated with 19th-century paintings . . . the suave, silent croupiers . . . the *salles privées,* where the tables were surrounded by elegantly dressed men and women and where one could catch a glimpse of a princess or duke, or a well-known member of New York's jet set . . . the roulette, crap, chemin de fer and baccarat tables in these salons where ordinary bets were in the $2,500 range and where a baccarat hand could be worth $50,000 or more.

Here was glamor, here was excitement, here was royalty and wealth, here was a dream world, a world of fantasy and illusion. Here, circulating among these people in these surroundings, one could imagine oneself to be one of them—significant, important, powerful. And playing among them would be even more exciting, more intoxicating, heightening the illusion that this is where one belonged, that this should be part of one's life, that the having and the betting and winning of large sums of money was the magic medium by which one could escape from the dross of ordinary life and ordinary people.

Although the return to real life in Minnesota after the vacation quickly dimmed the memory of Monte Carlo, the fateful impact had been made. A craving had been initiated for the relief, escape and illusion that the visit to Monte Carlo had given him. From then on, although Monte Carlo itself could never be duplicated, Bert sought to relive the experience in casinos in the United States and the Caribbean. In time, gambling itself, regardless of the setting in which it was done, had generated a craving of its own. The gambling had become compulsive, pulling him into a cycle that brought him little pleasure and great pain, but from which he found it impossible to escape.

Many things go into the making of a person, shaping his personality, motivating him, giving him goals and direction: heredity, the standards and values of his culture, the aspirations and demands of parents and the way in which the mother and father relate to the child—the last being probably the most potent influence of all.

Bert's father was a stern, inflexible man who set high standards for himself and high expectations for his children. Rigid, moralistic and self-righteous in his attitudes toward pleasure and play, he imposed severe restrictions on his children. Bert could never be pure enough for his father or accomplish enough to suit his father's perfectionist standards. As hard as Bert tried, he always fell short, never being able to win from his father that for which every son yearns—approval, acceptance, recognition, the pat on the back, the squeeze of the arm, the grin that indicates,

"You're all right. I really think you're great. I really like you, and I'm glad you are my son."

A child treated in this fashion begins to see himself as his father sees him, as not quite having "what it takes" to be a success or to "amount to something"; the image rankles and must be effaced. Child, youth and adult, he spurs himself on to ever greater efforts, not enjoying what he is doing, frustrated and resentful, feeling that no matter how much more he tries, it is just going to be no use. Yet, he must keep on driving and driving, to meet his father's expectations, which he has incorporated as his own.

Life is grueling, unfulfilling, pleasureless, depressing. He must find some relief and escape, some way of bolstering his low self-esteem and improving his poor self-image, his feeling that he is unwanted, unimportant, helpless. He may find it in alcohol, or in drugs. Or he may find it in gambling, as did Bert.

Among compulsive gamblers, Bert's case is not unique. When we look back into the lives of gambling addicts, we find a distinct group who went through very much the same thing that Bert did, unable, ever, to satisfy the expectations of a perfectionist, rigid, moralistic father; developing, as a result of this, a view of themselves as inadequate people for whom success and approval is always out of reach; striving throughout life to find success and validation; becoming competitive work slaves, guilt ridden, anxious and depressed; winding up ultimately with the illusory fulfillments of gambling.

Angelo T.

Angelo T. is 63. He is counting the days since he placed his last bet, exactly eight weeks and three days. Each day, he says, is agony. He is restless, dejected, morose.

Thirty-eight years of my life gone to hell, wasted, and for what? I still owe $48,000, and I'll never be able to pay it. My poor wife—she's 60—still has to keep on working in order to pay off my debts. I've got a little pension, but we need that to live on, and we're collecting a little rent from the house she made me buy. Thank God she put it in her name and never let me touch it.

All I've ever given her is worries, aggravation, torture . . . 38 years of gambling and 38 years of misery from the first day she was fool enough to marry me. Not a single month of happiness. All she ever wanted was to live a quiet life, enjoy her family, her relatives, her friends. She never asked me for anything. She wouldn't touch a nickel from my gambling. I'll never understand why she stuck with me; maybe it was our religion; maybe it was the children.

I've figured it out, and in these 38 years of gambling, I've lost over a million dollars. I've paid more than $225,000 in interest on loans I made. Last year alone, the interest was $8,600. What I could have done with that money! What I could have done with my life! What a happy life I could have made for my wife and two kids!

But I tell you, even right now, with all this misery I'm telling you about, if you were to put $500 in my hands, and if I would let myself do it, do you know where I would be? I'd take off for the track like a shot. I'd forget all about the misery and suffering in a minute and I'd be happy. That doesn't make sense, does it? You think I'm crazy. Well, that's what it is, real insanity. It's like taking drugs. They put you through hell, but you've got to have them; it's the only time that you're really happy.

Angelo grew up in a working-class district of a large industrial city in the East, the youngest of seven children born to an immigrant couple. Theirs was a neighborhood of tenements, except for a block or two of old frame houses owned by people who had been able to put aside enough from their wages as day laborers and factory workers to realize their life's dream—a house of their own and a little piece of ground where they could grow flowers and vegetables.

Angelo's family lived in one half of a two-family house; the other half was occupied by a rent-paying tenant.

The house had been purchased with part of a settlement the father received after his leg had been crushed on the job by an iron girder. Unable to work any longer, the father spent his days sitting on a bench in front of his house or watching the men play ball in the park or play cards in a store-front social club. Embittered and ashamed, he had to endure the sarcastic comments of some of his neighbors and acquaintances about "men who are not men any longer" and whose wives had to go out to work to support the family, as indeed Angelo's mother did have to do, taking a job as a sewing-machine operator in a small dress factory in the neighborhood.

Angelo was 10 when his father was injured and his mother had to go to work. Taking care of Angelo and the other young children during the day became the task of older sisters and a brother who were still living at home. The oldest child, a girl of 20, was married, and the next oldest, a boy, was going to school at an out-of-state Catholic college, supported by a scholarship from a civic organization.

Even before the injury, Angelo's father had had little time for the children, little to give them in the way of affection. Life's burdens were too heavy. The dream of "a happy life in the new country" had turned into a bitter struggle to keep his family alive during the Depression, and there were many times when he yearned for the little stone home on the hillside where he had grown up, even with the hunger and deprivation, even with the beatings from his father, an impoverished peasant laboring to eke out a living from the arid soil.

Defeated by life and embittered, like his father before him, Angelo's father let out his frustration and anger in ugly quarrels with his wife and scoldings to the children. At times when he could no longer contain his misery, he would lash out, physically, at his wife and at the older children, eating himself up with remorse when his rage was spent. After the injury to his leg and the beginning of his enforced idleness, the father's angry explosions were replaced by sullenness and withdrawal. His emotional alienation from the family was complete. He lived among them a silent, scowling shadow; he paid little attention to them and they paid little attention to him.

With nothing to which he could attach himself at home, Angelo sought his supportive ties on the outside and found them in a neighborhood gang of boys his own age and in a group of older boys, 17, 18 and 19, who hung out at a poolroom. Angelo was too young to be the friend of these older boys, but they liked him and let him hang around, sending him out on errands and throwing him a quarter or half-dollar for a tip. There, Angelo learned not only about gambling and bookies, but also about crime.

One day, the older boys, in what they thought would be a great joke, asked Angelo—then 14—if he would like to come along with them. He had been a "real good kid" and they would like to give him a radio. Delighted, Angelo said yes. But once in the car and on the way, he became suspicious when he noticed the boys whispering to each other, looking at him and laughing. His suspicion turned to fright as he realized that they were not driving through the lighted, busy part of town where the stores were located, but through a dark and deserted warehouse section. When the car stopped in front of a warehouse and one of the boys took a crowbar from under the car seat, Angelo realized he was going to be an unwilling participant in a break-in. Terrified, he huddled in the back of the automobile while the others went about the business of breaking in. In about 10 minutes they came out, each carrying several cartons; then they went back and came out with several more. On the way home, one of the boys lighted a cigarette and Angelo was able to read the lettering on the boxes: "Acme Radio Company."

From then on, the boy was wary about getting into anything criminal and found other, less dangerous things to do that still were stimulating and exciting and had an element of risk. His gang, boys of his own age, would get into street fights with gangs from an adjacent neighborhood. They would break into the storeroom in school and make a shambles of the school supplies. They would drink beer and travel to another part of the city, where they would harrass and assault students at an art school. They would stay out late at night trying to pick up $5 and $10 tips running errands for known gangsters. They would pilfer small items from local stationery and food stores and threaten the store owners with the Mafia if they should call the police. They would find out where big crap games were taking place and, pooling the money, would gamble.

When word of Angelo's escapades got back to his mother, she screamed at him, called him "a worthless bum." "Why," she implored, "can't you be like Anthony [Angelo's oldest brother] and make something of yourself? Why can't you be like your cousins [pharmacists and owners of a drug store]? All you can do is make trouble for me." She threatened to throw him out of the house but never carried out her threats. She wept, pleaded with him, invoked the intervention of the saints, but nothing helped. Angelo went on his way doing what he wanted to do, managing to keep from being caught.

When Angelo was 16, his father died of a stroke, and with that the last remaining restraint on Angelo was gone. His oldest brother, who had become an attorney and then married, was too far removed, physically and emotionally, to exert any influence on the boy, even if he had wanted to. Surprisingly, the boy's schoolwork did not suffer. In fact, he was one of the better students at the commercial high school he attended.

Angelo's gambling started when he was 12, but it was an innocent sort of gambling known to every boy who grew up in a working-class section in the East in those days—pitching pennies, penny rummy, penny poker, nickel craps. It was entertainment, nothing more. But by the time he was 16, gambling had become for Angelo and his friends their major recreational activity.

There were the football cards we could buy in high school. You bet a dollar and you could earn a hundred. There were the crap games on the streets and in the alleys in the market [an outdoor wholesale food market, sprawled out over several streets]. All the guys knew where they were. Or you could go to the pool parlor or the bowling alleys and place a bet on anything—ball games, horses, the numbers. Or you could go to the club house or the taverns where the older guys hung out and play rummy, poker, shoot craps . . . whatever you wanted and as much as you wanted to bet.

After school and on evenings, Angelo and his friends would move from one gambling site to another, betting quarters, half-dollars, dollars, as much as they could afford from their part-time jobs or from what their older brothers and parents would give them. "We would pool our money to look like big shots and bet maybe $25, $30. You could bet as little as that, but the guys who had the dough were betting $100, $500, $1,000.

When he graduated from high school in 1938, Angelo went to work on a factory production line, earning $25 a week, a handsome wage in those days. "They were paying only $16 or $17, but I was a hustler and I got my line to hustle and we made the top pay, more than anyone else. I gave my mother $10 for board and with the rest I went out and gambled."

Now his gambling arena expanded. In addition to the neighborhood games, there were the professional gambling houses on the outskirts of the city, and there were the baseball games.

We had a real good Triple-A league team there, and real gamblers would go to the game and sit behind third base, and we'd bet on anything—a hit, a walk, a strikeout, a run.

That's all we did—gamble—and I loved it; it was wonderful. I was the happiest man in the world. I always loved to win, but it wasn't that. It was the excitement. I loved the excitement, the betting, the winning, the losing. After the game or wherever we were gambling, we would go out to drink and eat, or to where there was entertainment. We would drive in to New York and go to Broadway. We'd go out with women and have dinner, drink wine and dance. You could go out with a few guys and go to a tavern, and sit and talk and play cards all night long. If you didn't have the money, you sat and watched. If you lost, you didn't go home and brood. The guy who won would carry you. Next time you would carry him. It was a great life.

In 1941, Angelo was drafted into the army and sent overseas. When he was not in active combat, all he would do would be to gamble. "I would gamble two, three days in a row . . . cards, dice . . . without sleep. I would take pills to stay awake. I could bet, win, lose $1,000, $2,000, $5,000. That was the way it went, day in and day out. I won and lost thousands, but I stayed even.

Angelo was discharged in 1945, at the age of 25, and that, he averred, "was when my misery began."

My girlfriend had been waiting for me, and as soon as I got out we made plans to get married. I had $12,000 left over from my gambling in the army, and we made plans for a real big wedding. Inside of three weeks it was all gone. Lucky for me we had to call off the wedding because of a death in her family. So we got married in a small, private wedding and they gave us money presents just the same, and she collected about $3,000. In a week that was gone, too; I had gambled it away. Now my wife knew what she had gotten into and she cursed the day we were married. But she couldn't do anything. We're Catholic and she didn't want the family to know.

From that time on, for the next 38 years, gambling was my entire life. Nothing else was important . . . not my wife, not my kids, my job, my brothers and sisters . . . nothing, only gambling. There wasn't a day I didn't gamble, even Thanksgiving, Sundays, Christmas, my kids' birthdays, my wedding anniversaries, Easter, Good Friday—it was a craze that got hold of me and wouldn't let go.

When I got out of the service, a cousin got me a job in a city department where I was boss and handed out construction and repair jobs to contractors of different kinds. I got a real good salary, but every dollar went into gambling. My wife worked, and she made me buy a house where we rented out two apartments. Her wages and the rent kept the family in food and clothing and paid the bills. She never saw a nickel of my salary, not once in 38 years. I was betting big then, and losing big, $5,000, $10,000, $15,000. I would borrow from the banks and the loan companies and the Shylocks. I got desperate because I owed so much, so I started to take kickbacks from the contractors. I made as much as $50,000 a year that way . . . but I lost every bit of it gambling, year after year after year.

You can't imagine what a torture that was, what a misery. When I lost I was depressed. When you owed money your mind wasn't on anything else. How am I going to get money to pay my debts? How am I going to maneuver? What move do I make? Where can I borrow? I would go around talking to myself, screaming at my wife and kids. I couldn't sleep. I would stay awake, worrying. I used to sit by the lake and just sit . . . not knowing what to do. I took my son's money out of the bank. I borrowed on our insurance. I couldn't face anybody. I went to get a loan putting a second mortgage on my house, but I couldn't do it without my wife's signature, and I knew she would curse me if I asked her. So I got this woman I knew, and paid her a hundred bucks and got her to come to the bank with me and say she was my wife. I had stolen my wife's driver's license and identification cards, and this woman showed them and forged my wife's signature. I even sank so low as to borrow a few hundred bucks from my two nieces. If my wife knew about it, she would have put a knife in me. But my nieces kept it from her. I even went to work at night . . . two jobs. I held down two jobs for five years so I could get money to pay my debts and gamble . . . from 8 to 4:50 on one job; from 6:00 to midnight on the other, gambling ate up both salaries, in addition to the kickbacks. . . .

And so it went on until 1981, when Angelo retired.

Then suddenly, something came over me. I don't know what it was. I decided I had had enough. I figured I could live comfortably for the rest of my life. For over a year I gave it up. I would place small bets every day, but not the big bets any longer. I got into playing the stock market, and in two years I had over $160,000 in securities. My wife was able to put away $40,000 in CDs from her work . . . and then I started betting heavy again. What's the use of telling you all the details. It was the same old story. I sold my stocks—all of them—and lost the $160,000. I forged my wife's name on her CDs and cashed them and lost the $40,000. I stole her medical reimbursement checks and forged them and cashed them in. Finally, I was in debt $48,000; that was about two and a half months ago. I just couldn't take it any longer. I knew there was no way I could pay back that money. I even lost my heart for gambling. So I went to Gamblers Anonymous, and I haven't placed a bet in exactly eight weeks and three days.

But I tell you, even right now, if you were to put $500 into my hands. . . .

THE MAKING OF A SELF-IMAGE

"Why?" Angelo's mother had screamed at him. "Why can't you be like your cousins?"

Why, indeed?

They were the sons of a food merchant who had emigrated to the United States and who had, with the help of a friend, opened a vegetable store. For several generations the tradition in that family had been that of small businessmen and tradesmen—thrifty, hardworking, ambitious, with an eye always to improving their lot. Poverty or want were unknown to the children who had grown up in the family during the previous four generations. In their homes there was never an air of uncertainty about what tomorrow or next week or next year might bring. Things were good. Everyone expected them to be good and to continue that way. The men in the family were proud of themselves, and they were admired by their wives and children. Pride, confidence and a feeling of worth were handed down from generation to generation as a family heritage. In this atmosphere, Angelo's cousins had no difficulty shaping a good self-image and strong self-esteem. They absorbed the sense of worth and pride radiated by their parents. They lived within sensible rules laid down by their parents and learned that when you lived this way, life could be predictable. They were cherished by their parents and so they cherished themselves. With all this assurance, they had no need to prove themselves through spurious excesses of work, hostile competition and arrogant demonstrations of importance and power, or to create fictitious, illusory self-images through the medium of alcohol, drugs or gambling.

Angelo, by contrast, grew up in an atmosphere of misery and despair. The family's poverty would not have been enough, by itself, to undermine his sense of self-worth. There are poor families in which the children feel confident and proud because their parents feel confident and proud, because the parents do not take their misfortune as proof that they themselves are worthless. Angelo's father was already defeated when he himself was a child, beaten and rejected by his father, the scapegoat (together with his brothers and sisters) for his own father's feeling of failure and defeat. This heritage he handed down to Angelo, through beatings, ridicule, rejection, emotional neglect. He was unable to project, because he himself did not have it, the confidence and pride that his son could have emulated and incorporated into his own personality. What Angelo saw was a beaten man, his masculinity in question because he was unable to earn a living for his family; it was this, rather than strength, confidence and pride that the boy incorporated into his own personality.

Some of this corrosive influence might have been ameliorated had Angelo's father been able to show the boy love and concern and through this made him feel he was liked, wanted, approved, a worthwhile person. But how could he, when he was so emotionally depleted himself?

Had there been some opportunity for Angelo, as there had been for his oldest brother, to escape from this morass and to establish his self-worth through some worthwhile, creative accomplishments, this, too, might have altered the outcome. But for Angelo, there was no way out. Still, he had to survive. He had to do the best he could with what he had, to make the most he could out of his circumstances. Lacking a true sense of self-worth, self-respect, importance and masculine assertiveness, he sought to create it in two

ways: first by his antisocial, almost-criminal pranks, challenging the authorities, showing what a tough, brave, "macho"
man he really was; and second by gambling. How big and
manly he felt, hanging around the "real" big gamblers, the
pros and the hoodlums, all older than he, aping their adult
ways, making a display of "big-time" betting. Gambling
made him feel, grown-up, adult. Gambling made him feel
important. Gambling made him feel powerful.

He didn't have to struggle through years of hard work
and patient waiting to achieve this. It was there for him
instantly, without delay, without effort. All he needed was
some money and a place to gamble, and, like magic, there it
was—an illusion of course, but people can live by illusions,
allowing themselves to believe what they want to believe,
ignoring the unpleasant and painful aspects of reality.

And there was the fun, the excitement, the pleasure of
this life. Going out with the gang. Drinking, dining, wom-
en. Sitting around, playing cards all night, talking, winning,
spending, enjoying. Who even had time to think about the
reality of growing up, about getting a job so he could make
a good wage, get married, start a family, make a home for
his family, live a normal life like the others. Life was too
much fun, too exciting for him to be bothered with that.

Then, just about the time he had reached the age when
such plans and decisions had to be made, the army snatched
him up and sent him into another life that spared him the
need to make his own decisions, to assume responsibility for
himself. The army took care of all that, made all the
decisions for him.

On his return from the army, Angelo was faced with
the reality of civilian life. He got a job, was married and
made plans to raise a family. But it was much too late for
any important changes to take place inside himself. He had
chosen his lifestyle long before, and the pattern was fixed
and solidified. There would be a real home and real wife
and real children and a real job, but all these would have to
fit into Angelo's world of unreality and illusion as best they
could.

Bert, the banker from Minnesota, represents a group of
compulsive gamblers whose unsatisfactory relationships with

perfectionist, uncompromising, cool and distant fathers kept them from developing a sense of self-worth and importance; who sought to find this in gruelling hard work and competitive striving; and, failing to find it through that course, turned to the illusion-filled world of gambling, hoping they would find it there.

Angelo represents another group of compulsive gamblers, whose low self-esteem and sense of powerlessness and worthlessness come out of unsatisfactory relationships with frustrated, defeated, punitive fathers, men who are unable to transmit a masculine, assertive self-image to their sons because they do not have it themselves, who, because of their own misfortune and despair, are unable to give their sons the caring and affection that would make the sons feel cherished and approved.

These sons, first as children and then as adults, turn to gambling as their first recourse because gambling gives them the illusion that they are masculine, adult, worthwhile, important and powerful, and does it instantly, without struggle, hard work and delay. The escapist world of gambling also fills their life with fun and excitement and frees them from the unpleasant and burdensome demands of reality.

There is a third group whose poor self-image and low self-esteem drive them to find self-validation and power in gambling and who ultimately become compulsive gamblers. Those in this group are neither self-effacing, self-driven conformists such as Bert the banker, nor rebellious, pleasure-seeking fugitives from reality such as Angelo. They are of a personality type that is characterized by conceit, arrogant contempt for others and the exploitation of others to satisfy their own needs. They are driven to gamble and to acquire great amounts of money because this, they believe, will demonstrate their superiority (to compensate for an overwhelming sense of inferiority) and enable them to wield power over others (to compensate for their unbearable feeling of powerlessness). How does this fit in with the picture of the compulsive gambler as a friendly, sociable, outgoing, generous fellow? We shall see.

Frank N.

As the train started, Cordell N. pressed close to the

train window and, waving his hand, tried to catch the attention of his son whom he had just left standing on the platform. But Frank, a tall, well-built, attractive man of 29, was already walking away toward the exit.

The father, 53, looked sadly at the retreating back, wishing his son would turn to wave goodbye. But it was no use, he knew, and he accepted it with resignation.

Only 36 hours had passed since Cordell had arrived in this little Arizona town, rushing to the scene with a certified check for $4,500 to save Frank from being prosecuted for passing a worthless check. A year earlier, it had been a $5,000 debt, which he had paid to keep the bank from foreclosing on Frank's home. Before that, he had jumped in and found a job for Frank after he had been fired for suspected misappropriation of funds. And before that he had intervened to placate the parents of a girl Frank had made pregnant and who was pressing him to marry her. And before that it had been another crisis, and another, as far back as he could remember.

He wondered whether any of these things would have happened, whether Frank would have turned to gambling, had he not been stricken by rheumatic fever during his freshman year in high school and forced to give up his football and tennis and to withdraw from school for a semester during his long illness and convalescence.

He could not erase from his memory, even now, 15 years later, the look of despair and anger he had seen in his son's eyes when he had gone to visit him in the hospital on the day the doctor had told the boy that his illness had left him with permanent damage to the heart and that he would have to give up sports and all other strenuous activities. He could see even now, with searing anguish, the accusation in the boy's expression, as though the father were somehow to blame for this calamity.

But this was not a new role for the two of them. They had played it often before—the son blaming, the father feeling guilty for difficulties and problems in which the father had played no part at all. It was a role the mother had modeled for the boy and which he had readily adopted.

All her life, Mrs. N. had been disgruntled and dissatis-fied, with unrealistic expectations about what life owed her and the kind of a man she would marry. Her marriage to Cordell was a grudging compromise, and instead of being happy that she had won a kind, concerned, hardworking, devoted husband and family man, she made him the butt of her bitterness and frustration.

The birth of Frank, their only child, was a blow to her. She had desperately wished for a girl to become her friend and confidante. Also, she felt the birth bound her forever to a husband and a life she did not want. She didn't really want this child, resented him, even hated him at times. But whenever she found herself feeling this way, she was over-come with guilt and did everything she could to compen-sate. As do many parents who have such a conflict, she pulled the child close to her, indulging and spoiling him. She sided with him against friends with whom he quarreled, neighbors whom he annoyed, teachers whom he provoked, and his father whom she herself had set up as an adversary. She made the child feel that he was the most important creature on earth, that he could have anything and do anything he wanted.

Little Frankie repaid the debt by staying close to his mother and becoming her friend, ally and confidant. Later, however, as he grew older and realized how his mother was using him, and the power this gave him over her, he began to manipulate her in return, to gain advantages even beyond those her guilt-inspired overindulgence motivated her to grant him. When, for example, he wanted to go to an expensive, exclusive camp to which some of his wealthy classmates were sent, his mother gave up a long-planned trip to France with her sister. And when he wanted to show the boys in his neighborhood that his family was "better" than theirs, he did not let his mother rest until she had, much against her will, prevailed upon her brother to arrange the family's admission to the country club, at a cost the family could not easily afford.

Frank's hold on his parents became even more perni-cious with the guilt he was able to arouse in them because of the physical handicap and social deprivation the rheumatic fever attack had brought him.

Thus, underneath the facade of a civilized and peaceful family life, a silent drama of mutual suspicion and anger was being enacted incessantly. Resenting her son and wishing he had never been born, the mother was driven by guilt to compensate with extravagant expressions of love and with limitless indulgences. Aware that beneath her show of devotion his mother did not really love him, the son concealed his anger and resentment and made her pay by demanding more and more. Ensnared in this trap, the mother grew to dislike her son more intensely, even while showering him with favors. Cast by his wife in the role of an inept weakling, the father became the butt of his son's contempt and derision. Yet the father needed love from someone and so continued to court his son by helping him escape the consequences of scrapes he got into, hating him at the same time for being bound to him in this fashion.

Thus was born a cynical, affectionless personality, a boy covering his loneliness, fear and insecurity with an arrogant, contemptuous display of superiority, driven to manipulate and control others in order to compensate for his feeling of being helpless and without power to control his own life.

In high school—after Frank had returned there following his recovery—fellow students felt the sting of his tongue and the fickleness of his friendship and fled from him. When teachers and the school counselor became aware of what was happening, they conspired, without Frank's knowledge, to engineer his inclusion in clubs and social groups. For a while, Frank would relax in the warmth and security of companionship, and the better traits in him would blossom. But it was impossible for this to last because he was unable to accept the new friendships as genuine and lasting. So low an opinion did he have of himself that he thought his friends were being "nice to him" because of the suffering he had endured in his illness and the handicap with which it had left him. Tortured by his suspicions, Frank would turn on his new friends, criticize them and quarrel with them, try to show them up as less intelligent and less knowledgeable than he. And the inevitable would happen—they would discard him. Then Frank would move to a new circle, and in time the same thing would happen again. The loneliness and rejection were unbearable. Yet he was unable to control his behavior—nor did he understand what it was that was driving people away. The fault, he felt, was with the others. He did not realize that the problem was within himself.

There were only two ways Frank could relieve the gnawing anguish of his loneliness and the bewildering frustration of his inability to make and keep friends—through drinking and gambling.

He had had no experience with alcohol at all prior to his rheumatic fever attack, and his gambling had consisted of a weekly bet of 50 cents or a dollar on football cards. There was little change in these interests until about two years after his return to school. A friend he had made in class invited him to a party, and there he had his first drink ever, a can of beer, followed by a second. "It was like a miracle," Frank later recalled. "I had gone to the party dejected, scared that the kids wouldn't like me, kind of sour, with a chip on my shoulder. After that first can of beer I had another, and man I was floating. It was fantastic. That rotten feeling was gone. I felt wonderful. I was relaxed. I kidded around with guys and with girls and laughed. I even found a nice-looking girl who liked me, and we went into another room and made out."

Then there was another party and another where we drank beer and reexperienced the euphoria of his first drinking adventure. At one of these parties he met an older boy who had come to work at a plant in town after having dropped out of college in his freshman year. This new friend had "been around," and invited several of the boys to come with him to an illegal gambling house. Frank was now working after school and had money for gambling.

The establishment to which this young man took his younger friends was not by any means a posh Las Vegas casino, but for Frank who had never been exposed to anything forbidden and glamorous before, it was a scene of unimaginable beauty. The house, once the home of a wealthy manufacturer, had been built in the late 1800s, and those who had restored it had kept the original ornate paneling, woodwork, wallpapers, mirrors and ceiling moldings. Aside from the gaming tables—dice, cards and roulette—the furnishings and draperies were of the period, and Frank felt he had walked into the past. He let his imagination obscure the reality that the gamblers were hardly the gentry who might have gathered there in days gone by.

This was fantasy, and Frank drank it into his being. The effect was more intoxicating by far than that first alcoholic drink a few months earlier.

The alcohol gave me a great high, but nothing compared to this. Not only that, after a while the alcohol made me sleepy, made me feel dull. This place and the gambling kept me keyed up, sharp, alive, excited. I walked over to the dice table and saw thousands of dollars change hands with a roll of the dice. Then I walked over to the card tables and the roulette and saw the same thing taking place—men and women, calm, cool, deliberate, tough, thinking for a second or two, then placing their bets, hundreds and thousands of dollars. I saw one man win $15,000 at the dice table, cash his chips, collect 15 thousand-dollar bills and walk away with them.

I knew then and there this was for me. The whole scene. I tried my hand at the roulette table and won $100. I took that to the dice table and won another $300. By the end of the night I had won $1,000—the first time out. Can you imagine what that did to me? A kid of 17 with $1,000 in his hands, when I had never had $50 of my own before.

When we were ready to go, I asked the other fellows how they had done. Most of them had lost $15 or $25. One had won $150. Here I was with $1,000 . . . king of the hill. Inside myself I laughed at them. They were dumb, clumsy, inept. I was sharp, smart. I was a genius at gambling right from the start. Can you imagine what a sense of power that gave me?

On the way home, I was silent, kept to myself, so I could dream about the millions I was going to make, how important a man I was going to become, how I would no longer need to worry about people liking me or not liking me. They would fight each other to be invited to my home, my parties, my yacht. I would be able to have my pick of women and there would just be one or two men friends, and they would be there, available, ready to come to me when I wanted them and needed them.

Frank's euphoria was deflated when, the next time out, he lost $500 of his $1,000 winnings, and for days he went about depressed. But this did not discourage him. He had drunk the heady wine and had dreamed the heady dream, and the pursuit of this dream was to become his life's goal.

The gambling continued throughout his four years in college and then his three years in law school, and beyond that into his law practice and into his married life.

He had been married only two years when his wife divorced him; not because of his gambling, which he had managed to keep under control, but because, when he was losing, he would treat her with derision and contempt, as he had done with his friends in the past, in times of frustration and despair. Then he had married again, this time a woman who was a heavy drinker and who was able to escape into drinking when Frank became abusive and when his losses drove him into heavy borrowing and then into stealing and writing fraudulent checks.

By the age of 25, Frank was a confirmed compulsive gambler—an addict—and by the time he was 29, he was already living a life of desperation and despair, arriving there in pursuit of his impossible dream: to become powerful and important so he could lord it over a world he could not master and over people whose friendship and allegiance he could not win.

Bill R.

Most compulsive gamblers are friendly and sociable. However, there are the exceptions, the loners.

When we look into the backgrounds of the sociable gamblers, we find that even though there was a lack of abundant parental love, concern, constancy and security out of which could come a good self-image and a strong self-esteem, there was, nevertheless, something there to which they could cling, out of which they could fashion some strategy for emotional survival.

In the life of the loners, we find that even that shaky and imperfect foundation was missing. Lonely, bewildered, frightened as children and adolescents, they were emotional orphans, struggling to maintain some semblance of psychological integrity amid the turmoil of their parents' lives, trying to retain the feeling that life was worth living at all. Such was the life of Bill R., as recounted by his sister, the oldest of five children. Bill was the next to youngest.

One of his sister's earliest memories was that of her father coming home drunk when the rest of the family was seated at the table for dinner, cursing his wife for not having waited until he got home, then upending the table and kicking the wreckage of the food, knives and forks and broken dishes into every corner of the room.

"That was not as rough as it ever got," she recalled. "There were times when it was even worse. He would beat her and he would beat us, and she would fight back at him with a club or a wrench or whatever she got hold of. She got so worn out and desperate, she would scream at us and slap us if we asked for anything or if we got her upset."

She spoke with bitterness about both her parents. That the father was to blame, there was no question. But she felt her mother could have done more to protect the children. On reflection, however, she acknowledged that a person so beaten down by the physical and verbal abuse and worn down by taking care of so many children under such conditions could not possibly have had enough strength to do very much for herself or the children.

"She probably hated us, too . . . my father, her life, the children, everything. Sometimes she would be nice to us for a little bit, then it would get terrible again. I couldn't wait to get out." She left when she was 17, found herself a furnished room and went to work in a bakery.

Bill was a cuddly, friendly baby and a playful, even happy child. He was too little for them to hit, and they had to love something so they were good to him. But that didn't last. When he was five or six, his disposition changed and he became a whiny, pesty child and then they started to treat him the way they had treated all the rest of us.

Then as he grew older, Billy's personality changed again. He became silent and withdrawn, not wanting to play with his brothers and sisters or the other children out in the street or in the schoolyard. He would go off by himself and poke around in the alleys and backyards, picking up junk and selling it for a few pennies when the junkman came around with his truck. Once, Billy found an old radio that somebody had thrown away, but it was still playing and Billy was smart enough to find an outlet on the roof of the building where we lived [a five-story walk-up tenement], and he built himself a little shack up there out of some old crates, and he would go up there by himself and listen to the radio for hours.

Billy did have some friends in the neighborhood and in school, but he would kind of fade in and fade out. Sometimes, he'd play with them on the street—kids' games— and look like he was having a good time. Then he would quit them, and when they came around to the house to call for him, he would say he didn't want to play. I think he was afraid the kids didn't like him, and that was silly, because they did. I remember once how upset he got when one of the kids he went to school with had a birthday party and Billy wasn't invited. Billy didn't say anything to me or to any of my brothers and sisters ... certainly not to my parents ... he would never talk to them about anything.

But I noticed one Sunday he came back into the house when he was usually out on the street, and took his radio and went up on the roof. He never went out on the street at all after school for a whole week after that. Then one of my friends asked me why Billy hadn't come to her brother's party. All his friends from the neighborhood and school were there. I told her I didn't know and later I asked Billy. He wouldn't talk about it, just clammed up. Later I found out. Tommy, the kid who was having the birthday party, had forgotten to ask him ... just that ... had just forgotten to ask him. Billy must have thought Tommy and the other kids didn't like him and that they deliberately left him out.

* * *

Somewhere, in his hunt for junk, Billy found a stack of old science fiction paperbacks, and that, his sister recounted, caught hold of him "like a fever." After school, he would rush through his school assignments and then go off into the bedroom where he and two brothers slept and plunge into one of the books. When he had exhausted those, he found some others and brought those home, too.

Then she noticed that he was bringing home "wires and gadgets and pieces of old radios," and when she asked him what he was making he said he was going to build a "space communicator" that could pick up signals from other planets. She dismissed this as just "childish imagination and play," until one night she was awakened by a noise and heard the apartment door opening. She was able to catch a glimpse of Billy, who was about 12 years old then, going out into the hall. She followed him quietly to the roof and to his little hut, where he sat down, lighted a candle, and started to turn the knobs of his "space communicator."

Not wanting to frighten him, she returned to the apartment and waited. Billy came down a half hour later, and she went back to sleep. In the morning, she told him she had seen him and followed him to the roof. He was angry and sullen and told her to mind her own business and not be spying on him.

I thought he was going to become a scientist—he was smart; the kids knew it from school and the word got around—but he didn't become anything... just a truck driver and a gambler. He didn't like to study and he didn't work hard on his homework, so he got bad grades, and when the teachers tried to encourage him to do better, he would get nasty with them, and after a while they let him alone. His classmates let him alone, too, because he wasn't much fun. This I got from friends who got it from their kid brothers. They said he would sit in class with a mean look on his face and at lunchtime he would go off and eat by himself.

Starved as he was for affection, Billy would not accept it when it was offered to him by his teachers and classmates. Indifferent and punitive treatment from his parents had made him fearful and suspicious, not only of them but of everyone. He had become a loner, not by choice, but out of hurt and fear. Reality was too painful. Fantasy was safer, more satisfying. In his fantasy world of "space communicators" and science fiction magic, he would identify with the masterful space creatures who bridged galaxies and light-years to spread their power and make their conquests, to win or carry off beautiful female creatures from Earth or other planets. And what solace he could not find in the fantasy of fiction, he was able to find in the illusory life of gambling.

His gambling started early, when he was 12. By the time he was 15, he was heavily involved in card games and craps. There, among his young, tough gambling cronies, he could loosen up and feel comfortable, safe and at home. There he felt important. There he did not need to depend on anyone, just himself. There *he* was in control, making the moves and the decisions. There his hurt and his fright were gone. He did not need to struggle any longer with the bitterness of real life, nor content himself with the flimsy satisfactions of outer-space imaginings. Now he had a new life, in which he could immerse himself entirely, from which he could draw deep gratification, retaining just enough contact with the other reality to earn money to finance his gambling.

At the age of 16 Bill dropped out of school and went to work as a helper on a moving van. The pay was good and the work was irregular, all of which suited him wonderfully. Now he could go to a game or the track, bet with a bookie, sit at home and drink beer, follow the game or listen to the results from the track on radio or television.

By the time he was 20, Bill R. was fully addicted to gambling, betting on the horses, on college and professional football games, on baseball and basketball games, every spare hour during the day, every day of the year, gambling away his earnings, everything he could borrow from his fellow employees and everything he could steal from the cash receipts he handled in an electrical-appliance store where he worked evenings and weekends (except when he had to give it up for a while after being stabbed in a fight with a bookie's "runner").

Bill R. typifies a large number of unfortunate people who, frightened, lonely, beaten down and bewildered, find their way into a life of gambling.

Bill came from a home where he and his siblings were either ignored or abused by a drunken father and a joyless, downtrodden mother. Others, similarly destined, come from homes where one or both parents are absent or suffering from a serious psychiatric illness or in trouble with the law or are themselves compulsive gamblers. The homes from which these people come are characterized by fighting and turmoil. Discipline is unreasonable, inconsistent and frequently brutal. The children are a burden on parents who cannot manage them and do not want them but still have to feed them and take care of them. Children who come from such a setting grow up feeling unwanted and unloved. Subjected constantly to mistreatment at home, they expect mistreatment from others. They shrink from intimate relationships for fear that they will be hurt. They are extremely sensitive to rejection and so withdraw into the safety of isolation. They are anxious, unhappy, depressed. Gambling provides some relief from intolerable, loveless life. It gives them at least some sense of identity and significance, of being recognized and approved; it provides the only gratification that revives in them the joy of living and the desire to stay alive.

WHY PEOPLE BECOME COMPULSIVE GAMBLERS: SUMMARY

Our explanation of compulsive gambling and its causes has to do with three basic emotional needs of every human being—affection and approval, recognition and self-confidence. When these needs are fulfilled—when a person feels that people like him, want him and recognize his worth; when he has confidence in his capabilities—he can be happy, contented, effective, creative and give of himself to others through love, concern, emotional support and mutual interdependence.

If these needs are not fulfilled—if a person feels inadequate, rejected, helpless, and overwhelmed by life—he will struggle to overcome these handicaps, to attain acceptance, recognition and control of his life. To do this he will devise strategies that may carry him to heights of achievement, importance and fame, or sidetrack him into a life of fantasy, illusion and escape.

The yearning for fantasy, illusion and escape is not at all abnormal. We fill our lives with these from children on—with fairy tales, novels, plays, music, dance, participant and spectator sports, hobbies, poetry, daydreaming. If we didn't have these and life were stripped down to the practical tasks of making a living, dealing with illness and death and overcoming problems, contending with our meaner natures and our cruelties to each other, it would be unbearable indeed. We create fantasy and escape to make life more enjoyable and livable.

Resort to fantasy, illusion and escape is not abnormal when it occupies just some part of our lives, when it is an "extra" in a life that is devoted mainly to the practical realities: providing the wherewithal for survival; protecting ourselves, our families and society against disease and destruction; creating a productive and humane civilization.

It is abnormal when it takes the place of reality, when it renders the individual incapable of dealing with the inescapable, practical tasks of life, when it becomes the whole of one's existence. This happens when the individual is overwhelmed by reality and feels incapable of dealing with it. Such a condition may come about through a genetic defect of the personality. Or it may come about through the undermining of the personality by stressful conditions in the home and indifferent or destructive treatment by parents. Or it may come about through a combination of both factors.

In the case of the children who become compulsive gamblers, we believe it is a combination of both. We believe that the person who becomes a compulsive gambler is born, not with a genetic trait for compulsive gambling, but rather with a vulnerability of the personality, which is then acted upon by parental indifference, neglect, hostility or abuse, producing a person with low self-esteem, poor self-image, feelings of inadequacy and inferiority, an incapacity to deal with life's problems and a need to find relief and escape, self-justification and fulfillment in fantasy and illusion.

We can only go as far as postulating a genetic vulnerability of personality, because there is no research yet by which this genetic component can be proven. But in so speculating we are following the position that psychiatry accepts with respect to other personality disorders. Clinical observation of compulsive gamblers, and some limited research, have thus far disclosed four types of family situations from which a vulnerable child is likely to emerge with low self-esteem, a poor self-image, a feeling of helplessness to deal with life's problems and a predisposition to find escape and relief in the fantasy and illusions of gambling—as illustrated in the previous pages by the cases of Bert J., Angelo T., Frank N. and Bill R.

Group I: Conscientious, hardworking boys, driving themselves competitively to meet the perfectionist standards of strict, moralistic parents. The search for perfection and parental approval is constant; the goals are always out of reach. Expression of fear, doubt and anger are suppressed by excessive parental control. Life is without fun, excitement, joy.

Group II: These are restless, erratically, hardworking, rebellious youngsters, the sons of unhappy, frustrated fathers who have been disappointed in life and present an image of defeat to their sons. Unable to find strong male identification with their fathers, these boys seek it in masculine, "adult," aggressive experiences. Instead of love and concern, these boys receive criticism and punishment. Deprived of love and caring from their parents, they lack the foundation on which to build respect and esteem for themselves. Having failed to establish warm, close, meaningful relationships with their parents, they are unable to do so with others.

Group III: These are demanding, complaining teenagers, friendless and overbearing, insisting on immediate gratification of their desires at all costs. They insist on being the center of attention, and they regard others with contempt. Generally, there is not a good relationship between their parents, although they may pretend to have a happy marriage. The mother casts the father in the image of an ineffective weakling and encourages the son to do so, too. The mother and father dislike the boy, but are guilt-stricken because they feel this way and try to make up for it by indulging and spoiling him. This does little to overcome the boy's feeling of being unwanted, unloved and powerless, and so he compensates by arrogance, ruthlessness and domination.

Group IV: These are bewildered, frightened boys—loners searching for acceptance and recognition. The only relationships they are able to form are superficial ones with other gamblers. They come from homes in which the parent or parents are absent or are suffering from a psychiatric illness or are alcoholics or compulsive gamblers themselves. The home is characterized by fighting and turmoil. Discipline is overly harsh and inconsistent. These boys are regarded by their parents as worthless. The boys do not know the meaning of being loved. Extremely sensitive to rejection, they withdraw to the safety of solitude. They flee from dependent relationships with others for fear they are going to be discarded and hurt. They are unhappy, anxious and depressed.

Out of such family situations (and research may disclose that there are still others) come the boys who seek escape and relief and the self-justifying fantasies and illusions that they find in a life of gambling.

But why gambling? Why not one of the many other directions a person can follow to find relief, escape, fantasy?

We believe that the person who becomes a compulsive gambler is driven in that direction instead of the others because in addition to the possible genetic vulnerability of the personality, and the undermining family situations of the types that we have described, there are several additional factors present in his life.

1. He is by temperament an energetic, highly charged individual needing stimulation and excitement, welcoming risk, challenge and adventure. All these are fulfilled in gambling.

2. His experience leads him to view money and the things money can buy as the most important things in life, more important than ethical, humanitarian and esthetic values. Gambling is the quick, easy way to obtain the money that, he thinks, will buy him acceptance, respect, recognition and power.

3. He is given to "magical thinking," the belief that he is endowed with some mysterious power that will not let him lose, that will win him fortune and recognition. Gambling provides the perfect stage for the projection of this illusion.

4. While his lifestyle is escapist in nature, he is not willing to escape completely from the world of real things and real experiences and move into the dream life created by alcohol and drugs. He wants to be able to create the fantasies and illusions with his own hands, by his own decisions and actions, and to savor the products as sensually and as keenly as possible. Gambling permits him to do this—to keep one foot in the world of reality and the other in the world of fantasy.

Relief From Anxiety and Depression

People who become compulsive gamblers turn to gambling for more than self-affirmation and the illusion of importance and power. They turn to it also for relief from the anxiety and tension that are so much a part of their lives.

But why to gambling? Why not to alcohol—the means used for this purpose by tens of millions, young and old? The fact is some *do* resort to alcohol also; there are a few cases of double addiction—to gambling and alcohol—and even triple addiction—to gambling, alcohol and drugs. But these cases are rare, representing only a very small part of the total.

Why this is so, why most prospective compulsive gamblers seek relief from anxiety and tension in gambling rather from in alcohol, we do not know. There is as yet no scientific answer. However, we can get a preliminary idea from the reports of the compulsive gamblers themselves. When asked "Why not alcohol?" they will say such things as:

Alcohol was not part of my upbringing or background. My folks didn't use it much, and there wasn't much occasion to use it in our home, except for a celebration or religious holidays. Even after I grew up and left home, I would drink only on special occasions. I didn't like parties or other get-togethers where the big thing was drinking and getting high.

Alcohol never did very much for me. I would drink a beer or a glass of wine or a cocktail when we went out to dinner, or when we were invited to a party. It was pleasant, relaxing, but that's all. I've heard some people who drink tell about what a terrific high they get from drinking, how great it makes them feel. It just never did that for me. I guess I've got the wrong body chemistry.

I liked to have a few shots. It eased me off and slowed me down. But it would make me dull and sleepy; and I hated that. For me, the big thing was feeling alive, excited . . . feeling the adrenalin pumping . . . getting the action. I got my highs from the action, the excitement. You can't gamble when you're drunk or even when you've had a few drinks. It dulls your senses. It throws off your judgment. You do stupid things when you've been drinking, and the one thing a smart gambler does not want to do is to be stupid, to do stupid things.

I've had an aversion to drinking and drunkards ever since I was a kid. I used to see my mother get intoxicated and it disgusted me. I promised myself I would never let that happen to me, and I haven't. I don't think I've had 20 drinks in the past five years. I just don't care for it.

From Gambling to Addiction

A fundamental law of behavior is this: An act that

brings pleasure, satisfaction or relief from pain will tend to be repeated and ultimately become fixed as a habit. This is the principle used by animal trainers. When the animal does what the trainer wants it to do, the animal is rewarded with a tidbit. Anticipating the reward, the animal will repeat the act until it becomes a habit. Similarly, parents and teachers reward a child with cookies, praise, a pat on the head for doing something they want the child to do. Anticipating the pleasure of the reward, the child will repeat the act or word or multiplication table until it becomes fixed as a habit.

The same thing happens with gambling. The gambler finds that gambling makes him feel liked, accepted, important, powerful—things for which he has hungered—and that it also relieves his anxiety and depression, making him feel relaxed and contented. Since gambling brings these rewards, the gambler (like the child with the cookie) will repeat the act until it becomes a habit.

But habits, once they become established, do not necessarily continue to wax in importance and to dominate a person's life. That this does happen in the life of the compulsive gambler is due to the fact that his need for self-affirmation and relief from anxiety and depression—the rewards that gambling gives him—is omnivorous. It is never satisfied. It continues to demand greater fulfillment, even as it is being fulfilled. The process does not level off. It continues to mount and accelerate, and as it does, gambling crowds out everything else, becoming the most important thing in the compulsive gambler's life.

At the same time, something else insidious is taking place. Resort to fantasy and illusion removes the gambler further and further from reality and realistic solution to his problems. But evasion does not solve his problems; they become worse, and in the meantime, new ones are created. This, in turn, intensifies the craving for relief and escape in gambling and removes the gambler further from reality. The vicious cycle keeps on spiraling and draws him deeper into the morass.

Gambling continues to inject fantasy and illusion into the normal processes of thought and feeling, weakening bit by bit that part of the ego whose task it is to maintain contact with reality and direct behavior into rational and realistic channels. The ego, in this weakened state, is unable any longer to exert control over impulse, and impulse takes over as the controlling force.

When impulse replaces rational, cognitive control over thinking and behavior, when behavior and thinking become compulsive, then the state of addiction has been reached.

CHAPTER FOUR

The Phases in the Life of the Compulsive Gambler

PSYCHOLOGICAL DISORDERS CAN BE INFINITELY MORE COMplex than physical illnesses, but we know that they, too, follow a predictable course, from inception to conclusion, with identifiable symptoms and other manifestations appearing at each successive phase.

Compulsive gambling has not been studied for long enough to permit the charting of a precise "life history" of this disorder. Nevertheless, the research done to date has disclosed that compulsive gambling does follow a rather clear-cut course, separated, after a preparatory period, into several phases—I. *The Winning Phase*, II. *The Losing Phase* and III. *The Desperation Phase*—and that certain characteristic things happen in each of these successive stages. We would expect that the development in any individual case would follow, in general, the progression outlined here.

THE PREPARATORY PERIOD

In order for an illness to become established, it is necessary that the patient, or "host," be in a susceptible condition. Obviously, not everyone succumbs to influenza when there is an epidemic of this disease. Only those succumb who are vulnerable at the time because of low resistance or because of a defect in the immune system that combats microorganisms causing disease.

Likewise, not everyone exposed to gambling becomes a compulsive gambler. The ones who do succumb, we believe, are vulnerable because of a combination of traits of temperament and personality.

These are:

- a fragile ego incapable of withstanding rejection and disapproval;
- a tendency to be impulsive;
- a tendency to be overanxious and depressed;
- a low tolerance for frustration and a need for immediate gratification;
- a tendency to cling to magical thinking and a sense of omnipotence, which others relinquish on growing up;
- abounding energy, restlessness and an extraordinary need for excitement, stimulation and risk.

When a person with these traits is subjected, in childhood, to the following conditions, the likelihood is great that that person will become a compulsive gambler:

1. Parental indifference, neglect, rejection, abuse (singly or in any combination), which impair the child's self-esteem, make him feel unloved, unwanted, unimportant and powerless, and generate in him a drive to compensate for and overcome these acutely painful feelings.

2. An environment in which (a) the main emphasis is placed on money and the prestige and power associated with it; (b) gambling is readily available; (c) people gamble or drink as a way of dealing with life's problems and pains.

Let us now picture what might happen to such a child.

He comes out from his home into the surroundings of neighborhood and school, frightened, unsure of himself, mistrustful of others, not knowing whether he will be accepted or rejected. He tests the situation gingerly, ready to pull back in an instant if necessary. He makes some friends but does not allow them to come too close to him emotionally, or he to them, for fear he might be hurt.

To protect himself further, to make sure that nobody is going to hurt or reject him, he starts out on the task—later to be his lifestyle—of becoming the sort of person he thinks people will applaud and admire: tough, strong, smart, superior, a little "superman."

Restless and charged with energy, he gravitates toward sports or toward bodybuilding, his aim being to display his superiority and thus gain approval and recognition. Or, if he is of a studious turn, he will devote himself to his studies and attempt to demonstrate superiority in that area. Besides being a test of his intellectual prowess, it is also a show of endurance. He can "hang in there and tough it out" with the really difficult subjects and bring in the high grades. For him it is the same as "bringing in" a big fish or an athletic trophy. Not only that, he can do it with "one hand tied behind his back." He can do it while holding down a newspaper route before school, a stockroom job after school and a gas station job on weekends.

He doesn't realize that that is not the way to win acceptance and friendship, that people like you and accept you because you are kind and considerate, easy to get along with, lots of fun—not because you are a "big shot." He doesn't yet know something he will learn later, that friendship and acceptance do not always come with recognition and acclaim, that there are many important people who are also very lonely.

Further, he carries on his campaign with braggadocio, arrogance, egotism and sneering at "inferiors"—behavior that produces the very opposite of what he is trying to achieve. Instead of encouraging people to like and accept him, it tends to provoke them to reject him. Frustrated, bewildered, frightened, lonely, not understanding why this is happening, he searches desperately for something, anything that will relieve this terrible pain.

He does not intentionally seek out gambling and say, "Aha, here is something that will do it." The encounter with gambling is accidental. It is something the boys in his neighborhood are doing and so he tries it, too. When he does, he finds it a very gratifying experience. It's fun. It's exciting. There are kids there who like you. You've got a ready-made circle of friends. You don't have to test yourself or prove yourself. All you've got to do is get up a half-dollar or a dollar and gamble along with them. You've got someplace to go and somebody to be with.

Little by little, as he moves more deeply into gambling, the bitterness of the years of loneliness is wiped out. He has entered into a new existence, a new world, where he no longer feels unsure of himself, unwanted, lonely, defenseless. Some of the people he discovers are other youths who have arrived there by a route similar to his, and he makes friends with them. Many of the people he finds there are adults, and by identifying with them and the "adult" thing they are doing, he expunges the feeling of being a frightened, bewildered and helpless boy. Circulating in this atmosphere, he too feels grown-up, masculine, masterful, strong.

The world of adult gambling is still new to him, somewhat intimidating, and so he moves about quietly, unobtrusively, observing. He ventures a question now and then and begins to learn some of the fine points. He places a few small bets, quietly, gaining more confidence with each one. He now feels more comfortable. He feels he belongs. He talks to his cronies and they compare notes. He is now one of them. He is now a gambler.

THE WINNING PHASE

With this, he has moved out of the preparatory period and has moved into the Winning Phase.

This phase generally begins inauspiciously. Not having much money, he will bet only small sums, satisfied just to have the camaraderie and excitement, a place to go and something to do. At the beginning, he may stay with the sports cards, poker games or crap games. As he gets a little older, he may venture out to the track for an afternoon or evening, or begin to place bets with bookmakers.

To do this, he has to have more money and so he seeks

other sources—a part-time job, selling some of his possessions, pilfering a few dollars from his mother's household
money, lying to his older brother or his parents about
needing money to buy a baseball uniform or sports equipment. With this extra money he can bet more and win more.
He comes away at the end of an evening of gambling not
just with $10 or $20, but with $50, $100, $200. Nothing
like this has ever happened to him before. He looks with
amazement at his two or three hundred-dollar bills and
cannot believe this is happening to him. This is more money
than he's ever seen, let alone possessed.

With winnings of this kind, he gambles more frequently and for larger amounts. His bets have moved from the $5
and $10 level into the $50 and $100 level . . . and he is only
17 or 18!

Suddenly, money takes on a new significance. Before,
money meant only the things you could buy with it. Now
money is something else. Money is importance. When
you've got money, people crowd around you, admire you,
tell other people about you. Money is friendship. When
you've got money to spend, people want to be your friends.
Even without friends, money can keep you from being
lonely. If someone rejects you or doesn't like you, you can
stick your hand in your pocket, clutch that roll of bills and
say, "Who needs you? I've got money."

Money is medicine. It's tranquilizers and antidepressants, uppers and downers, sedatives and stimulants. If
you're feeling worried, agitated, restless, it relaxes you,
gets you feeling comfortable and calm. If you're feeling
dejected or blue, it will energize you, set the adrenalin
flowing, give you the greatest highs, put you on top of the
world. This isn't just a figure of speech. Money actually
does this for some people, perhaps even for most.

Think of the times you were feeling low and then
something nice happened to you. You got a call from a
girlfriend or boyfriend. You received an invitation to a party.
You got news that you were accepted to the college of your
choice, or were going to get a promotion at work. In an
instant, your mood changed from "down" to "up," from
"low" to "high." You suddenly felt good, pleased, happy,

even ecstatic. That doesn't happen just in your head. It happens first in your body. When that "good thing" occurred, your brain and endocrine systems started to manufacture natural antidepressants that caused the elevation in your mood.

In many parts of our society, money has become the symbol for everything good that can happen to you. The possession of money, of and by itself, can set off the internal biochemical reaction that elevates your mood, makes you feel "great," happy, euphoric.

Consider now the vulnerable teenager we are talking about—the boy who's been experiencing rejection, neglect and abuse most of his childhood and early teenage years and is moving about from day to day in a dejected, joyless state, feeling anxious, dispirited, low. Nothing has been happening to make him feel good, to generate the mood-elevating substances in his body.

Then, suddenly, his life experience changes. He finds a setting where he feels at home, safe, comfortable, where people like him and accept him. Then, on top of that, he encounters the magic of money . . . and he feels important, powerful, in control, superior. His brain and endocrine system start pumping out their natural stimulants and antidepressants and he starts to experience wonderful feelings he has never experienced before.

Is it any wonder he is smitten with gambling?

But what happens if this boy, or young man, doesn't win when he starts gambling? What if he loses, as many are bound to do?

If he loses and continues to lose he's most likely going to turn to something else. His battered self-esteem is just not going to be able to take the additional beating of constant losses. He may stay away for a while and then try it again. If he wins and keeps on winning, it is very likely he will stay. If he loses again and keeps on losing, he is going to flee . . . perhaps to alcohol, perhaps to drugs, perhaps into introspective daydreaming and fantasizing, perhaps into an aggressive, violent lifestyle, perhaps to suicide. But he will not become a habitual gambler, and consequently he will not be able to become a compulsive gambler.

It is generally those who win early and consistently in their gambling career who become the compulsive gamblers. Having caught the "fever" and experienced the excitement and the magic of money, they come back to gamble some more. The longer they continue, the more adept they become at the particular type of gambling they have chosen. They study the angles and the odds, much as the professional gamblers do. They learn the art of controlled betting, differentiating themselves from the reckless gamblers who bet on every hand or every throw of the dice or every race. They are able to garner substantial winnings, to buy themselves the things they have always wanted and to improve their standard of living.

But gambling is still accorded only a small role in the totality of their life. The rest of life continues much as before. Success at gambling may even advance the individual in his other pursuits. With his new confidence, he may change to a better job or better his grades in school or take on the responsibility of getting married.

The longer the winning edge is sustained, the more confident he becomes and the larger are his bets. Nevertheless, his betting does not become excessive nor does it throw his financial affairs into a state of imbalance. He manages to keep his betting within the range of what he can afford and what appears reasonable, viewed from the perspective of his total holdings.

After a while, gambling becomes integrated into his overall behavior pattern, readily available as an outlet and response on occasions when his self-esteem undergoes a battering and when he is especially in need of comfort and reassurance.

The "love affair" with gambling blossoms, generally, at that time in life when the young man is facing new, ego-threatening experiences and when he may be especially in need of something to fall back on in the event he suffers a rebuff. It is remarkable with what frequency and repetitiveness we find, in studying the lives of compulsive gamblers, that the first serious occurrence of heavy gambling, or a return to heavy gambling after a letup, occurred in the anticipation of or in the aftermath of a jarring emotional experience affecting the individual's self-esteem.

Typical are these incidents:

He had applied to enlist in the marines but he was turned down. He then enlisted in the navy but never got over his rejection by the marines. He started to gamble heavily as soon as he got into the service.

I wanted very badly to get into an Ivy League university, and I tried to pull every string I could. I got letters of recommendation from my father's business associates, my high school football coach, the bishop of my church. This is not unusual. Many college applicants do this and it often works. Why it didn't work for me, I don't know. I guess I just didn't have what they wanted. That made me feel very bad. When they let you know why, you can rationalize, give yourself some excuse that makes you feel better, blame them for making "such a stupid mistake," work to make up for the shortcoming and hope you can try again, if not that one, then another one almost as prestigious. But when they leave you in the dark, you start imagining every sort of crazy thing, and you start feeling real lousy, depressed. The next thing, you're looking for something to get you over that feeling, to bolster up your ego and so you start to gamble.

I wanted the job at the L.,M.&N. law firm desperately. Anyone chosen by that firm was automatically regarded as a "top pick," one of the best in the new crop of law school graduates and hence the envy of all the others. I wanted it badly. I needed it. I was feeling pretty low and it would have worked a miracle. But they turned me down, and one of the fellows with whom I had gone to law school got it. I was sick. I took a job with a good firm, but not anywhere near as prestigious as L.,M.&N. I had eased off on my gambling, some. This threw me right back into it, heavy.

It must have had some connection with his disastrous love affair. He had known this girl from high school on. They dated steadily and they were definitely set on getting married. But her parents were opposed to him and they didn't want her to marry him. They did everything they could to break it up, but the girl wouldn't pay any attention to them. It was very tough on John knowing they didn't like him. He was kind of insecure about himself anyhow, and the one thing he could fall back on was that Jennie liked him and wanted to marry him. She was very pretty and very popular and she could have had her pick of some of the class leaders. But there must have been something special about John that attracted her, and she wouldn't have anybody else. But her parents did prevail. They got her to agree to go away to college in another state. John would have gone there, too, but his folks couldn't afford it. So he had to go to the state college near home. The inevitable happened. Jennie met another man and they got engaged. That broke John's heart and his spirit. Right after that, he was into gambling up to his ears.

I was always a very jealous person. When I was dating in high school and my girl would dance with another fellow, I couldn't stand it. I would go off and sulk, and once I even walked out of the dance and left the girl there, I was that upset. It was crazy, because you have to expect that sort of thing. You can't expect a girl to stay attached to you like a Siamese twin, just because you're dating. I guess you could call me insecure. I was still that way when I got married, and it drove my wife crazy. If we went to a party and she stood and talked to a man for two or three minutes, I was right there, breaking into the conversation and trying to drag her away to another part of the room. It did finally happen to me; not just in my imagination, but the real thing. I found out my wife was having an affair, and that's when I really blew. I left the house and drove out to Las Vegas and stayed there for over a week, gambling day and night.

I started to gamble heavy at about the time my wife had our first baby. I don't know what it was. Maybe I was jealous of the baby; I didn't want to share my wife with anybody, not even my own kid. I was wanting her to continue to pay attention to me, all the time, like before the baby came. But you know she couldn't do that. She had to be with the baby and take care of him and love him. I knew that her love for the baby didn't take away anything from her love for me. I knew it in my head, but you try to tell that to a person who doesn't feel good about himself to start with. Maybe it wasn't jealousy. Maybe it was the idea of the added responsibility. Before it was just her and me. Now it was a family, someone else to worry about, to take care of, to support.

The acceleration of gambling as the result of an ego-shattering experience is likely to introduce a frenetic quality in the gambling for a while, but as the hurt of the rebuff subsides a more casual rhythm is likely to be resumed, at a somewhat higher plateau with respect to frequency and size of wagers.

Then, somewhere along the line—earlier for some, later for others—something happens that changes the course of the gambling career and of the gambler's entire life. *He makes his first big win.* His winning may have been in the range of $100 to $500, and this time he wins $5,000. They may have been in the range of $500 to $1,000, and this time he wins $10,000. Or they may have been in the range of $1,000 to $5,000, and this time he wins $25,000. Whatever the ratio, the significant factor seems to be the size of the win in comparison to the individual's annual earnings. To win as much as a half year's or a whole year's earnings in one hour can be a staggering, truly mind-boggling experience. Winning this amount of money, in just a flash, does something to his perspective. He starts to think, "It happened tonight, why can't it happen again and again and bring me 10, 20, 100, 1000 times as much? Why keep on working for the pitiful salary I've been earning, or the skimpy returns from my business? I should be able to do this again and again, right along."

Here, to this gambler, is proof of something he "knew" all the time—he actually has the skill and savvy to do it. Here is proof of something he suspected all along but had not allowed himself to believe—he has a magic touch which will win for him every time and make him, ultimately, a millionaire. Why bother any longer with his job? Gambling, itself, could be his career. He might continue with what he is doing, but that would be only secondary. Gambling would take first place.

The big win is the booster on the rocket that tears him loose from the gravitational forces of reason and reality and sends him flying into a weight-free flight of illusion and fantasy where there are no limits to what he can do and become.

His expectations and his optimism soaring, he turns his attention to his new career, gambling. That doesn't mean that he gives up what he is doing—going to college, or working in an office or a factory or at a profession. That part of life continues, and, if he is married, so does his life with his wife, but these are not as important as they were before. More and more time and attention are given over to gambling. Before, it was an evening at the track; now it is two or three evenings and an afternoon during the weekend. Before, it was a few bets on football games; now it is a dozen, and Sundays spent glued to the television screen. Before, it was an occasional trip to Atlantic City or Las Vegas; now such trips take place every few weeks.

He goes to parties and to the movies and the theater as before; to the beach or to dinner with his wife or friends as before; but his mind is someplace else. He's wondering how the races came out or which team is winning. He's thinking about how much he's going to win today and how much he's going to bet tomorrow. During intermission at the theater or while the others are having dessert at dinner or while his nephew is reading the Torah at his Bar Mitzvah, he sneaks out to a telephone and calls his bookie. He's in bed with his wife and she's trying to stir up his sexual interest, but he won't be distracted. He's got to finish watching the ballgame on TV and wants to know why she can't wait until it's over. (Before, he used to complain she wasn't sufficiently responsive to his sexual advances.) His doctor has just finished examining him and has told him his blood pressure is dangerously high and that he's going to have to find ways to reduce his stress. He asks if there's a radio in the office; he needs to get some results.

Fellow students, fellow employees or business associates, as the case may be, are starting to wonder about him. He's not as available as he used to be. There are "things he has to do," but he doesn't tell them what these "things" are.

His wife, if he's married, is getting annoyed at his cooling interest in her. They are not yet quarreling. He is still trying to placate her. If he thinks it unwise to let her know the extent of his gambling, he makes up stories about where and why he spends so much time away from home. If he isn't concerned about her knowing, if he thinks he can draw her in with him as an ally instead of having her as an adversary, he tries to please her by getting her things she's wanted for herself or for the house. He buys her jewelry and fur coats. He gets her the dishwasher and the dining room suite. He sells the old house and they move into a much larger one. He buys her her own sports car to run around in. He invites her to come with him to the ballgame or track or casino. He takes her on special weekends where she can entertain herself with sightseeing and shopping while he is taking care of his gambling.

If his work does not require that he keep a low profile, he himself assumes a showy lifestyle, and friends and neighbors start to wonder where his money is coming from. After a while, he is unable to resist the temptation to tell just his closest relatives and friends. He reveals that he's become a master gambler and that what they see are the fruits of his enterprise. He boasts about the kind of money he has won and how easy it has been for him to do it. He makes sure they know it's not just a matter of luck, that it has taken great skill and know-how. He boasts about his prowess in gambling the way a manufacturer might boast about his sales and profits or an architect about the skyscraper he's creating.

Having moved into gambling as a career, and a successful one, he is now brimming with new-found confidence and egotistical self-esteem. He now feels the importance and power that his large winnings have brought him. He is no longer lonely. He doesn't need, as much as before, the companionship of his gambling cronies. He is now doing almost all his gambling alone.

For a year or two or three, he just keeps sailing along. There are times when he loses, of course, but he is able, through his adroit playing, to win far more than he loses. He has truly become a "pro." He knows all the tricks of the trade: the odds, when to bet and when not to bet, when to bet more and when to get out.

THE LOSING PHASE

Sooner or later, however, the time comes when the balloon in which the compulsive gambler has been floating is punctured and he plummets, suddenly, to earth.

He has been on a winning streak (overall) for years. He has been increasing the size of his wagers steadily and now may be betting thousands or tens of thousands. He can do this because he believes he is invincible. He's convinced he cannot lose. He's seen other men losing $25,000, $100,000, $500,000, a million in one night. But that is never going to happen to him.

But it does. He starts to lose, and he loses fairly consistently. It may be no more than a turn of the law of probability. More likely, it is the result of his cockiness and his belief in his omnipotence; he has become careless and rash. At any rate, the losses persist, and the effect is devastating. In no time at all, a large sum of money which was firmly and permanently (he thought) his no longer belongs to him. The "house" or the track or the bookie has it. He is angry, bewildered, frightened. What has happened to his magic? What has happened to his expertise? Is he really the "pro" he thought he was or was he just kidding himself? Quickly, he rallies and starts to rationalize. It had nothing to do with his expertise. How was he to know that the ace pitcher or wide receiver was going to falter in the last seconds of the game? How was he supposed to know that a sudden storm would come up and turn the track into a mud pond? He'd be much more careful next time, concentrate much harder on the salient factors. This thing, by God, wasn't going to happen to him again. He'd start regrouping tomorrow and get back on his winning track.

But right now, tonight, he is going to have to do something about getting back at least part of what he had lost. Otherwise it will eat at him and he will not be able to sleep. So he doubles his bet and loses again. He tries once more and loses.

"That's it," he declares to himself. "That's all for tonight." His luck is just not running right tonight, and he'd better quit and start fresh the following day. So he leaves the game or the track or the casino and goes home. He is sullen and irritable with his wife or roommate or girlfriend or parents. He goes to his room and broods, starts checking the races or games for the following day and figures out the bets he's going to make. Then he calls his bookie and places his bets, or writes them down and saves them for the following day.

The following night, he tallies up the results of the day's gambling and finds he's still far behind. So he doubles his bets for the following day, figuring that this time he's going to wipe out his losses entirely and maybe even come out ahead. And again, he comes out behind.

Now he's truly frightened and depressed. He can't understand what's happening. Instead of cooling off, sitting back for a day or two, regaining his calm and studied approach, he becomes anxious and agitated. He brushes aside the very cautions and techniques that have won for him before. He is too rattled to study the percentages, too impatient to sit and figure them out. He starts running scared and betting on impulse. And again, he comes out behind.

He may not be aware of it, but a new and catastrophic element now dominates his betting style. Before all this happened—before the losing streak began—he was gambling to win. Now he is gambling to recoup. He is doing what gamblers call "chasing"—the frenetic pursuit of lost money.

The pursuit is fired by many fuels. There is the loss of the money itself and what that money could have bought for him. There is the loss of what the money symbolizes—

importance, prestige, acceptance, recognition, friendship, power. There is the loss of self-esteem and of the feeling of invincibility. Until the lost money is recovered, the loss remains as ineradicable evidence that he is not as good a gambler as he had made himself out to be, that he does not possess the magic gift that he believed was keeping him safe from the vicissitudes to which other gamblers are vulnerable, that he is just a "poor sucker" like the rest of them, an epithet he had sneeringly applied to gamblers who were losers instead of winners. There is also the loss of face with the other gamblers. He is not close friends with any of them, having moved away from them in his flight to uniqueness and superiority. But he knows that they are now going to sneer at him behind his back. And there is just the plain sharp pain and chagrin of loss, the kind anyone feels when he loses or is robbed of something substantial: money, jewels, an automobile, an object of art, anything he values greatly and of which he is now bereft.

His obsessive gambling—his addiction—has now been in force for a number of years, but the motivating force has changed. Before, it was propelled by the euphoria of winning and the devouring desire to perpetuate it. Now it is propelled by the depression and anguish of losing and the overwhelming need to quell these feelings. There is only one way he can do this: continue to gamble, even more persistently and more heavily than before. He is hooked to an endless chain from which he cannot tear himself loose.

His whole life is now given over to the chase—the pursuit of his lost money. Evenings he used to spend with his family are now spent at the track or at an illegal poker or dice game. To avoid the fight he knows would ensue if he told his wife about where he is going, he lies. He tells her he is going bowling, to a bar with friends, to the shop to check the inventory, to the office to straighten out some accounts, to visit a sick friend or to see an uncle who has come to town unexpectedly. To cover up his absences from the job or the office while he goes to the track or a card game or while he sneaks out to call his bookie or goes somewhere to listen to the radio to get the race results, he lies. He's not feeling well. His child is sick. He's got an emergency at home. He's got to get to the bank before it closes. Lying and covering up become an integral part of his interpersonal relationships. This resort to lying is as basic a symptom of compulsive gambling as are any of the others.

What is remarkable is how compulsive gamblers are able to get away with their lying month in and month out—that they are able to concoct stories that their relatives, coworkers, employers and business associates believe; that all these others are so gullible that they can be fooled consistently without suspecting anything, or if they do suspect something, without doing anything about it.

Compulsive gamblers lie about where they go when they're gambling. They lie about how much they're winning or losing. They lie about what they do with their wages or other income that they are siphoning off into gambling. They lie—but this comes later—when they begin to cash in their stocks or redeem the children's bonds or sell the wife's automobile, furs or jewelry. They lie in order to get the wife's consent to the sale and then they lie about what has happened to the money. When they begin to borrow, they lie about why they need the money.

Lying becomes so much a way of life that they begin to lie about things that have nothing to do with their gambling or with money. Lying becomes more natural to them than telling the truth, even about innocent things, when there is no need to deceive.

Consider these comments by compulsive gamblers:

My wife came home from work and I was watching TV. She asked me if I had gotten the things at the supermarket. I said yes, they were in the refrigerator. I knew I hadn't gotten them. I knew she would look in the refrigerator and not find them there. I knew it would make me look like I was crazy, but I lied just the same. I haven't the faintest idea why. It had just become a habit.

My neighbor—a very good friend—asked me if I had watched the fights on TV the previous night. I had watched them, but I said no. I told him that somebody had broken in while my wife and I were away and had stolen the set. I was going down to the store that night to get another one. That was an absolute cock-and-bull story, and I didn't have the slightest reason to make it up. I knew that when he came over to watch a program with me, he would see the old set still there. What good did it do me? What was I trying to do? You tell me; I don't know. Lying had become second nature, and I just lied for no reason at all.

My uncle asked me about my son, Tom, how he was doing at school. I told him Tom had quit school and had decided he wanted to make his living as a carpenter, and that he was working now with a crew that was building houses upstate. This was insane. It was absolutely untrue. Right there on the dresser was a letter that I had gotten from Tom that very morning, telling me about how great he was doing and that he had decided he wanted to study law when he got out of college.

Back now to the compulsive gambler's devastating losing streak and his frantic chase after the money he has lost.

Week after week, he continues to plunge and to lose, to plunge and to lose. Certainly, there are winnings along the way, but the winnings are never enough to wipe out the accumulating losses and so he must bet more steeply and more insistently to recover the new losses piling up on the old ones.

As he turns to his convertible assets—securities, real estate, jewelry—the feel of the new money restores his confidence. Maybe this will be a new beginning, he thinks. Maybe now his luck is going to turn and his magic touch will return. The temporary respite enables him to calm down and bet more thoughtfully and carefully, and when he wins once or twice he is sure that his misery is at an end, that he is on the way to recovering all his losses.

But, inevitably, the losing starts all over again, and in a month or so he is back again in the depths of despair, deflated, depressed, miserable, sullen, frustrated, angry, impossible to live with. He is no longer thinking so much about big wins nor is he as confident that he is going to recover all his losses. Now the important thing is that he have money with which to gamble. Where to get it?

There is still another resource. He has borrowed before for other purposes. Why not borrow now to gamble? There are banks, finance companies, lots of them. Certainly, he can get more money that way.

One might think that with his large holdings gone—the assets he might have used for security—the compulsive gambler would have difficulty in getting a loan. When you raise this question with them, they laugh. "You can't imagine how easy it is," they say, "even for good-size loans. It might take a little doing, but it's never a big problem at all." One compulsive gambler gives this account to illustrate.

I had been doing business at this bank for years. That's where I had my checking account. I knew one or two of the behind-the-rail officers, casually, through occasional transactions—opening a money market account, purchasing Treasury bills, buying travelers' checks, that sort of thing. This loan was going to be a big one. I wanted to get at least $25,000 and so I had to move carefully. There was one officer I thought would be best to work on—a nice, friendly fellow, about 35, who, I figured, was trying to get ahead in the bank. I had watched him a while on several occasions, and I could tell, by the eagerness and friendliness with which he greeted the customers, that he was somewhat insecure and that he would welcome a friendly approach. I figured, also, that he would be mightily impressed when I told him about my important government job.

With all that in the back of my mind, I cooked up an excuse to talk to him. I told him I wanted to know whether I could buy a "Ginny Mae" [government-insured mortgage trust] through the bank, and if there was a certificate involved and would they hold it for me in their vault. While we were sitting there chatting about this, I told him how much I liked doing business with this bank, how nice and helpful the officers and the tellers were. Then I got the conversation around to personal things—I asked him how long he had been in the banking business, what college he had gone to, was he married, did he have children. I knew that somewhere in the conversation we would turn up some mutual acquaintances, and we did, and we chatted about them a while. I learned he liked to play golf, and I asked if he wanted to come to my country club to play, as my guest; he was delighted.

I left it at that for that day, and then that Saturday we played golf, and the week after we played again and I invited him and his wife to be our guests for dinner at the club. All this while I never even mentioned anything about a loan.

Then, one day, about a week later, I invited him to lunch downtown, at an elegant restaurant near my office. During lunch, after we had had a couple of martinis and were both feeling nice and mellow, I raised the subject of a loan. I told him that I needed $25,000 to build an extension on my house. He had been to my house already, so I could describe to him just where I wanted to build the extension and what extra rooms we were going to put into it. He thought it was a great idea, that it would make the house a lot more valuable in case I ever planned to sell it. I didn't even have to ask him about initiating the loan. He suggested it himself. He said, "Why don't you come down to the bank tomorrow night—we're open late and I'm going to be on duty. I'll work the whole thing out for you." He was so eager to please, I didn't even have to open my mouth. I had cased it right on the button. I knew just how to handle him, and he came through just the way I expected. The next day I went to the bank and saw him, and in less than 15 minutes I had a check for $25,000.

He then went on to relate, how, with this check for $25,000 in hand, he felt like he had just made a big win. This is a strange phenomenon, common to compulsive gamblers. Other people, on placing a loan this size, might feel distressed at being in debt for so much, worried about repaying the loan, concerned about the things they would have to give up in order to make payments. Not so the compulsive gambler. Here he has proof again that no matter how desperate his situation, he can still find a way out. He still has skill and savvy and his magic touch. They have not abandoned him.

Now, once more, he has thousands and thousands of dollars, and how beautiful they look and feel. No matter that they are dollars he has borrowed. His depression and his agony vanish. He is on top of the world again. His ebullient mood returns, and his friends and relatives can't believe it. This is the man who has been avoiding them, giving them short shrift, staying away from parties and family gatherings. Now, suddenly, for no apparent reason, he is the same old friendly, sociable Joe or Harry or Pete.

His wife can't believe the retransformation, either. The days of "wine and roses," of gifts and holiday trips, of luxurious anniversary and birthday surprises have long been gone. For months she has been putting up with his silence, irritability and carping, his absences on nights and weekends, his discourtesy to her relatives, his total absorption with gambling. Now, suddenly, he is cheerful again. He laughs and jokes and asks what show she would like to see, what restaurant she would like to go to, when she would like to call in the painters to start repainting the house. She doesn't know what has happened to restore him. She prays it isn't gambling. She doesn't care if he doesn't ever buy her another thing, so long as he's nice to her again, so long as they can start enjoying life together the way it was before he got so deeply into gambling. She doesn't know that he's lost all the money he ever won, that he has cashed in his securities and gone into debt with the bank.

For a while, it seems as if her wish has come true. For a week, 10 days, two weeks, there is sunshine and joy. Life is good again. With money from his loan he has started to gamble again, and for a while things have been going right for him. He knows, now, that his luck has returned, that he's back on the winning track, that things are going to be as good as they ever were. He starts dreaming again of some more big wins, of a return of the tens or hundreds of thousands of dollars he has lost.

Inevitably, he loses this money, too, and the misery begins all over again. Now he must try to get another loan, and again he has no difficulty doing so.

As remarkable as their ability to get loans without security and their insouciance in borrowing is the ability of compulsive gamblers to get loans from as many as half a dozen sources at one time, juggling and balancing them, getting money from other sources to repay them and to start borrowing all over again. One compulsive gambler gives this account.

I was into this bookie for $4,000 and he was pressing me hard. So I went to another bookie who knew me, figuring I could win with him and pay off the other guy. But I lost $1,200 with him. I figured I could stall him for a while, but the other guy was still breathing down my back. It was a Friday night, I was on the night shift and I was eating dinner at a little Italian restaurant in the neighborhood. While I was eating, this guy came over and asked me was I Steve R. and I told him I was, so he said to go into the men's room with him and I did, and he closed the door and put a knife to my throat and said, "You son of a bitch, you pay up or they're going to find your body in the river."

I knew this guy was a small-time collector for the bookie and that he wasn't going to do anything. He had done the same thing with some of the other guys, and we all knew that he never made good his threat. He was trying to show the bookie that he was doing his job, and when we paid up he could claim that we did it because he threatened us. Actually, I don't know of one case where the bookies would have somebody killed for a couple or three thousand dollars. If you're talking about $25,000 and $50,000, well, that's another story. That's where the Mafia itself is involved, big-time bookmakers and loan sharks where hundreds of thousands of dollars are involved, and for that they would knock you off.

I wasn't really scared, but I went home and told my wife and she was scared. She hated me because of my gambling and what I had done to her and the children, but she was afraid they'd kill me and she didn't want that to happen. So she went to the bank where she had her own account from her wages and drew out $4,000 and gave it to me to pay back the bookie.

I gave him the money, and he let me bet some more. In a week I owed him $4,000 more. I knew I couldn't go to my wife again, so I went to a loan company. They had checked the place where I was working and found out I had been working there a long time and was earning a good salary. So they lent me $5,000, and I signed some papers so they could garnishee my salary. I didn't have to tell them why I needed the money. They couldn't care less. They were charging a steep interest and making a good profit. Actually, they loved to lend me money. I could get it whenever I wanted it—just walk in and sign a paper. If I lost the money they lent me and I didn't want them to garnishee my wages on the job, I would go to another loan company and borrow and pay back the first one. There was the time when I was juggling five loan companies at once.

But I got sick of the high rates they were charging, so I decided to go to the bank to get a loan. My credit was good at the bank because when we were married I went there to borrow to buy furniture and I paid them back. So I could get $3,000, $4,000 whenever I needed it, so long as I paid it back. When I got hung up with this bank, I went to another one where I had once borrowed a few thousand dollars to buy a car. My father-in-law had cosigned for it, and I had paid it back from my salary, so my credit was good there, too, and I would borrow from them. When I borrowed from a bank, I'd give them some cock-and-bull story about doctor bills, painting the house or buying new furniture, and they believed it, or just didn't care. They weren't giving me a loan for nothing. They were making money on me, too. At one time, I had three loans going with three banks.

Most of the time I was able to pay them off, because I would go to the track or I would bet with my bookie and win a few thousand and pay it back. But at one time I was owing $10,000, and for me that was a terrible amount. That was better than a whole year's wages. With that kind of debt, the pressure was terrible. I couldn't squeeze the banks and loan companies for any more, so I started to go to my relatives. They knew my situation. They knew that I was hooked on gambling, but I would go to them and cry; I would tell them the loan sharks were after me and that they would kill me if I didn't pay, and while it wasn't true in my case, there were stories in my neighborhood about this happening and my father-in-law was frightened about me being killed and leaving his daughter a widow with two little children, so he would lend me a thousand. Then I would go to my brother and do the same thing and then to my mother-in-law, who had her own account and didn't let her husband know, and then to my mother. Each time I promised them I would pay them back—which I never did—and I promised that this was the last time, that now I was cured, that I would pay back the debt and that I would never gamble again. When I was telling them this, I even began to believe it myself. But you know, the minute I got away with the money in my hand, I was back at the track, gambling.

THE BAILOUT—AND THE DESPERATION PHASE

The bailout—the point at which a relative comes up with $1,000, $10,000, $50,000 depending on the family's economic level—generally marks a turning point: the end of the Losing Phase and the beginning of the Desperation Phase.

The Losing Phase may have lasted 5, 10, even 15 years, a stretch of time in which there has been incredible borrowing, betting, juggling and repaying, and in which the compulsive gambler has managed, somehow, to remain afloat. But with the first substantial bailout, the process accelerates sharply along the downward path.

Why the bailout has this effect, we do not know. It may very well be that with the bailout money in hand, and feeling immensely relieved, the gambler's despair turns to euphoria and he convinces himself that even when he was on the brink of disaster, his "lucky star" would not let him be destroyed. It is a sign that he is invincible, that at last his luck has turned and that he is on the way up again, that now there will be another string of successes, the way there was at the beginning. Now he will not only be able to recoup everything he has lost, he will be on the way to making the fortune he had always dreamed about.

When this does not happen, when in fact he plunges and loses even more quickly whatever money he has been able to scrape together, he is cast into even deeper depression and despair, and he is driven by his addiction into doing things he would not have dreamed of doing before. One after another, the moral and ethical restraints that had kept his behavior within civilized, rational, and legal bounds, vanish, propelling him into one desperate move after another, each one worse than the preceding, including acts that are blatantly criminal. While this is happening he knows that the time of reckoning will come, that he is going to have to face the consequences, but he is powerless to withstand the overwhelming force of his addiction. He must gamble and gamble and gamble. There is no way he can hold back.

Michael P.

When Michael P. graduated from high school, he went to work for a Wall Street firm as a messenger, with the aim of becoming first a customers' man and then a full broker. He wanted to follow in the footsteps of his father who had, as a broker, amassed some $10 million by the time he was 45, mainly through competent investing.

Advancement was slower than Michael had expected; frustrated, he turned to gambling, hoping to speed his movement toward his ultimate goal. Promotion to the job of customers' man finally came when he was 22. By that time Michael was heavily involved in gambling, both in the customary gambling setting as well as in his securities trading. One might have thought that trading in securities would have satisfied the young man's need for excitement and financial advancement, but it wasn't quite enough for him. There wasn't enough action. It didn't stimulate his adrenalin flow the way gambling with dice or cards or the horses did. Further, securities trading was a solitary pursuit and a colorless one. The gaming rooms, the track and the Atlantic City casinos and their denizens were much more stimulating than the drab surroundings in his Wall Street office and the dull people with whom he worked. The gains from his Wall Street activities, both as an employee and as an investor, served mainly as a reservoir into which he dipped regularly to finance his gambling activities.

Michael kept his gambling a secret from his father and from his fellow employees, disciplining himself severely to restrict it to evenings and weekends, except for an occasional discreet telephone call to his bookmaker from his office or during lunch.

As Michael picks up his own story, he has been losing steadily and heavily, owing $7,000 to a bank and $15,000 to a bookmaker.

I had never been in this kind of fix before—owing so much to a bookmaker. I had managed to spread it around—$5,000 here, $3,000 there, juggling from here to there and not letting any debt get so big that I couldn't find some way to borrow and pay it. Up to this point, I had been able to keep well ahead in the market. I knew a trader in an over-the-counter house, and he would let me know when a new issue was coming out. I would buy it from him before it went on the market, and so I was able to make a profit on the issue as soon as it was traded. He wasn't supposed to do this, but we exchanged favors. Whenever I ran really short in my gambling, I could count on him to help me make a fast couple of thousand to pay off a debt.

But now it seemed everything was against me. My friend had been fired. The market was acting crazy, going up when it should have been going down and going down when everybody was expecting it to go up. At this point, I was desperate. I figured I could stall the bank on its loan, but this was a big-time bookmaker I was dealing with and he was after me for the $15,000. He had allowed me to push it from $5,000 to $10,000 to $15,000. But now he wanted his money, and he was threatening to get me into trouble unless I got him the money. He didn't care where I got it. He knew about my father (my father is still in the market with a large, prestigious firm), and the bookie threatened to go to my father for the money. That would have killed me, and I pleaded with him not to do it. I knew also that if my firm ever got wind of my gambling, they'd fire me in a minute.

I was desperate, and I went ahead and did something I would never have done otherwise. It was stupid, crazy, but remember I was desperate, and when you're like that you're not thinking straight anymore. One night, my wife and I and the kids were visiting my father for dinner in his Park Avenue apartment. After dinner, while we were sitting and talking, he got a telephone call and went into his study to answer it. He didn't bother to close the door, because, after all, he was with family. What he didn't know was that a member of his family was a gambling addict. I didn't intend to overhear the conversation, but I couldn't help it. He was kind of excited and he was talking loud. My father is on the board of a big corporation, the XYZ Company, and the conversation had to do with a deal they were planning, something nobody knew anything about, including me, up to that point. The XYZ Company was planning to take over the UVW Corporation, a smaller outfit, but one with a lot of promise. They were going to announce the negotiations early the following week. That was a Thursday night when I heard this.

The rest of the night there was only one thing on my mind. I was going to buy $15,000 worth of options—calls—on the UVW stock, figuring it would positively shoot up when plans for the merger were announced. Considering my father's involvement, this would be a risky business if it ever got out, but I figured I could wiggle out of it somehow if it were exposed.

The following day—Friday—I bought $15,000 worth of calls on the UVW stock. Come Monday or Tuesday, when the news came out, I would not only be able to cover the $15,000 for the options but make maybe $30,000 or $45,000 besides. What a break, I thought. Now, all my problems would be solved. I would be out of the bind and have plenty of money to gamble and recoup.

I guess you can figure out what happened. Monday morning the news broke, but not the way I expected. Some man who owned about 15 percent of the UVW stock was fighting the merger. When the reporters got hold of the story, they dug into the UVW's finances and found the firm a lot shakier than anyone had ever suspected. When that got out, about three o'clock, the UVW stock dropped six points. I was wiped out. The following day I was going to have to deliver a check for $15,000 to my firm to cover the cost of the options. All I had was about $2,800 in my trading account with them.

I was practically out of my mind. I didn't know what to do. I was thinking of committing suicide and was trying to figure out what would be the quickest way. There was only one other choice left—to go to my father, confess everything and ask him for the money. I knew that would be the end of our relationship forever; he would never have anything to do with me again. Being a gambler and dishonest were probably the two worst things anybody could be, in his reckoning. I was terrified at the idea of facing him; it was even worse than suicide, but I just didn't have the courage to kill myself. So I called him on the telephone at his office and said I needed to see him about something very urgent.

You should have seen the look on his face when I confessed about my compulsive gambling, my debt to the bookmaker and my buying the options based on overhearing his telephone conversation. He didn't say a word, just looked at me with such loathing, disgust, contempt that I wanted to die. But I could see what was going through his mind: what would it do to him if it came out in the press that his son was a compulsive gambler and that I had traded on the basis of information originating with him. He may have wanted to tell me to go to hell, but he couldn't. His own reputation was at stake.

When I had finished, he sat there looking at me another few seconds, still saying nothing. Then he opened his drawer, pulled out his checkbook, wrote out a check for $15,000 and handed it to me. Then he buzzed his secretary and told her to come in for dictation. He didn't even look up at me as I put the check in my pocket, got up and walked to the door. It was as though I wasn't even there.

After leaving his office, I went to my bank, deposited

the check and wrote out another check for $15,000 to my firm.

While I was still in my father's office, and on my way to the bank to deposit the check, I was desolate, disgusted with myself, depressed. Again I was thinking of suicide. But once I had deposited that check and written another for $15,000, which I then gave to the cashier at my firm, I suddenly felt free and light again. A terrible weight had been lifted from me. It was a magical sort of change; I was astounded at how quickly it had happened, but I wasn't about to start being analytical and wondering how and why it came about. It felt so good. I didn't ask any questions.

Michael's euphoria didn't last long. The $15,000 from his father had saved him from a scrape with his firm, but there was still the debt to the bookmaker—the debt that had prompted his disastrous plunge into options. Again, the feeling of desperation seized him. He *had* to get this money. The bookmaker wouldn't achieve anything now by going to his father, but he could make trouble for him with his firm. Where to turn? The banks had had it with him and wouldn't lend him anymore. There wasn't a relative left who would lend him any money. There was only one thing left. He knew his wife had several pieces of jewelry in their safe-deposit box at the bank—a bracelet, some brooches and several rings she had inherited from her mother and grandmother, jewelry she never wore because she thought it was too showy. She hadn't had occasion to go to the box for years and probably wouldn't for another several years. He knew that when she did find out she would probably want to leave him. Their relationship was not the best, as it was, mainly because of her displeasure with aspects of his personality that had come to light after they were married. This would be beyond anything she could tolerate, he knew. "But," he said, "I could no more keep from doing it than I could will my heart to stop beating or my kidneys to stop functioning. I had to do it. I had to pay back the bookie. I had to have more money to gamble. Don't forget, I was an addict."

The sale of one ring and a bracelet brought him

$23,000—much less than they were worth. When this money was gone—$15,000 to the bookmaker and the balance lost in gambling—he went to the safe-deposit box again and sold the remaining pieces for another $14,000. This, too, went in a matter of weeks.

"Again I was caught in a dead end with no place to turn. I had to have more money. I had to gamble—even if I had to hold up somebody or kill somebody to get the money."

Michael wasn't quite ready for something quite so desperate; the stratagem to which he next resorted was bizarre if not quite that drastic. One evening, when he had lost the last $3,000 he had in cash and then had run up another $9,000 debt with his bookmaker, he drove to Connecticut to the home of his wife's sister, a wealthy young woman and a member of an elite social circle. Michael knew that his sister-in-law's husband was away at the time on business, and that he would find her gullible enough to believe any story he could concoct. What he would tell her he did not know, but it came to him on the way up. It was a wild tale about his wife's infidelity with a shady character who was threatening to expose her in her social set and with her parents, unless Michael paid him $10,000.

His sister-in-law was tense when he got there, not knowing what she was going to hear. When he told her, she was horrified. She could not bear the thought of a family scandal. Further, she felt extremely vulnerable because she herself was carrying on an affair and knew that Michael suspected it. She was frightened that Michael might tell her husband unless she gave him the money. She might have wondered why Michael was so eager to protect his wife and cover up her infidelity. She might also have made a telephone call to her sister to verify the story. But she was too flustered and too frightened to act rationally and, without any hesitation, wrote him out a check for $10,000. Michael's weird mission had succeeded.

Next in his precipitous descent came the kiting of checks—cashing a worthless check at a bank where you are known and, before that check has cleared, covering it with another worthless check from another bank, then while that one is "in the air," covering it with another, etc., hoping that when you come to the end of the chain, you will have enough money from other sources to make good the outstanding balance. This Michael was able to do for several months, without getting caught; but the time came when he simply did not have the money to cover the check at the end of a particular "kiting" chain.

By this time, his next step—forging a check—was no longer out of the question. In fact, it was no more difficult to take than had been any of the previous steps. The last of his scruples was gone, not because he had entirely lost his sense of morality, but because the addictive pressure to get money for gambling was so intense, so relentless that nothing could have stood in its way, not even the knowledge that if he were caught he would surely go to jail . . . or, at the very least, that his wife would certainly leave him.

Forging his wife's signature on her personal account, he cashed a check for $10,000. When the monthly bank statement arrived, the forged check for $10,000 was there. Confronted by his wife with the forged check, Michael confessed to the act. The following day, his wife took their two children, went to stay with her father and started proceedings for divorce.

Three months later Michael was caught stealing $12,000 from the stock market portfolio of an aged woman whose account he was handling. Knowing that she was becoming senile, Michael had hoped that the theft would go undetected. Unfortunately for him, a relative had obtained custody of her assets and was conducting an audit of her account.

This time there was no reprieve. Michael went to jail for three years.

One might wonder why, in the latter part of the Losing Phase and in the course of the Desperation Phase, when the compulsive gambler is almost always losing, seldom winning—even given the ordinary odds of his particular gambling game—he is not doing any better.

As we said earlier, when the compulsive gambler starts to lose he becomes frightened and bets less carefully and intelligently than he did before, giving up the only real advantage he ever had. Even with this advantage lost, he still might not come out so badly did he not also start betting in a way that only the most inept and ignorant gamblers follow—betting by hunch or superstition. We must keep in mind that this has been a sophisticated gambler, who, when he was still in control of his gambling, was able to pick and choose and place his bets according to his best judgment. But by the time he arrives at the end of the Losing Phase and the beginning of the Desperation Phase, all that is lost. He is desperate and his betting is desperate. He no longer has the composure and control to reflect, to weigh, to choose. His betting behavior is now frenetic, spastic, unreasoned, panicky. He bets on a horse because the trainer has the same name as his godfather or because the jockey's colors are the same as his high school colors or because he had a dream about water and the horse's name is Bucket of Rain. He will bet impossible 30 to 1 or 60 to 1 shots, even knowing that the horse hasn't come in better than fifth in the last 20 starts. He has a "hunch" that, this time, this horse is going to surprise everybody and come through. He listens to other bettors while he's in line waiting to place his bet, and if he hears someone touting a particular horse he will bet on that horse and discard his own choice. He will adopt utterly senseless "systems," such as calling for another card in blackjack if his total is under 16 and his last card is red, or staying if his last card is black.

The rest of his behavior, simultaneously, becomes as unreasoned and disordered as his betting. He may induce friends, relatives, fellow employees to come into a fraudulent investment scheme he has cooked up, hoping to repay them later from his winnings, or planning to flee to another state if he loses and his fraud is discovered. He may become utterly unprincipled and unscrupulous in his treatment of other human beings, retaining not even a scintilla of his former sense of honor and decency. Here are some illustrations.

I was at the track with a gambling buddy and we put a $20 exacta box combination together, and the exacta hit for $480. My friend, Bill, went down to cash the ticket and when he didn't return in 20 minutes, I got really nervous. I went down toward the cashier's window to look for him. When I got down there, there was an ambulance and they were loading somebody into it. I asked a man what happened, and he said somebody had had a heart attack. I pushed in closer and they were just closing the ambulance doors, but I was able to get a look and it was Bill. I was shocked for a second and just stood there dumbstruck. Then I saw the ambulance pulling away. Do you know what I did? I ran after the ambulance and started banging on the door and screaming, "Where is the ticket? Where is the goddamned ticket?"

I was standing in line waiting to cash my ticket. It was a long line, and a little old woman—she must have been 70—said there was something wrong with her leg and she couldn't stand on it and would I cash her ticket. It was a $2 ticket paying $20. I told her, sure, I'd be glad to and she went over to the side and sat down to wait. When I cashed the ticket, I took a look and she had closed her eyes and seemed to be dozing. I got lost in the crowd and snuck off with her $20.

I had been cashing a lot of bad checks, small ones for $20 or $30, at drugstore, gas stations, with friends, and I was generally able to get away with it. But this one guy wouldn't let me get away with it. He got out a warrant, and the police came one night and I had to go to jail. There was no money in the house so my wife couldn't bail me out. In the morning she came to see me and I told her to go to my mother to get some money. She was back about two hours later and bailed me out. We were out there, standing in front of the police station, and I asked her where the rest of the money was. She asked me, "What rest of the money?" "The money to bet with, you stupid bastard," I screamed at her. "You mean you only got the $100 to bail me out?"

Now picture this, if you want to think about how real crazy you can get. My wife didn't even have enough money to buy food for the kids; her father had to come with bags of food. They had just turned the electricity and the telephone back on; my father-in-law paid for that. The landlord was threatening to throw us out because I had gotten hold of the money her father had given her for three months' rent. Okay? With all that trouble squeezing in on me, and with me still facing a rap on a bad-check charge, and just getting out on bail, I'm standing there cursing my wife because she didn't get me money to gamble with, and post time only 20 minutes away.

But wait. You think that's bad? I figured I could still make the late afternoon races or the night races, but I needed the money to bet with. So I left my wife standing there and drove out to my mother's house. When I got there, she was surprised to see me because she didn't understand anything about bail and she didn't know what the money was for that she gave my wife. She thought I was still at the police station. So I explained it to her, and I told her about the bad check that I had to make good or maybe I would have to go to jail. I pleaded with her to give me $200 so that I could pay the check.

My mother was 80 years old. She was all bent over from having worked at a sewing machine in the factory most of her life. I had already gotten $35,000 from her. That was what she had left from her savings and what she got out of my father's insurance when he died. I had cleaned out all that. And now she was living on her Social Security with a little pension. She started to cry and pleaded with me, "Ralphie, what do you want from me? I gave you everything. Now you want to take the food out of my mouth. No. I can't give it to you."

I didn't even hear what she was saying. I had to have the money. So I got on my knees and began to cry and I promised her by all the saints that this was the last time, that I would just pay off that check and my gambling would be finished. I would go straight and my wife and kids would get all my salary. And she believed me. She went down to the bank with me and cashed her Social Security check and gave me $200. An hour later, I was at the track.

* * *

What the Situation Is Like at Home

One can well imagine, when things have reached this stage, what the situation is like at home.

In the Winning Phase, the compulsive gambler manages to participate to some reasonable extent in family life, despite his preoccupation with gambling.

In the Losing Phase, there is no longer any family life as far as he is concerned. So consuming is his frenetic chase to recoup his losses that he hasn't the time, patience, energy or interest to do anything with his family, to take his wife to dinner, to attend parents' functions at school, to help his children with their homework, to visit relatives, to just sit with the family and watch a police serial or sit-com on television. How can he? When he's at home, he's watching two or three ball games simultaneously on television, with the sound turned down, while listening to another game on the radio and checking every 20 minutes on the telephone for the race results.

When he's not at home, he's at the track, or Atlantic City or Las Vegas, or at an illegal card game or dice game. Or else he's at a relative's house, or at a finance company, a bank or a loan shark trying frantically to raise some money to cover his losses and his other debts. Or he's hiding out somewhere, frightened, trying to get away from a bookmaker's collector or from the police.

His wife tries to talk to him, to get him to pay some attention to her, to the children, to his responsibilities, to the unpaid bills, but he is entirely out of contact. It has been so long since he has had any interest in sex that she doesn't even bother to think about it. His children no longer expect anything from him; they just want to stay out of his way. He is snappish, irritable, surly. Comments or questions about his gambling throw him into a fury. Interruptions while he is watching a game or getting the race results provoke explosions of rage.

With the beginning of the Desperation Phase, things get even worse. He is virtually out of control. He alternates between periods of explosive anger and periods of zombie-like behavior. His explosions of rage are no longer confined to verbal abuse. Now he is throwing things, smashing glass and china, smashing the furniture, striking out at his wife and children. In his zombie-like phase, he walks about muttering, talking to himself, blind and deaf to what is going on around him, sitting for hours either watching television or staring sightlessly ahead of him, or lying in bed.

His wife cannot stand it any longer, and she has taken the children and left him, either staying for a while with a relative or setting up an independent residence and proceeding toward a divorce. The job or the business are long gone now, and he is totally alone—without work, without friends, without family. He has no money with which to gamble. Nobody is left who will give him or lend him a dollar. He walks about his empty apartment or house with nothing to do, no one to speak to. He is jittery, agitated. He cannot even sit still to watch television. He is deeply depressed. He is given to fits of uncontrollable sobbing.

His sleep is shallow, miserable, filled with nightmares. He has no appetite, and when he does eat he depends on whatever is left on the shelves or in the refrigerator. If he does go out to buy himself food, he pays little attention to what he gets; he no longer has any interest in keeping himself operating physically. His clothing is soiled, and he cannot muster up the energy or interest to do something about his personal appearance. He goes unshaved for days and doesn't bother to bathe.

If someone should knock at the door, he reacts with terror and hides. The ring of the telephone throws him into a panic. He is so "strung out" he cannot stand it and tries to quiet his nerves with alcohol or tranquilizers such as Valium, if he can get hold of any.

By this time, gambling is no longer an issue. He does not have the money, and he could not mobilize his physical and mental resources to gamble even if he did. He is feeling so miserable, so lost, so depressed, that even gambling cannot entice him any longer. All he is looking for at the tail end of the Desperation Phase is relief from his unbearable depression.

What happens to him after that? He may, if he is fortunate, seek help at a psychiatric center or a treatment center for compulsive gamblers, or he may find his way to

Gamblers Anonymous. Failing that, he may wind up in a mental hospital, psychotic, or in a general hospital, physically spent. He may disappear from view, becoming a vagrant, floating from one town to another, from one porter's or dishwasher's or crop picker's job to another. He may attempt suicide. (One out of every five compulsive gamblers does attempt suicide, a rate vastly greater than that for the population as a whole.) Or he may die of an accident or from a shooting or knifing, or of an illness that, in his debilitated condition, his body is unable to withstand.

CHAPTER FIVE

Compulsive Gambling and the Family

THE DEVELOPMENT OF COMPULSIVE GAMBLING MAY BE likened to that of cancer. Starting slowly and quietly, it gives no indication of its presence. Its very early signs, pertaining mainly to personality and temperament, are barely distinguishable from normal behavior and would, if detected at all, indicate no more than a generalized emotional problem—nothing specific to gambling. Then, as the years go by, telltale symptoms begin to appear that would, if recognized, flash a high-level warning that a deadly malignancy was in the making. To the untutored eye, however, they still appear as minor excesses in gambling behavior that, though deviating from the customary, are still not great enough to arouse alarm—suspicion and concern, perhaps, but not alarm. They are still within the range of acceptable behavior and not too difficult to tolerate and rationalize. Thus ignored, the disorder gradually grows until it bursts out in the first open, ugly manifestation of a virulent malignancy. Countermeasures of various kinds are taken, but they cannot halt its advance. In short order it spreads out and affects every person with whom the compulsive gambler is closely involved—his wife, his children, his siblings and parents, his other relatives, his friends and business associates.

While all these people are affected, the most intense and destructive impact is felt by the immediate family, by the gambler's wife and children. It is the nature of emotional disorders that when one member of the family is afflicted, the effects are felt by all the others. There are few, however, in which the impact is felt with such severity as in the case of compulsive gambling.

Just as it is possible to chart a predictable course for this addiction as it develops in the gambler, so is it possible to chart a predictable course for the effects of the addiction on the spouse. The progression may be divided into three fairly distinct phases: I. The Denial Phase, II. The Stress Phase and III. The Exhaustion Phase.

THE DENIAL PHASE

The term *denial* as it is used in a psychiatric context does not meant knowing something and refusing to acknowledge it to others, or saying that something isn't so when you know that it is. In the psychiatric context, denial means refusing to acknowledge something to oneself, getting oneself to actually believe that there is no danger at all. It is a psychological mechanism that all of us use to a lesser or greater degree to avoid anxiety and fear. A good example is the attitude of many smokers toward smoking. They know that smoking is dangerous to their health, that it can cause cancer, heart disease, stroke, emphysema and other life-threatening illnesses. They have seen research reports providing mountains of indisputable evidence. But they are addicted to smoking. Rather than accepting the fact that, by their own actions, they are exposing themselves to serious illness and early death, and to escape the terrible anxiety this causes, they evade the issue. They refuse to read or listen to any more reports on the evidence against smoking. When they are unable to avoid the evidence they tune it out. They make themselves not perceive or understand what they are seeing or hearing. When others insist that they pay attention and discuss the evidence, they come up with all sorts of rationalizations. "It's only statistics. Anybody can twist figures around to make them come out the way they want them to. Look at all the people who smoke, and nothing happens to them. I'm positive it is not going to happen to me. It's a one-in-a-million shot and you take that kind of risk every day." Because they are unable to make themselves stop smoking, they create every kind of rationalization or excuse to minimize the danger, to convince themselves that the danger does not exist. This is denial.

Denial is a characteristic of alcoholism and of compulsive gambling, too. Even with the evidence of destruction and havoc spread before their eyes, the alcoholic and the compulsive gambler deny that they are addicted, that the devastation has anything to do with drinking or gambling. They can give you a hundred rationalizations to prove that it's not the drinking or gambling that has caused the problems but something or someone else.

So it is with the wife of the compulsive gambler (or the wife of the alcoholic). She, too, falls back on the evasive strategy of denial when she is confronted with the evidence that her husband has a gambling problem.

Jane McH.

Jane was 19 when she married Eddie. He was 22 and working as production assistant with a large printing firm. They had met at a party in the neighborhood and were married after just a few months of dating.

"What I liked about Eddie," Jane related, "was that he was so lively, so much fun.

He was very light-hearted and he could make anybody laugh. He had a wonderful sense of humor. We never just sat around. We were always going out—to the beach, to a dance, to parties, to restaurants.

The only time he went anywhere by himself was on Sundays—that's when we were still dating. He had a group of men friends and they played cards every Sunday. He didn't hide it; he didn't have to. Everybody played cards. It was something people did when they got together. It was sociable. My parents used to do it practically every weekend, and it was nothing, just enjoyment. Friends used to get together and play cards, drink a little, eat, talk, till two or three in the morning. I personally didn't care for it much. I would play once in a while when my uncle and aunt and cousins came over, but I wasn't particularly excited about it. It was all right, something to do. So when Eddie went to play cards on Sunday, I didn't give it a second thought. Not only that, he would give me the money he won and I would put it away for the wedding.

After we were married, he continued to play cards on Sunday, and then he started to play cards a night or two during the week. I didn't think anything of it even then. He worked hard during the day, and if he wanted to be with his friends to play cards, what was wrong with that? I had enough to do. I had girlfriends, and we used to visit with each other when the men were away in the evening, or go to a movie. Besides, I wouldn't have dreamed of telling him not to go or to question him. You have to understand that there was no reason for me to be suspicious or worry about his playing cards, anymore than if he was going bowling or to the movies.

Then other things began to happen and they did upset me, but I tried not to pay too much attention to them. I figured this was the sort of person I married, and I had married him for better or for worse and I would just have to put up with it. It started when he would say he would be home before midnight because he had to go to work early the next day, and then he wouldn't come home till two or three in the morning. Then he would tell me he was going over to visit his mother on a Sunday, and I would find out later, when I was emptying out his jacket pockets to take his suit to the cleaners, that he had been to Atlantic City. When I asked him about it, he would shrug his shoulders and say, "So what?" and rather than start a fight, I let it go.

Then one Saturday we had planned to go up to the lake to go boating and fishing. It was his idea; he liked to do that, and I didn't mind it either. I liked being in the country. When we were already on the expressway, he said we weren't going fishing. We were going up to Saratoga to

the races. I was angry because he made the change
without even asking me. But, I said to myself, let it be the
races. I had never seen Saratoga, and I had heard a lot
about what an interesting place it was.

It was just one thing after another I had to put up with,
but none of them was very much. Then something else
began to happen. One payday he didn't give me the
regular amount. He told me the union had just made a big
assessment because they were building a strike fund.
Next, he had to make a contribution to the support of the
family of a buddy who had been killed on the job, so he
couldn't give me the full amount. Then he had to make a
loan to his widowed cousin who was having an operation
and didn't have enough health insurance; all the other
relatives were chipping in.

These all sounded like legitimate reasons, but they were
coming up too suddenly and one after another. I should
have become suspicious then and insisted on checking it
out. But again I didn't want to start any trouble. Eddie had
a mean temper, and I had seen him take it out on other
people, and I was afraid. So I said to myself, "All right, I
don't like it, and it smells kind of fishy, but it isn't the
worst thing that could happen."

Besides, the picture was not entirely a bad one. In fact,
it was bright more often than not. That was when he was
winning, and in those days he seemed to be winning quite
often. He would come home one day and stick four or five
hundred-dollar bills in my hand and kiss me and say,
"See, I told you I would make it up to you." Or he would
come home and say, "Look out the window, I've got a
surprise for you," and there was a brand-new automobile.
Another time it was tickets for a one-week cruise to the
Caribbean. "Okay," he would say, "are you still worried
about my being away so much? I wouldn't be able to get
these things if I didn't get out once in a while and bet a
little. You don't think I could afford these things from what
I earn on my job? You don't want us to stay in a hole for
the rest of our lives, do you?"

Of course, I recognized the snow job he was giving me,
and I didn't feel comfortable going along with it. But what

was I going to do? Tell him I didn't like these extras and luxuries? It wasn't too hard to make myself like them and be happy with them and not think about where they were coming from.

Jane's experience is not unique. It could have been the story of any of the hundreds of women who have been interviewed on this subject by health care professionals, social service workers and research investigators.

First the innocent, unobtrusive forays into gambling, arousing no notice at all. Then the somewhat troublesome incidents that arouse annoyance, some concern, some suspicion, but are not serious enough to fight about and disturb an otherwise good and enjoyable relationship. The wives, at this point, are doing what most wives, and husbands, too, do in a marital situation when friction begins to occur. Unconsciously, they balance the minuses against the pluses and say to themselves, "These annoyances and frustrations are troubling, and they are something I didn't expect. But is it really worth getting that upset about them and jeopardize the rest of our marriage? Why not look at the other side of it and see how many good things there are? Count your blessings and you'll see how high they stack up in a pile against the shortcomings."

This state of affairs can go on for a year or longer without any abrupt change, only a gradual increase in the frequency and severity of the problem behavior. He used to go out just one or two nights a week to gamble. Now it is three or four. He used to play with the children at home, take them out to the playground, go shopping with his wife to buy clothing for them and furniture for their home. Now he has hardly any time for the family at all. He used to take his wife out to dinner, to cocktail parties, to dances. Now it is perhaps an occasional visit to friends, nothing more. He used to miss an occasional Sunday dinner with her folks. Now he goes only once every six or eight weeks. The relatives could always count on him to be there when there was a christening, a First Communion, a Bar Mitzvah, a wedding. Now he hardly ever shows up.

She had hoped it would get better, but instead it is

getting worse. She cannot let it go on any longer, the wife declares to herself. There are now too many "minuses," and the "pluses" do not look as good as they used to. She decides to bring up the issue. At this stage, while he is still winning fairly consistently, the husband's response is likely to be conciliatory. He will try not to let it happen so often, he tells her. He will take her out more frequently. He will spend more time with the children. He will resume going to her mother's for dinner. He sends her nephew a belated graduation gift or her cousin a belated wedding gift, and a very generous one at that.

As she observes his efforts to set things right, she breathes a sigh of relief. It's going to be all right now! She's glad she spoke to him; otherwise, nothing would have happened. And he was so nice about it, too. With things now moving in a positive direction, her attitude swings over in the other direction. She wonders whether she hasn't really been too hard on him. Wasn't she really exaggerating? Had it really been as bad as she thought?

For a while things continue to go well and she is convinced that she was wrong. Then the reforms begin to drop away one by one until, in a few months, it is as bad as it was before. This time, she says, she's not going to let it go and she's not going to be so nice. This is getting to be a real problem, and they are just going to have to face it. She confronts him with the issue. She says she's been talking to her relatives and friends and that they say he's got a bad gambling problem, that they ought to do something about it before their whole lives are spoiled. She wants him to cut out the gambling and get back to living a normal life, or else she is going to have to do something about it, not being very specific about what this "something" is going to be. In the back of her mind are some vague thoughts about leaving him. This time his response is not conciliatory. He is angry. He isn't going to be pushed around by her. He is entitled to some freedom. He is supporting her in good style and she has no reason for complaint. With that he storms out of the house.

When he is gone, she is shaken, frightened, sits down and starts to weep. What is she going to do now? What if he should get really angry and leave her? She was crazy to think about leaving him. He may not be everything a husband should be, but at least he is a husband and he is here in the home and the children have a father. She ruminates about other married couples she knows. Wasn't it just two weeks ago that her friend Ethel came over, weeping, bruises on her arms and face, telling about how her husband had come home drunk the night before and beaten her? What about her cousin Joanne? Her husband had walked out on her one day, without saying a thing, and left her with their three little children. And then there was her own sister Ginny. Everybody knew that her husband was running around with other women. It was shameful! Compared to those others, she reflects, her marriage is really a good one when everything is said and done. What right does she have to complain? The others were probably wishing that they could be in her boots. Now she's sorry she quarrelled with him. She wishes he hadn't stormed out. Now she can't wait till he gets home so she can make it up to him, and when he comes home she does.

Having thus fooled herself into complacence about her husband's gambling, the wife takes the next step—revising her expectations about her marriage so as to embrace her husband's gambling as part of a pattern she can accept. The adjustment made, the gambling no longer bothers her as much as before. She busies herself with her children, her friends, her housekeeping. She starts sewing new curtains. Or, if her economic level is high enough, she becomes interested in tennis or golf, joins a garden club, takes a course at the community college.

Meanwhile, she tries to take "a more positive attitude" toward her husband's gambling. She may even resume going with him to the track or to the casinos. There are cruise ships that take you on one-day, two-day or three-day gambling trips "to nowhere," and they can be lots of fun . . . sunbathing, swimming, fine food, entertainment. Why not? It's nice to get away and have a little relaxation. She even catches a little of the gambling fever and finds some excitement in gambling herself, or in watching her husband gamble and win. She wonders how she could have been so negative about this gambling. Now she sees no harm in it at all, or, if she still has some doubts, she pushes them out of her mind.

Then one day she's opening the mail and looks at the telephone bill. It's about double the usual amount and she wonders why. Maybe Joe had made some long distance calls to his sister out on the coast. But not for that much! And if he did, he would have told her about it. She checks the itemized calls and there's nothing unusual there, no large long-distance charges. Then she looks at the bill again, and sees it's for two months. The previous month's bill is in arrears. "That's impossible," she says to herself. "We always pay our bills on time. Joe is always punctual writing out the checks and sending them off." When Joe comes home, she waits until they've finished dinner and asks him about the bill. "That can't be," Joe says. "I sent that check off three weeks ago. It's these damned computers. They're always fouling things up." Then he tells her about a friend who got a telephone bill for $3,500, and when he checked it with the phone company, they found out the computer had messed up more than 1,000 bills before they spotted the trouble. Reassured, his wife tells him to be sure to call the telephone company from his office and straighten it out. She doesn't like something like that hanging over her head. "Sure thing, honey," he replies.

The following month, the telephone bill comes in and she quickly checks and finds that there are no longer any arrears. "It was the computer all right," she says to herself—not knowing that her husband had held back the previous month's payment and had then been able to cover it with some money he had won.

The incident is forgotten until another occurs. She's at the department store buying a new lamp for the children's room. After making her selection she goes to the cashier and tells him she'd like to have the lamp sent. He takes her department-store credit card and following a standard procedure checks it with the credit department. The cashier talks into the phone for a few seconds and then tells her that he's sorry he cannot make the sale. There is an outstanding bill for $280 for a bed and mattress purchased three months ago.

She is furious. There's a mistake. Their accounts are in error. Her husband paid that bill long ago. If the bill wasn't paid, why hadn't they gotten another bill showing the arrears? The cashier just shakes his head and says he's sorry, he doesn't know.

That night when her husband comes home from work, she confronts him immediately. Taken aback, he hesitates for a moment and then he collects himself. Yes, he tells her, it's his fault. He hadn't paid the bill. There's this man at the office, a real good friend who had done him many favors, and now this man was in trouble. He needed some money for an abortion and he was afraid his wife might find out. He needed a loan of $300. So Joe had given him the money. That made him short for the month and he couldn't pay the department-store bill. The friend had promised to repay him in a few days but hadn't done so, even up to now, so the bill remained unpaid. "Then why," she asks, "didn't the store send another bill showing the arrears?" "They did, but he gave the postman an excuse and got him to hold it out so that he could pick it up at the post office. Why hadn't he told her about this before? He explains it isn't the kind of thing he felt comfortable talking to her about—abortions, secret affairs and the like, even if they didn't have anything to do with him. This really *does* arouse her suspicions. This was something she hadn't even thought about before. Could it be Joe who was having the affair, and was it he, rather than his friend, who needed the money for an abortion? She doesn't even ask him these questions, but they eat at her and for the next couple of days she's on the point, several times, of asking him, but each time she holds back. What if he should say yes? What would she do then? So she decides to let the whole thing pass, and prays that it was his friend and not he, never even suspecting that there was no friend and no abortion, and that he had used the money to gamble and had lost it.

Two, three, four such incidents occur, and each time he lies and makes up some other excuse. Were this to have happened four or five years ago, she would have realized that she was being taken in and would have pursued each incident to its resolution, and would thus have found out why the bills weren't being paid, that he was gambling with the money and losing it. But by this time she is no longer dealing with reality as reality. She has put her reality-testing criteria aside, in order to protect herself from the truth, fearing that if she were to confront the truth, she would have to acknowledge to herself that her husband is a problem gambler and a liar. So she makes one compromise after another with reality, hoping blindly that somehow things will work themselves out and that everything will be all right.

It is possible for a person to continue in such a state of self-deceit for years, provided things remain pretty much the way they are and that nothing happens to upset the equilibrium. However, as we very well know, the addiction of compulsive gambling does not stand still. It progresses, becomes more serious, more intense, especially after it enters the losing phase. Somewhere along the line in the progression, something happens to shatter the equilibrium and jolt the wife out of her delusions.

With this development, the Denial Phase ends and the Stress Phase begins—the phase of confrontation with reality.

THE STRESS PHASE

For Rachel B., the shocks came thick and fast, tearing away her self-deceiving denial and exposing her to the tough and ugly truth of being married to a compulsive gambler.

It was during the Vietnam War and we had been married a little over a year. Arthur was drafted in 1966 and he was stationed at Camp X in Z state. We had no children, and I got an apartment near the base and went to work at a bank. He was doing a lot of card playing on the base because he was bored. He would also go to the track a lot and I would go with him. At first it had been amusing, but after a while I had no interest in it at all. I just went along to be with him. I also thought I could hold him back. If I was there, maybe he wouldn't bet too much. We had been having an occasional spat about his gambling, but nothing serious. I was just taking it, not wanting to worry him too much. I knew he was going to be shipped overseas soon, and I didn't want to make it any more difficult for him. Then these things started to happen. He used to get passes to be off the base in the evening and to be with me where I lived. One evening he didn't show up, and I was worried. I got in touch with the base and they told me that he was out on a pass and he would probably show up any minute. Maybe he had stopped in to have a beer with his buddies. I didn't pursue it any further because I was afraid I'd get him in trouble. So I waited, worried to death that something had happened to him. A little after one in the morning, he showed up. He said he had driven over to the adjoining state and had gone to the track. I was furious with him and started screaming at him about what a rotten thing he had done. Then, when I saw the hurt, woeful look on his face, I felt sorry for him and toned down my voice and anger. By this time he was sitting on the bed with his hands over his face and I heard him sobbing. He started talking and pleading with me to forgive h.m. He knew what a terrible thing he had done, and if I would forgive him he would never do it again. Well, you know how it is—a lovers' quarrel, and the next thing we were in bed. I thought that was that and forgot about the incident.

A few weeks later he told me he had to do guard duty over the weekend, that he would not be able to be with me. I thought nothing of it; after all, the army is the army, and that's routine. That Friday morning he returned to the base and said he'd see me Monday night. I didn't mind too much. I had housework and shopping to catch up on. While I was looking through the drawer where I kept my records and papers, I noticed that the papers for our automobile were missing. That worried me because I'm an anxious person and can't stand it when something like that is missing. So I called him at the base to ask him about it. The sergeant said he was out on a weekend pass. I was about to blurt out, "But he said he had guard duty," but again, I was concerned about getting him in trouble and kept quiet. I was frightened to death. Where could he be? I started to imagine things about his being in trouble with gamblers or loan sharks and getting killed, the way I had read about other gamblers in the papers. I was beside myself and didn't know what to do. I called my mother, and she and my father tried to reassure me.

Finally, I quieted down and got hold of myself and decided there was nothing to do but wait. I would hear from somebody soon—the police, a hospital, Arthur himself. Sunday night he called. "For God's sake," I shouted, "where are you? What happened to you?" He was in Miami. He had taken a plane to Miami Friday night and had gone to the track. He had lost all his money and couldn't get back. He wanted me to go to the airport and pay for a ticket and they would issue one to him down there. When I hesitated, he pleaded with me to do it. If he didn't get back that evening he would be AWOL. If I had known then what I know now, I would have told him to get back the best way he could, and if he was AWOL that would be too bad. Let him take the consequences. That might have been the best thing for him, being thrown in the brig. That might have made him face reality. But no, I was still a sentimental fool, and I did what he asked me to.

When he came to see me after he got back to the base, I wouldn't let him speak. I was furious with him. What in heaven's name was happening to him? What had made him do such a thing? Only a crazy man would do this thoughtless thing. Was he going out of his mind? If so, he needed to go to a mental hospital. Maybe I ought to tell his captain and they'd send him to a mental institution instead of sending him to Vietnam. . . . When I stopped, he tried to explain. He was shaken, remorseful, penitent. He knew what a horrible thing he had done. He didn't know what had made him do it. But he knew it would never happen again. He would get hold of himself and he would never put me through this again. And don't you know, I believed him. I guess I wanted to believe him. I wanted things to be right again. Each time I thought, "This time it's going to be okay." He was sobbing and weeping and I felt sorry for him and guilty about having come down so hard on him. After all, here he was waiting to be sent over to Vietnam any day, maybe to be killed in combat. My thinking was so messed up, I even started to feel guilty about his gambling, to think that maybe I had something to do with it. Maybe I wasn't a good enough wife; if I had been, maybe he would not have gotten into gambling. Maybe if I had been more interested in him and shown him more love, he might have stayed home more and not stayed away so much to gamble. That night, too, ended up with our making up and going to bed and making love.

It wasn't until later in the week that I remembered about the automobile ownership papers, and I asked him. "Oh, that," he said, "I had to show them to the provost marshal." "But we've already done that," I said. "I know," he answered, "but there was some mixup and he wanted to see them again." That, of course, was a lie. A few weeks later I checked and found he had taken the papers to get a loan of $1,500 to take that trip to Florida and gamble.

Two or three weeks after that, it was our wedding anniversary and he said he would like to take me to some elegant place for the weekend, and he made reservations at a well-known expensive resort hotel. I was flattered and pleased. The drive took us about three hours. When we got there, and I saw the hotel, I was thrilled. It was just as beautiful as the pictures in the brochure. We had a lovely, large room with a balcony overlooking the ocean. It was one of those heavenly southern nights, with a soft, warm breeze coming off the ocean, the scent of night-blooming flowers floating to us from below, a beautiful moon casting a silvery reflection in the water. This was truly a night for romance and love. We decided to have our dinner on the balcony, and he ordered us an elegant dinner with champagne and wine. In the magic of the night and the wine all my concerns about his gambling melted away, all my anger was gone. I felt nothing but tenderness and love. We sat out on the balcony for a while, and then, with the unspoken understanding of lovers, I got undressed and changed into my flimsiest negligee. While I was still in the bathroom, he shouted to me that he had just remembered and had to go down to the desk to straighten out something about our reservations. He suggested I get into bed and wait for him. He'd be up in just a few minutes. For a second I was slightly miffed at this delay, but I was still feeling mellow with the food and the wine, and I brushed my annoyance aside. After he left, taking the door key with him, I got into bed to close my eyes for a minute or two and to wait for him.

The next thing I knew I was being awakened out of a deep sleep by the loud barking of some dogs who must have gotten into a fight on the beach. The lights in the room were still on. I looked over beside me in the bed to ask Arthur what time it was, only Arthur wasn't there. I was frightened and called his name, thinking he was in the bathroom, but I got no answer. I jumped out of bed and looked at the clock radio. It was four in the morning. I looked around the room and in the closet to see if the jacket or trousers that he had been wearing were there. They weren't. Everything was exactly the way it was when we had unpacked. Arthur had either not come back after leaving to go "down to the desk" or else he came back, saw I was asleep and went off to gamble somewhere.

This time I knew that I had a really bad problem on my hands. After his last weekend in Miami, I wasn't frightened any longer. Just furious, in a rage, ready to tear him to pieces the minute he walked in. I couldn't go back to sleep, and I fixed myself some coffee and sat on the balcony and watched the night fade and the sun come up.

By seven o'clock, I had my bags packed and called a taxi to take me to the airport. He walked in just as the bellhop was coming to get my bag. Arthur was disheveled, grimy, unshaven, his shirt stained. I could smell his perspiration, and it was disgusting. He seemed stunned when he saw me leaving and started to plead with me to stay, that he could explain everything. I didn't even bother to listen to the rest of it. The taxi took me to the airport, and I bought a ticket to New York and phoned my mother and told her I was coming. There was a two-and-a-half hour wait for the plane, and I prayed that he would not come to the airport and make a scene there. He didn't, and I was thankful. During the wait, I had a chance to review everything that had been going on and found it hard to believe that all this had happened to me. When you are right in the middle of something you lose sight of what's happening. It's only when you stand off at a distance and get a chance to look at it objectively that you first realize what a disaster it's been. I decided right then and there that I had had it with him. I wasn't going to take anymore. That was it. It was finished.

My mother picked me up at the airport and told me he had been calling every half hour for the past three hours. He even had pleaded with her to try to persuade me to come back. The phone was ringing when we got to my mother's apartment, and I answered it. I listened to him for a minute, and then I told him he was wasting his breath, that I was through. If he wanted to gamble he could, but I wasn't going to let it ruin my life; and I hung up. He called again several times that day, and my mother answered the phone and told him I didn't want to speak to him.

The calls kept coming that day and the next, after he returned to the base. By this time I had simmered down a bit and was not quite so angry, only depressed. There was something else in the situation that I hadn't thought about but that was worrying me now. I was five months pregnant. That itself was disturbing. Also, the army had this rule that if your wife was pregnant, they would move you further back on the list for being shipped overseas to combat duty in Vietnam. They were sending the unmarried and childless men first. If I didn't come back to the base, the army might consider him as being without a wife and ship him overseas right away. The papers were full of the heavy casualties in Vietnam, and I didn't want his death on my conscience. I also didn't want my child born without a father. It was a terrible quandary, and I suffered over it for weeks. My mother didn't help any either: "Don't worry. He'll get over it. He's just worried about going overseas and getting killed, so he does crazy things. You'll see; if you go back, he'll behave himself." Between his pleading and my mother's badgering and my own conflicted feelings, I couldn't stand it any longer, and I went back.

A week after I returned to the base, I started to hemorrhage, and an army ambulance rushed me to the base hospital to see if they could save the baby. But they

couldn't. My husband was on emergency army duty at the
time and couldn't come to see me right away. By the time
he got there, they were wheeling me back to my room. I
was devastated at having lost the baby. I wanted terribly
for him to comfort me. He just stood there looking. He
didn't say a word, didn't put a hand on my shoulder, didn't
even bend down to kiss me. Do you know what I did? I
began to cry and apologized to him, for having had a
miscarriage.

The Wife's Subjective Reactions

Three important things come through from Rachel B.'s
account. The first has to do with her sudden awakening to
the severity of her problem.

Jane McH., you will remember, was doing her best to
rationalize the effect that her husband's gambling was having on their family life. He was staying away nights and
whole days. He was ignoring and neglecting the children.
Friends and relatives were wondering why they didn't get
together as often as they used to and why she was coming
with only the children and without her husband. His gambling was depriving the family of things they needed. With
Mrs. B., even as things were getting worse, she was still
trying to make excuses to herself, to explain the situation in
a way that would enable her to avoid facing the truth and
dealing with it. This is typical. This is what most compulsive gamblers' wives do at this stage, at the end of their
husbands' Winning Phase and the beginning of their Losing
Phase. This goes on as long as the equilibrium is maintained.
But then there is a sudden change when the gambler does
something drastic, something that makes the wife aware that
she's got a serious problem. She's not faced just with the
problem of a husband who is neglecting his family and
relatives, but the problem of a husband so obsessed with
gambling that he is driven to commit acts that are destructive to himself and his family.

The second important aspect of Rachel's story has to
do with the wife's willingness, even after recognizing the
true problem, to accept the gambler's explanations; to accept his remorse as genuine; to accept his promise that if

only she will forgive him, he will not do it again; to believe that he is going to quit gambling and reform his life.

This, too, is typical. Why do wives do this? Rachel B. explained it quite simply and clearly. "I guess I wanted to believe him. I wanted things to be right again. Each time I thought, This time it's going to be okay." This is a perfectly normal and understandable reaction. When you're married and you have a husband and a home, this is your life, your haven. You want it to last forever; you don't want anything to interfere with it. Even after you've taken a severe buffeting, you still keep believing that the trouble is going to pass, that things will return to normal again, that the husband who is causing all this trouble will somehow straighten himself out so that things can be the way they were before. This sort of thinking goes on in many cases almost to the very end, even after the compulsive gambler has cleaned out the family's savings and other resources, let the telephone and utilities be turned off, forged checks, committed thefts and spent time in jail.

The third aspect has to do with guilt. Often, abused women feel guilty about what is happening, as though they were somehow to blame and had brought this problem on themselves. Take the case of Rachel B. After being put through one crisis after another, you would expect her to know where the blame lay. For a while she directed it where it belonged—at her husband. But in hardly any time at all, she was blaming the situation on herself—maybe if she had not nagged him so much, maybe if she had been a better wife, and so forth. Even more striking was her need to apologize to her husband for having lost their baby through a miscarriage.

This guilt—blaming themselves for the calamities brought down on their heads by their compulsive-gambler husbands—is typical of the wives in these marriages. This phenomenon also occurs with the wives of alcoholics. There are two possible explanations. One has to do with the family background of the wives. In a very large percentage of cases, the wives come from homes in which there was considerable disturbance of one kind or another—alcoholism, compulsive gambling, mental illness, desertion by a parent, divorce, abuse or just a pervasive climate of friction and strife. In such homes, children may be subjected to outright physical punishment or, at the very least, scolding and ridicule. Criticism, accusation and fault-finding have been part of their daily psychological diet. They don't know what it means to be praised and cherished, to feel good about themselves. Subjected to this sort of treatment they come to think of themselves as "bad," as not worth being cared about and loved, as meriting only criticism and blame. When things go wrong between their parents, they blame themselves for what has happened, even though they could not possibly have had anything to do with causing the trouble. They have been conditioned to feel guilty and to react, reflexively, with guilt whenever there is a problem of any kind.

The other explanation has to do with the strategy the compulsive gambler uses to divert the blame away from himself. In the early stages of marital friction as a result of problems brought on by gambling, the compulsive gambler attempts to be conciliatory, to placate, to convince the wife that there really is no problem, that his gambling is within normal bounds. However, when it becomes clear that his gambling is no longer within normal limits and that it is piling one disaster after another on his wife and children, he gives up the placating and "sweet reasonableness" approach and goes on the offensive. He becomes abusive. Who does she think she is? What right does she have to be telling him what to do? He's earning the money and supporting the family, and no one is going to tell him how he should spend it or what he should do with his spare time. If she doesn't like it, she can find herself a new husband, and he wishes she would; he's sorry he married her to start with. And if she thinks it's going to be so easy to find another husband, she ought to take a look in the mirror and see how unattractive she has become. Furthermore, if she would spend a little more time taking care of the house and the children she wouldn't be having to pound on him. Look at the house, he says. The children's things are all over the place, and you don't even pick them up. You're bringing them up to be careless, selfish slobs—and so on and so on, digging up every possible complaint or accusation he can find to throw at her.

She is shocked, astonished, frightened. She didn't expect this, didn't know he could be that way. She tries to defend herself, to hurl back some counter-accusations about the kind of man he's become, about what his gambling has done to their marriage, how it is ruining her life. He counters with additional accusations and insults, puts on his coat, slams the door behind him and takes off for the track. Defenseless, beaten down, bewildered, she is back where she was as a child—the subject of brutal treatment, accusations, blame, abuse. She responds with the reaction of childhood—she feels guilty about what has happened, that somehow she is to blame.

Accompanying the utterly baseless feeling of guilt, something equally irrational occurs. We must remember that prior to the problem gambling, there was, generally speaking a strong, positive relationship between the two. He has courted her, made her feel special and prized and then married her. They loved each other and felt happy when they were together. When he is in the Winning Phase, he showers her with gifts, surprises, vacations and other bounties. She has no notion that he is doing this out of his own need to prove himself a "big shot," to demonstrate to her how lucky she is to have married him. She thinks these are demonstrations of love and caring and is drawn closer to him. Then when the troubles and the quarrelling begin, when his preoccupation with gambling pulls him away from her and he loses interest in her, she feels hurt, rejected, abandoned. On top of everything else, this is a crushing blow to her ego. The situation arouses in her a feeling of low self-worth, of inadequacy as a woman and a wife, of having failed in her marriage. This is felt even more keenly when her husband's interest in sex begins to wane. She thinks it is because she is now less desirable. She does not realize that the very same thing would be happening no matter who she was, that he is just no longer interested in sex.

Regardless, she feels rejected and scorned, and in her bitterness and resentment she lashes out at him with renewed force; when she does, he has another excuse to storm out of the house to gamble.

At Her Wit's End

Now comes the time when her husband is caught up in the frenzied chase, the heavy borrowing, the draining of the family's savings and other resources, the dunning letters and phone calls from creditors, the threats from the bookmakers, the running to relatives to get money for bailouts, the loading on of second and third mortgages to get money for bailouts, the forging of her signature to get money for bailouts.

She is at her wit's end. Life, at this point, has become a day-to-day struggle for psychological survival, to keep from going out of her mind. She has considered leaving him but is still not sure that this is the only option she has left. Perhaps there is still some hope that he will straighten out. She invokes the help of his relatives, and one after another they try to intervene. They wait until he is in a dejected spell and cannot muster enough initiative to go out. Then they come over and talk to him, try to make him see what he is doing to himself and his family, appeal to his sense of decency and responsibility. To no avail. Then she tries to get a clergyman to do something, and he, too, tries to no avail. She tries to get him to go to a psychiatrist, but he refuses.

She makes desperate, pitiful attempts at controlling his gambling, calling up his gambling cronies and begging them to stay away, calling the loan companies and banks and pleading with them not to lend him any more money, hiding his automobile keys so he won't have transportation to the track, putting their childrens' bonds and savings books in her father's bank security box so he can't put his hands on them, refusing to cook for him unless he stops gambling.

One after another, the pleasures of living have been dropped from her life. They no longer go out together, anywhere. She and the children have been going to visit the relatives without him, but even this has become infrequent; she is ashamed to face her people. She is too tense, too much on edge, to listen to their attempts at reassurance and consolation. She cannot stand the laughter and gaiety of her sisters and brothers and their children, when she herself is going through such misery. She is embarrassed to face her parents after having had to come to them for money to bail him out, to pay her bills, to keep food in the house. She doesn't go to visit her friends any longer because she is so ashamed. From time to time an old, trusted friend comes over and she pours out her heart and weeps.

The Impact on the Children

In the beginning, when their father is still winning, his gambling is a boon to the children. His good fortune awakens in him his protective, parental instincts; he reaches out to them and they blossom. He buys things for them they have always wanted, to the point of absurd extravagance, and takes them to places other childrens' parents cannot afford. He loves them, and they love him.

But as he begins to lose, his mood changes and so does his relationship with the children. Absorbed in his gambling and chasing, he no longer has time for them nor any interest in getting them things or taking them places or doing anything for them. The children sense this change and are deeply injured by it. They are bewildered when they try to get his attention and he ignores them, when they do something that used to make him laugh and he doesn't even pay any attention, when they try to hold his hand or sit on his lap or elicit a hug and a kiss and he turns away from them.

They are even more upset when he is no longer just neglectful and indifferent, but now scolds them, pushes them away, even slaps them. They can't understand what is happening. Scolding and punishment are associated in their minds with "being bad," and they think it is something they have done; otherwise why would he be scolding and punishing them? They do not have the capacity yet to sympathize, as they will when they grow up, and so cannot have any idea that it is something in him that is making him so ugly and mean, and not anything that they are doing.

They become frightened but do not know how to express this fright, so they shut it away inside themselves. They become angry at the father because he is behaving this way, because he has turned away from them, because he is no longer loving and interested; but they do not know what to do with their anger. They fear that if they express it—if they show their anger—he will dislike them and punish them even more. They are afraid of their anger because it is such a powerful, strange emotion. So they repress their anger, try not to show it, not even to feel it.

It is not so bad while their mother is still able to handle the gambling problem without getting too upset herself, when she is still making excuses for her husband, trying to "understand" him and even to be sympathetic with him. She still has her composure, and she is able with her own love and caring to make up for what the children are beginning to miss from their father. She may have no idea what is bothering the children. She may just observe that they are making greater demands on her attention, that they are a little more sensitive to hurt and rejection than they used to be, that when she is too occupied to play with them or listen to them, they are now silent and sullen, something they never used to be. Yet she is still there as a buffer, and she is still able to shelter the children when they turn to her, upset and hurt.

What happens, though, when the mother herself is being buffeted by her husband's irrational behavior, struggling to keep the home from going under, dealing with the threats of creditors and the inquiries from the police, trying to protect the few assets they have left and keep them out of her husband's reach, trying to keep her sanity in the fact of her husband's stormy, abusive attacks and his withdrawal? She is no longer able to give the children the protection, attention and love they need. She herself is so exhausted and distraught that she is unable to be patient and tolerant. She cannot meet their extra demands for her time and attention, and when they keep on insisting, she reacts with frustration and anger. She, too, begins to pick on them, criticize them, blame them for things they didn't do. With no one to turn to now, with no release for their pent-up fear and anger, they internalize these emotions, which now begin to take their toll in a number of different destructive ways.

Little children become cranky, difficult, negativistic. They cry and whine. They begin to have eating and sleeping problems. They wake up with nightmares and night terrors or walk in their sleep. They refuse to sleep by themselves any longer or with the lights out, and now they insist on getting into bed with their mother. They become either rambunctious and cantankerous or silent and withdrawn. Their physical resistance wears down and they come down with colds, the flu and other illnesses. They develop phobias, anxieties, enuresis, facial twitches. If they are already going to school, they get sick in school and have to be sent home, or they get sick in the morning and so cannot go to school. In school, they become inattentive, lethargic, troublesome.

(By the way, when we describe the problems that the children of compulsive gamblers are prone to, we do not mean that all these things happen to all the children affected. These various psychological reactions are common in small children under severe and prolonged emotional stress from any source. Some children of compulsive gamblers will manifest some of these, others will manifest others, depending on the personality of the child and the particular situation in the home.)

With older children, we may expect many of the same sorts of reaction we have mentioned, but in addition they may react in the mode of troubled teenagers: truancy, running away from home, drinking, using drugs, sexual promiscuity, theft or other antisocial acts. Or they may become depressed or develop psychosomatic illnesses such as asthma, headaches and gastrointestinal disorders.

Something else is likely to occur, something common in situations where the mother and father are in conflict: The children will take sides with one parent and blame the other for the trouble. The compulsive gambler will be quick to detect his tendency and use it to turn the children against their mother, telling them it is all her fault, that she is always "on his back," nagging him, starting the quarrels and the fights. He will try to persuade them that there is nothing wrong with his gambling and that if their mother would only let him be, he would not be gambling so much and everything would be all right. If he still has money to spend, he will buy them extravagant gifts to win them over.

If he no longer has the money, he will remind them of all the wonderful things he bought them when he had it. Children are gullible and are easily won over to the side of this man who is so nice to them now—willingly pushing out of their minds the way he has been neglecting and scolding them. They turn against their mother and repeat the things their father has told them—that she ought to stop nagging him, that she ought not to be so tight with the money and let him have some to gamble with. They may even go further, using the advantage to manipulate their mother to their own advantage. ''You push me with my homework just the way you push Dad with his gambling. You don't let me stay out with my friends. You jump on me when I have a can of beer with my friends. You never get me the things I need, like Dad does. You don't really care about us the way he does, you don't love us. Dad loves us and we love him.''

You can imagine the effect of this on the wife who is struggling to keep herself and the children alive and the family from falling completely apart. However, the alliance between the children and the father does not last long, since, when he starts to lose again and finds himself in a desperate spot, he will once more turn on the children the way he had turned on them before. When this happens they are likely to swing over to an alliance with the mother. While this might be a comfort to the mother, it is unhealthy for the children, since they need to be free of alliances with either parent and not to be used in this way by either parent. An alliance with a parent imposes a heavy emotional burden on the child; sooner or later it will arouse in him a feeling of guilt for having turned against the other parent. The more deeply the child is enmeshed in the struggle between the parents, the more likely he is to develop an emotional, behavioral or psychosomatic disorder.

THE EXHAUSTION PHASE

Human beings have just so much endurance—even the strongest of us. When the blows keep coming one after another without letup, and they keep on getting not lighter, but worse, and there is no solution, no way out, there comes a point where you can't take it any longer and you go to pieces. That is what happens to the wife of a compulsive gambler.

No way out? you ask. But she does have a way out. Why doesn't she leave him, get out from under the whole mess and start life all over again?

Tell that to a woman who is going through it, and her answer might very well be, "That's a lot easier said than done. You can never know how difficult that is unless you've been through it yourself."

To understand the predicament of the compulsive gambler's wife and how nearly impossible it is for her to escape, recall Ruth Kohler's situation, as described in the Prologue.

Friends had asked her how she could have continued to live in that hell for so long without fleeing, and she had remained quiet, pretending she didn't know the answer. How could they know what it was like to be in a maelstrom, whirled about and pinned down by powerful, paralyzing forces, unable to generate enough counterforce to move even an inch, let alone to break out of its control? The crises and the traumas had followed one another with such rapidity that there was no time even to think about life on the outside, or life the way it could be. It took everything she had in emotional strength just to cope with each episode and get over it, to survive just for that day.

And when there was respite from the turmoil for a day or two or for a week, the relief and the peace were so precious she didn't want to do anything to disturb them. She would begin to hope that this might continue, that there would be no return to the agony, that this time her pleas and entreaties had taken hold and that something inside him had changed. But then, inevitably, it would start again, and so it would go on: the plunge into hell, then the relief and hope; the plunge into hell then the relief and hope. There were indeed times, she recalled, when the unendurable stretches had lasted so long without relief that she knew that in order to survive she would have to take the children and flee. But where? His parents? Her parents? For a week or two perhaps, but after that, what? How was she going to make a life for herself and the children? Where would the money come from? Who would hire her after she had been away from work so long? And how would she be able to stand the loneliness? How would she be able to muster up the strength and initiative to make a new home and start a new life? It was at those times, when it was impossible to stay and just as impossible to leave, that she contemplated suicide . . . but then what would happen to the children?

And then, difficult as it may be to believe this, the reason more wives do not leave their compulsive-gambler husbands is that, even after they have been through this nightmare, many still have hope that he may yet give up his insane gambling. And this, too, may be difficult to believe; many wives say, when questioned, that even at this stage of desperation and exhaustion, after all they have been through, they still love him. They remember the days when he was winning—the dinners at luxurious restaurants, the jewelry and the fur coats he bought for them, the vacations and the cruises, the exciting parties he gave, the lavish parties on Derby Day or during the World Series or on Super Sunday. There is a memory of the old times, and the hope is reborn that they may yet come back again.

His dramatic demonstrations of abject remorse work on her, too, to keep her from leaving. He swears by everything that is holy, on the life of his children, on his mother's grave, anything he can think of—that this time he will give it up forever, if only she will not leave him. With her still there with him, he has a chance to beat this horror, but with her gone, he is doomed; he will never have the strength to be able to fight this horrible obsession alone. He gets down on his knees and weeps. He arouses in her the deep sympathy of a mother for a suffering child. And he is able to persuade her to stay, no matter how many times he has made the same pleas and given the same promises before and broken them.

Again, we draw an analogy with alcoholism. The alcoholic does the very same thing: remorse, pleas for forgiveness, entreaties that his wife not leave him. There is one basic difference, however. With the alcoholic, the remorse and the agony and the promises are sincere. He truly feels what he is saying. The fact that he cannot keep his promises is not the result of insincerity but rather of his inability to break free of the addiction.

The entreaties and promises of the compulsive gambler are ever so much more dramatic than those of the alcoholic, but not a fraction as sincere. Granted, he, too, is in the grip of his addiction and does not have the power to free himself. However, even as he is pleading and weeping and promising, he is not thinking how hard he is going to try this time to give it up and how blessed it would be to be free of his addiction. He is thinking about what else he can say to manipulate her so that she will not leave him. He is not agonizing—as is the alcoholic—about things he has done to his wife and children, how low he has dragged them and himself. He is agonizing about not being able to get back to his gambling. He wants the situation to remain stabilized so he can concentrate on getting more money to gamble.

This does not mean that the alcoholic is basically a "decent" person, while the compulsive gambler is basically a "con man." It has to do with the nature of the addiction. In the case of the alcoholic, that which makes him behave as he does is the alcohol in his system and the action of the alcohol on the brain. When the alcohol level in his blood is high—when he is on a two- or three-day drinking bout—he is capable of virtually anything against his wife, children and others. His conscience is inoperative and he has no control over his behavior. When his drinking bout ends—when he gets too sick to drink any more, or falls into a stupor—the alcohol level in his bloodstream drops, until in half a day or more, there is no longer any alcohol left in his body, and he goes through the horror of withdrawal: the shakes, anxiety, depression, hallucinations, etc. When that is over and he has sobered up, he becomes fully conscious of what he has done. If he cannot remember, his wife and children tell him and show him the shambles of his rampage. He is, for that while, in full, conscious control of his behavior. His conscience is operative again and punishes him mercilessly. He is in agony over what he has done and frightened of the retribution. The remorse and penitence that come out of this are genuine. The fact that he will go back to drinking again—because he is addicted—does not alter the fact that at this point he means what he says about reforming.

The compulsive gambler does not have a foreign substance in his body that acts on the brain to paralyze the conscience. There is no rise and fall of such a substance in his bloodstream, with consequent alternating periods of sanity and intoxication. What affects his behavior, what produces the need to gamble and to keep on gambling, is the psychological urgency of the drive to recover the money he has lost and to find relief from his unbearable tension and depression. There is never a time when this drive is not operating full force, and hence there is never a time during which he is restored to sanity, a time when he becomes fully aware of the immensity of his problems. Hence, when he expresses remorse, it is not truly to beg forgiveness, but rather to buy more time to gamble so as not to have to face the final retribution.

So the wife forgives him once more, hoping there will be some respite, but inevitably he relapses and it begins all over again, and again she is faced with an impossible situation.

There comes a point where she cannot stand it any longer and she begins to come apart. It has been a long time since she has been able to get a good night's sleep, but now her insomnia gets even worse. She goes to the doctor for sleeping pills, and these help her for a while, but after a week or two, they no longer have much effect and the sleepless nights of tossing and turning and worrying return. She goes back to the doctor for stronger tranquilizers, and he prescribes some for her. This gives her some peace, but not for long, and she has to start increasing the dosage. She begins to suffer severe headaches, diarrhea and stomach disturbances.

She begins to do strange things. Here are some illustrations.

When he was out of the house and the children were asleep, I would come down into the kitchen and scream and curse him for what a rotten person he was, wishing a car would hit him and he would die. I would take the pots and pans and bang them on the counter. I would pick up dishes and cups and smash them on the floor. I would pace the living room and dining room and scream. I would talk to my poodle and say, "I hate him. He's a bastard. I hope he dies." I didn't have the serenity to sit down and watch television or read. I wanted to kill him. But then I would have to go to jail. I wanted to commit suicide, but I couldn't do that because of the children. I dragged him to the priest, but the priest couldn't even get him to promise to stop. I went to church four nights a week making novenas; and he went to the track. I cursed God for letting this happen. I would sit down and doze off and wake up screaming, "My God, the children are dead!"

I screamed at him and told him he wasn't going to go to the track; that I would kill him if he did. I even picked up a knife. Then when he ran out, I ran after him, and he was in the car and had started the engine. I ran in front of the car, right there in the street with all the neighbors watching, and screamed that I wasn't going to let him drive to the track, that he would have to run over me to do it.

I was out driving, when my mind went blank and I didn't know where I was. This was a route I had driven a thousand times, but this time I didn't recognize anything. It was as though I was in a strange place, and I thought I was having some kind of nightmare, that this was happening in a dream. Then I heard cars honking and saw cars passing me and people leaning out of windows and screaming things at me. I was frightened to death and I pulled over to the side and shut my eyes and waited for the nightmare to go away. I could feel myself trembling. I was so scared. Then I heard a man's voice. It was a policeman. He told me someone had stopped at a toll booth and told them that I was weaving and that my car was out of control and that he had gotten a radio call to try to stop me. I told him what had happened, and he called my sister to come and drive me home.

I got into terrible fights with my brothers and my parents. They were doing everything they could to help me, paying the rent and buying us food and buying clothing for the children. I must have been getting paranoid. I told them they really didn't care about me, that they were just doing this to humiliate me; I even accused my brother Joe of giving my husband money behind my back so he could gamble. I accused my best friend, Connie, of tattling behind my back and gossiping with the neighbors and saying that it was all my fault that this was happening, that if I had treated him right, he wouldn't be gambling and making all this trouble. The more she tried to prove to me that this was nutty, that she wasn't doing any such thing, the more I accused her of just trying to cover up her disloyalty. I'm sure they were about ready to pack me off to the loony bin.

I would get up at 5 or 5:30 in the morning and couldn't get back to sleep. So I got up and wandered about in the house from one room to the other, just picking up things and putting them down, pulling out a book and putting it back. Then I would go out in the yard and walk around in my nightgown, not even realizing where I was; then I would come in again. Then the children would get up, and when they came down my daughter would have to remind me that it was not Saturday or Sunday and that they had to go to school and that I hadn't even started breakfast. I would start to get out the things for breakfast and forget what I was doing, and my daughter had to shake me to get me back to what I was doing. I couldn't even make the breakfast right. I would crack an egg and throw the whole thing, egg and all, into the garbage. If I finally got an egg on, it would sit there and burn. In the middle of their breakfast, I would sit down in a daze until they screamed at me to finish making their breakfast. Then when they were gone, I would wash the dishes two or three times, pull things out of the cabinets and put them back, then pull them out again and put them back. . . .

I was riding up in the elevator where I work, and all of a sudden I got this horrible feeling that I was trapped and that if I didn't get out I would suffocate and die. There were other people in the elevator with me, and I started crying and pleading with them, "Please stop the elevator, please stop the elevator, I've got to get out. I can't breathe. I'm going to have a heart attack." They must have thought I was crazy. Luckily, the elevator had just come to a stop and the door opened and I got out. It was the eighth floor, and my office was on the twenty-seventh floor. I walked up 19 stories. From then on I wouldn't get on an elevator and I had to quit my job. After the elevator I got a phobia about department stores, and I had to stop going to them. Then I got a phobia about even being out on the street, and I practically became a hermit in my home. I could go out only if my mother or an aunt or a friend went out with me.

If, by this time, the wife is not already convinced that she is losing her mind, her compulsive-gambling husband, teetering on the verge of insanity himself, is helping to push her in that direction. His thinking is so badly impaired that he is convinced that there is nothing with him, that his wife is making this all up, and he proceeds to tell her so and to badger her so badly that she begins to believe it herself:

It's true that I'm neglecting you and the children. I've been a good provider, and I'm taking good care of my family. All I'm trying to do now is to get back on my feet so I can make life good for us again. You're accusing me of not being interested in you and the children, and of being cruel to you. It's not true. There's something wrong with your thinking. You ought to go see a psychiatrist. You're blaming the trouble between you and me on the gambling. Well, the gambling hasn't got anything to do with it. We're fighting because we should never have gotten married, because our personalities don't fit, because you're a hostile, dissatisfied person who wouldn't be happy with anything or anybody. You're just a malcontent, and you'd make trouble for anybody married to you. Nobody could possibly live peaceably with you. Look at what's happening to the children. They're failing their subjects and playing hookey. That's because you're upsetting them with your quarrelling. If you would let there be some peace and quiet in the house, they wouldn't get so upset. Maybe instead of staying home and making trouble for us all, you ought to go out and work and earn some money, and stay out of our way, and we'd all get along better.

Whatever weaknesses and vulnerabilities she may have, he will pounce on them and assail her with them, thus evading the real problem of his gambling and the disastrous state to which it has brought the family. Tragically, she is so beaten down, so worn out, that she can no longer distinguish between his accusations and reality, and she begins to believe the things he is telling her.

Driven to the point of despair, to a feeling of utter hopelessness and helplessness, the wife may finally make one desperate effort and tear herself loose from the web in which she is entangled, or she may suffer a mental breakdown and have to be hospitalized, or she may take to alcohol or drugs, or she may attempt suicide; this last is the way out chosen by at least 1 out of every 10 women married to a compulsive gambler.

CHAPTER SIX

The Female Compulsive Gambler

HOW DO WOMEN COMPULSIVE GAMBLERS DIFFER FROM their male counterparts? Do they gamble at the same games? Do they bet and lose as heavily? Do they steal and embezzle the way some men gamblers do and go to jail? What are their personalities like? Are they "feminine"? "Masculine"? Does the addiction progress in the same way as it does with men? Do they "hit bottom" the way many male compulsive gamblers do? Are the causes of their addiction the same?

Unfortunately, the answers to these questions cannot be given with nearly as much assurance as in the case of male compulsive gamblers. There simply has not been any research on female compulsive gamblers, and not a sufficient number of them have come for help for us to be able to draw reasonably safe conclusions. All we know about them, at this stage, is what we have learned about the handful who have come for treatment or who have attended Gamblers Anonymous meetings, and from interviews with several others. Hence, we can give only impressions, not conclusions; and we ask that the reader bear this in mind in evaluating this information.

What sort of people are the female compulsive gamblers? There is nothing that immediately distinguishes them from other women, by way of appearance, temperament or personality. There is no way, from general appearance or manner, that one could tell a woman is a compulsive gambler unless she tells you she is. Not even watching her at the gambling tables or at the track could you distinguish her from the other people there. She will be quite keyed-up and intense with each spin of the roulette wheel or show of cards or surge of a horse, but so are most of the thousands of other gamblers there. Perhaps, if you were able to watch her hour after hour, day after day, week after week you would be able to observe her persistence as she sustains one loss after another, the look of anguish and chagrin on her face as the croupier rakes in her chips or as her horse drops back into fifth place, the momentary relief when her horse or number or hand wins, and then the lapse into gray dejection as she loses again and continues to lose. The others win and leave or lose and leave, but if you were to come back three or six or eight hours later, you would see her still hanging on—provided she has not lost all she had to bet with for that day or night.

But, in that respect, she is not different from the male compulsive gambler, who will behave in practically the same way, except that he may mutter, stomp, curse, pace, leave for a while then come back again and throw himself, grim-faced, into the betting once more until his cash or chips or credit is gone.

Away from the track, casino or gaming room you may never know this woman does much gambling, let alone that she's got a gambling problem. She just will not talk about it. She's still living by society's rules and expectations and, in spite of the impact of the women's liberation movement, these are still generally different for women than they are for men.

Although gambling is something almost everybody does, it still has a taint of social opprobrium. When people say, "That one's a gambler," or, "That one gambles too much," the implication is accusatory, derogatory, demeaning. It says in effect, "That person ought to be ashamed."

SOCIETY'S DOUBLE STANDARD

Yet, withal, society does make allowances—for men. In this as in many other respects, society has a double standard, one for men, one for women.

A man can be "a gambler," and while this is not something to be admired, it is also not a cause for ostracism. People may shake their heads and make some mild comments of disapproval when it's a man, but they manage to find a way to explain it, understand it, tolerate it. But not so when it comes to a woman gambler. There is a quality of dissoluteness, immorality and indecency that people read into it, exceeding even that attributed to women alcoholics.

Knowing this, women compulsive gamblers do everything they can to hide their problem not only from their husbands but from everybody else. They see themselves the way they think other people regard them—with loathing and contempt. They are ashamed even to come for treatment, and they keep putting it off as long as they can. This may also be the reason why there are so few women in Gamblers Anonymous. Even though they know they will be among others with the same problem, as badly off or even worse off than they are, they hesitate to come because they expect they may be rejected and looked down upon by the men who are themselves compulsive gamblers. Even in that setting, among other "sinners," they feel more "sinful" than the men—not because the men who are there make them feel that way but because they have been taught from childhood on, that there are things that men may do that a woman may not do, that are "indecent" for a woman to do—and so they react automatically with shame even in the presence of men who have committed the same act.

Those who do come for treatment carry this feeling of shame right into the treatment setting. The difference is apparent in a second. No matter how badly depressed the male compulsive gambler may be, no matter how much havoc he has wrought on himself and his family and with creditors and the law, he still, somehow, manages to retain a "hang-tough," combative, challenging attitude, almost a cockiness, as if he feels he is justified in what he has done, that there is really nothing wrong with him, that the problem is everybody else's fault.

In contrast, the woman who comes for treatment is subdued, withdrawn, frightened, abject and almost cringing in her demeanor. The male compulsive gambler finds it difficult to admit he has an illness because he's still egotistic and "proud." The woman finds it difficult to admit she's got an illness because she's ashamed. She would rather be anyplace else but there, facing the therapist and other members of the staff. She feels she's a pariah, a leper. She can't understand how anybody would even want to bother with her, a "fallen woman."

This attitude is engendered in many cases by the irrationally punitive attitude of the husband. The husbands of compulsive gamblers, generally speaking, regard their wives with contempt and disgust. They would almost rather the wife be an alcoholic or even a prostitute. They see the wife not only as dissolute and immoral, but also as a thief. They accuse her of betraying the trust that he and the children have put in her as wife and mother—the one who is "supposed to keep the family together."

As much as the wives of compulsive gamblers may hate and detest their husbands for the harm they have done, they still do not condemn them as immoral sinners; they still find it possible, ultimately, to see the compulsive gambler husband as a sick person and in most cases to find a way to forgive and to rebuild. They almost always are willing to come to Gam-Anon meetings and to take a hand in the husband's rehabilitation.

The husbands of compulsive gamblers are, with few exceptions, unable to do this. They are much more likely to seek a divorce. Very few are willing to come to Gam-Anon meetings or to do anything to help the wife to recover.

Has This Served as a Deterrent?

Society's attitude toward the female compulsive gambler is reprehensible. Yet it may actually have been serving as a deterrent, keeping her from going to the extremes that men do in order to get money to keep on gambling.

Stealing, embezzlement, check forgery and check kiting are common among male compulsive gamblers. In only two of the cases that have come to our attention did the women compulsive gamblers commit that sort of offense. In one case, the woman, assistant comptroller of a manufacturing company, embezzled $7,500 of the firm's funds. In another, the woman was apprehended having taken money from a P.T.A. bank account, which she, as treasurer, was handling. She had been borrowing small amounts—$25, $50, $100 at most—and replacing them scrupulously either from winnings or from loans from friends. The "borrowing" was detected when a new slate of officers was elected and a new treasurer took over the account.

Women compulsive gamblers are much more hesitant about borrowing from friends, because they do not want the friends to know that they are gamblers; when they do borrow, they keep the reason a secret, lying not so much to manipulate and connive but rather out of their concern about being found out. Nor do they become as insensitive as men do to the feelings and needs of others. Men compulsive gamblers, as we have noted, will, when they have become desperate, borrow from their dearest friends and relatives, with no thought at all about when and how they are going to pay back the debt. When the woman compulsive gambler borrows, she is painfully aware of her indebtedness and agonizes about being able to pay it back.

In sum, there does not appear to be as extensive a dissolution of conscience and social responsibility among women compulsive gamblers as among males, nor the near-total abandonment of all restraints and scruples. It would seem that social pressures on a woman act to reinforce her hold on herself and to give her stronger control over her impulses. Society expects men to take more liberties, and so they do. This, of course, is purely hypothetical. It could be entirely biological; it could be that males are biologically more aggressive and will therefore commit aggressions more easily than women. Or it may be a combination of the biological and sociological factors.

There are also economic limitations on the excesses to which most women compulsive gamblers can go. Many are housewives and, in most cases, do not have sources of money other than their husband's earnings. This limits the amounts of money they can get their hands on and hence the amounts they can gamble. Getting loans from lending institutions is much more difficult for women than it is for men, except for those women who have independent incomes and have established their own credit.

Further, since few families depend on the wife—even where she is working—as the main support of the household, there is not as much chance that the family will be stripped of its possessions and brought to the point of financial desperation, as is the case with so many male compulsive gamblers.

STARTS LATER, DOES NOT GO SO FAR

The addiction is progressive with women as it is with men, but with women it does not go so far. The social and economic factors we have discussed put a brake on the descent before it reaches total destruction. "Reaching bottom" appears to be an entirely different phenomenon with women than with men. The "bottom" for women comes when they cannot stand the guilt and shame any longer—total emotional exhaustion. It is then that they come for help, either to a professional or to Gamblers Anonymous. While they do leave a trail of problems in their wake, it is nothing like the havoc and destruction generally found with the male compulsive gamblers.

Social factors have their impact on the woman compulsive gambler in still another respect: the age at which they start gambling at all and the age at which they start to gamble compulsively.

In almost every case, men who gamble compulsively started gambling when they were in their early teens—not necessarily heavy gambling, just the casual sort that is common among teenagers in working-class and lower-middle-class families—"pitching pennies," matching coins, penny poker, "punch board," sports cards and the like. This is very much a part of the play activity of these boys and is not in any way predictive of a gambling career or even of a predilection for gambling. The girls in those same settings do not do this, as a rule. They are involved in other sorts of recreational activities that are suitable to girls according to the standards and customs of the community.

This may account for the fact that compulsive gambling generally has its onset much later for women than for men. Since gambling is not part of their social scene as teenagers and young adults, they have little occasion to gamble at all. It is only as they move from childhood and into settings where gambling for women is common that they make their first contacts with gambling, and generally at a much later age than men. The later the exposure to gambling, in general, the later would we expect the onset of compulsive gambling to occur.

The precipitating factors are often much less obvious with women than they are with men. In the case of men, generally, one can find some ego-damaging, security-damaging event that preceded the onset of heavy gambling, such as a financial loss, loss of a job, rejection by a college, failure in business, rejection by a woman, infidelity of a wife. With women, the trauma is likely to be much more subtle, the feeling of hurt and loss much more private and sometimes so obscure as to evade detection by all but the closest observers.

Angela V.

I never gambled in all my life—nothing, not a game of cards for money, not a slot machine, not even bingo—until five years ago. I was 34 then. I never even had any interest in it. Everybody else where I worked was playing the numbers, but I never bothered with it. The most I did was buy a raffle once in a while from one of the women at my church, or for some charity. I did it because I wanted to help. I really never expected to win, and I didn't, but that never bothered me. I just didn't expect anything.

Then this thing happened. People talk about seeing a number in a dream, and then betting it and winning. Well, I didn't see a number in my dream, but it was the night before my mother's birthday, February 26, and I dreamed about my mother. She's been dead for years, but I've never forgotten her. I think about her a lot, and I miss her. I have this terribly lonely feeling that makes me want to cry, and I think of my mother, and how I would want her to be alive now so I could go to her. That night I dreamt about her. I was a little girl in the dream, and my mother held me and kissed me, and then I woke up and I was very happy. I expected to go into the kitchen and see her there, but then I realized it was only a dream, and I felt very sad again, and I cried and called for her. My husband had already gone to work—he owns a meat market—and I was alone in the house. I used to work as a hostess in this very nice restaurant, but I developed a bad condition in my leg, and the doctor told me I would have to stop so I haven't been working for more than seven years, just staying home and taking care of the house. We don't have any children. I wanted to have children, but we couldn't.

Anyhow, that day after I had the dream, I sat down to read a book, and when I opened it up to where I had the bookmark, it was at page 226. Two twenty-six; that's my mother's birthday—February 26. I thought that was some coincidence, and forgot about it. Then, when I went out to get my car out of the garage to go shopping, there was a car parked across the street with three numbers on the license plate: 226. That bothered me. I am not superstitious, but superstitious things frighten me; they bother me. That day, I saw that number two more times, and I was upset.

I had this funny idea that my mother was trying to say something to me. I'm very religious. I go to church regularly. I thought maybe this was a sign of some kind. Maybe it was God trying to tell me something about my mother. Anyhow, this feeling began to build up inside me, like a pressure, like something I had to get rid of, and I got the idea that I ought to play that number. So I went to the store and bought a lottery ticket. I watched for the number on television that night. It was 226. I won $2,000.

Then other numbers began to bother me the same way. They weren't connected to anything like a birthday or anything special. I would just see them three or four times in a couple of days, and I would bet the number and win. I continued to do that every few days, and I continued to win. I wouldn't win every time, but I won many more times than I lost. By the end of three months I was ahead about $20,000, just the same way, betting numbers that bothered me. I know it's hard to believe, but I'm not lying to you. You can go and ask my priest. I was afraid. I thought it was some kind of an omen, a message. He didn't say yes or no but told me not to be afraid.

It came along just at the right time. We had just bought a house and we wanted to furnish it right, so with my winnings we bought a new dining-room suite, a new living-room suite, carpeting. I continued to win that way, and we really gutted the whole house—tore out walls, made rooms bigger, put in new, better stoves than came with the house, everything. By the end of that first year, we had practically rebuilt the inside of the house entirely; something that would have taken us years, we did in one year, all with my winnings.

Meantime, I was also helping out my sister. Her husband is struggling, and they have four children, so I helped them out. I promised myself that if this kept up, I would put aside money for their children's education. I also wanted to put money away for our future—my husband and I—so he wouldn't work so hard. I didn't want anything for myself, no jewelry or furs or a summer home or trips. The only jewelry I own is my wedding band and engagement ring and a gold bracelet my husband bought for me on our tenth anniversary, but that's all.

I just kept on betting and winning, and I was convinced I just couldn't lose, that God had given me some kind of power. I believe that through God everything is possible, and that it was His will, that he wanted me to do these things for my husband and sister and other people to make up for the way my mother had suffered. I didn't get all excited when I kept winning, running and telling everybody. I kept it to myself, except for my husband, not because I was ashamed or anything else. I just saw it as a natural happening, the way other things in my life had come, good things and bad things, and just accepted it without getting all excited. If that is what God wanted for me, then that is what it was.

You could say my life has had a lot of ups and downs in it, but I take it the way it comes. I was born in a labor camp in Germany. The Germans had taken my mother from Lithuania, where she was born, and brought her to this labor camp. I was born there in the camp. My brother, too. We were both illegitimate, by some soldiers, but my mother never told me any more. We came to the United States in 1947, as displaced persons. I was just a baby; my brother is a year older.

My mother had a hard life. When we came here, she went to work as a housekeeper on a ranch in Texas, and we all lived in a little shack. When I was old enough—11 or 12—I had to work in the ranch house, too, doing chores and scrubbing, helping my mother. My brother had to do men's work on the ranch. When I was 14, I was raped by one of the ranch hands, but I was too frightened to tell my mother or anybody else, so I just kept it to myself. Lucky I didn't get pregnant, or they would have thrown us all out and we wouldn't have had any place to go. In 1960, my mother went to the hospital with cancer. She suffered terribly, and she died there in a few months. My brother and I were put in different foster homes. The foster home was terrible. They made me work like a servant, and the man tried to take advantage of me. They wouldn't let me go out with my friends, and they locked me in. I ran away. Then the agency found out about a family that came from my mother's hometown in Lithuania and they placed me there, and it was better there, but not much. They moved to West Virginia, and I stayed with them until I was 18, and then I met my husband and we were married.

I don't feel bitter about my childhood. It was hard, but I really didn't take it that way. I took it that that is the way it was meant to be. I never felt life or God owed me anything. I tried to be contented with what I had. But my brother was different. He was always angry about what life had done to him. He felt life owed him something. He carried a chip on his shoulder. Then he turned to alcohol and drugs. He's in a hospital now for his drugs. It makes me very sad because he's the only living relative I've got in this country.

I was worrying about him, too. A year after I started betting, I went to visit him in this mental hospital. It was terrible, him being in the middle of all those insane, frightening-looking people, and I knew I had to get him out of there and get him to some private hospital, and then build up his life for him, maybe buy him a small business that would keep him out of trouble.

By that time, a year after I started, I had won $52,000. That's right, $52,000. You can ask my priest; I would never lie to him. But most of that had gone into the house and into my husband's business. All I had left of that was $4,000, which I kept in a separate account. That wouldn't be enough for me to be able to do anything for my brother. I had to do something special. It was just coming up to my mother's birthday, and I thought that was an omen that I should bet her birthday number again, and that I should put a large bet on it, maybe $100, and then I could give all the winnings to my brother.

So I put $100 on the number and lost. That was two days before her birthday, so I waited until the twenty-sixth— her birthday—and bet another $100, and lost again. I wasn't upset; I just knew I had to keep on betting, maybe not that number, but maybe another number would be revealed to me, and I would bet that and that would win. So I was watching, and the number 814 kept on coming up on dollar bills, on my electric bill, on the zip code in a letter I got, and so I bet that for a couple of weeks, but it didn't win. Then I started to step up my betting, not just one number but five numbers at a time, and not just once every three or four days, but every day, and not just $25 for a day, but $100, $200 and $300 a day. But I kept on losing. Oh, I would win a number maybe once or twice a month, but that didn't last long the way I was betting. In a few months I had lost the $4,000 that was left over from my winnings. I had never touched a penny from the savings account my husband and I had together. There was $10,000 in that account, and so I started to dip into that account. And I continued to lose.

Before, when I was winning, I used to tell my husband, "Joe, I just won again for $2,000 or $3,000." And he would just be happy and say that was wonderful. He never said anything about my gambling then. He really didn't see betting on the numbers as gambling. He believed me when I said it was something God wanted. He was happy when we put the winnings into the house and into his business.

When I started losing, I couldn't come to him any longer and tell him about my winnings. But he didn't seem to notice the change. He was too taken up with his business. That was all right so far as I was concerned, so long as I was betting only from my leftover winnings. But when I started to take from our savings account, I became terrified he would find out. I was in a panic from one day to the next, praying for the numbers to win so I could put back the money so he couldn't find out about it. He's a very emotional man. He's 15 years older than I, and he's the old-fashioned type, where a man has the right to treat his wife anyway he wants to, even to beat her if he wants to and nobody would even blame him for it. I had seen him get angry before, and it was terrible. I was afraid. But his being of the old school kept me safe for a long time. He would turn over the money to me, and I paid all the bills and kept all the accounts. The bank statements would come in every month, but he wouldn't even look at them. He left that to me. So I could keep on drawing on the bank account and he would never know. Inside of a year, I had cleaned out the $10,000. Then I went into some bonds and CDs we had. They came to about $25,000. I went through those—it took about another two years.

That was in addition to what my husband gave me for the house. I lost that money, too. I had to borrow from finance companies and friends so that my husband wouldn't know. I didn't tell my friends about the gambling, just told them that I was in trouble and that I needed the money, and they didn't ask me any questions. Four of these friends were women I had known for a long time; a couple of them I had worked with. There were also three men. I knew them from when I worked as a restaurant hostess, and we became friends. Nothing funny, or anything like that. I guess they just liked me or felt sorry for me, but whatever it was, I knew how to get around them. They were all big spenders, Mafia type, and that money didn't mean so much to them.

So I was able to keep it from my husband for three years from the time I started losing. But finally he found out. I got a call from my former boss at the restaurant. Her daughter, a girl of 20, had leukemia and they had her stabilized for about a year but now they were afraid she was going to die, and my friend wanted to fly down to Louisiana to be with her, but she had no one to leave in charge of the restaurant. Her manager was sick, and she couldn't trust the other waitresses or the cooks to leave the restaurant with them. She asked me to take it over for about three days, and I told her I would. I couldn't turn her down. She was a good friend, and she was one of the women who had loaned me money. I was afraid that if I wasn't home when the mail came my husband might see the bank statement and find out about the money. But it was a few days too early for the statement so I felt fairly safe. My luck! That month the bank installed a new computer system and changed the mailing date to four or five days earlier.

The statement came in the mail that day, while I was at the restaurant, and my husband saw it and opened it when he came home after work. I didn't come home until midnight, and he was waiting up for me. He had looked at the statement and found out there was only $400 there out of about $10,000 that he knew had been there, and there should have been more because he had given me more to put away, which I never did.

When I walked in, he started screaming at me before I even took my coat off. "Where the hell's the money? What the hell have you done with it?" He thought I had taken it and given it to my brother. Then I had to tell him I had lost it gambling on the numbers. He couldn't believe it. He told me I was a liar. He said it had to be drugs. He called me every kind of vile name and said I was a crook, stealing his money. He didn't say that when he was fixing up his business with the money I was winning. I tried to explain to him, to see if I could get him to understand what I was going through. I was crazy enough to think that he might even be sympathetic and shield me and help me. I guess that's just my romantic notion. I never had a father to care for me or protect me, and my mother was too worn out and sick, so it had to be me alone, by myself, nobody else to stick up for me. I was wishing my husband would do this, but he never did. It never was that kind of a marriage. You know the way the old-fashioned men are. They go out with their friends, to a restaurant or drinking, and they leave their wives at home. That's the way they are. They don't think there's anything wrong with that.

The one thing I wanted was to be part of my husband's life, but he wouldn't let me. He shut me out. When I complained, he couldn't understand what I was talking about. He told me I ought to be happy, having a home and a husband who earned a living and didn't go out with other women, which I know he didn't; he isn't that type. Talking to him about sharing his life with his wife was like talking a foreign language. It didn't mean anything to him. He thought I was some kind of a nut and told me to stop reading those silly novels, which I never did read.

I wanted to have a baby, so much, when we were first married, but he held it off. And then when he said all right and we tried, I couldn't conceive. I was ready to blame myself. I thought it was my fault, and I went to the doctor but before he would even examine me he said he had to have my husband come in to get a sperm count. I finally convinced him to come in, and the doctor told him his sperm count was low and he gave him pills for it. He took the pills, but he kept on drinking and the doctor told him he would have to stop because that would cancel out the effect of the medicine. But he kept on drinking. I would quarrel with him and we would have some awful fights but he wouldn't stop. So I just gave up; that was 10 years ago, and I just resigned myself to not having any children, ever.

So you could say it was just a marriage, not a happy marriage, not the way I wanted it, but what could I do? I had to be satisfied. At least I had a husband, and he did care about me, I guess.

But when he found out that I had taken the money from the bank account, I lost even that. He moved into another room and shut the door on me and didn't even let me in to sleep with him anymore. He stopped talking to me, except for a few words about things for the house and meals and other practical things. He even stopped calling me by my name and he couldn't look me in the eye. That killed me. I really got depressed then, because I didn't have even that left. I had nothing but emptiness and loneliness. I tried to fill it up with the church and my friends, but my friends were being kind of cool on account of the debts. I had to keep on gambling; it was the only thing I had, and I managed to get a little more money from selling the bracelet. Finally, there wasn't a place I could borrow a dime. The bank account was gone—he had taken my name off it. I couldn't go to my friends any longer, and the finance companies were after me because I still owed them. I was desperate. I thought about killing myself, but I couldn't. Then I found a way to get some money out of my husband's bank account, even with my name off it. I had the bank transfer money from that account to my old private account, and they didn't even catch on. You can't imagine what kind of scheming you can do when you're a compulsive gambler and you need the money, what kind of cunning and trickery you can think up. When I did that, I looked at myself as though I was outside myself looking at another person, a stranger, and I said, "How could you possibly do a thing like that?" It was against everything I had been brought up with. It was against my nature.

Then one of the bank bookkeepers noticed what was happening and notified my husband, who hadn't even been bothering to look at the bank statements. This time he was in a rage, and it was so bad, I couldn't stand it and I spilled out everything, which he didn't know about yet— the CDs, the bonds, the $30,000 debts to my friends. He called me a crook, a whore, an animal that never deserved to be born. He beat me, which he had never done before. Then he told me to get out of the house, that he didn't

want me there any longer. But I told him I wouldn't leave.
Then he said he was through with me. He was going to get
a divorce and that I better do something about getting
help.

I heard about GA but never thought about doing anything. But this time I got the phone book and looked up
their number, and I called them and they told me about a
meeting and I went. That was five months ago. I've been
going regularly, but I haven't been able to stop gambling. I
still squeeze some money out of what he gives me for the
house, and I told my friend at the restaurant and she
knows I can't stop so she's giving me some money to bet
with, even though she knows it's wrong, but she says she
can't see me suffer. I used to weigh 150 pounds, and now
I'm less than 100. I'm terribly depressed. I shake. I can't
sleep. I have no appetite. It's worse than death. Every
night I pray to God that he should take me and not let me
wake up the next morning.

I know I hurt my husband terribly. I can see it in his
eyes. I tell him that. But I also hurt myself, and I ask him
to understand that. But he can't. He can't understand
about this being a sickness. A man from GA asked to see
him and he agreed, but after that he didn't want to have a
thing to do with it. He shut his mind to it completely.

Suffering, self-blame, resignation, humility come out
with almost every breath—and most of all, insight and
self-awareness, a picture contrasting sharply with that of the
obstinate, arrogant, self-righteous stance of the average
male compulsive gambler in this stage of the addiction.
Here we see in sharp outline the personification of the
traditional contrast between the masculine and feminine
personalities. Both as mate to the compulsive gambler and
as the compulsive gambler herself, the woman comes out
submissive, suffering, caring, concerned, empathetic. The
man comes out in both these roles as tough, egotistic,
obstinate, punitive, unfeeling, unable to empathize.

This raises another basic question: Does this fundamental difference—be it biological or cultural—show up also in
the causes of the gambling addiction and in the way it

develops? Let us see. But before we go on, let us again caution that little is known yet about the woman compulsive gambler and that whatever tendencies or trends we note are only speculative.

COMPARING THE CAUSES AND DEVELOPMENT

To summarize what we have said about the causes of compulsive gambling in males:

In childhood, this person is subjected to indifference, rejection, or outright abuse, as a result of which he grows up feeling inadequate, insecure, unliked, worthless and helpless. In order to compensate for these unbearable feelings, he does things through which he tries to prove to others that he is superior and for which he should be liked and admired. He does not realize that this is not the way to win acceptance and approval, that people like someone because he is a pleasant, decent, caring person, interested in others besides himself. He sees that important people are acclaimed in our society, and thinks this is the way to go. He sets his goal at becoming the best, the most important person in whatever area his capabilities lie—athletics, studies, mechanical skills, making money.

But when he achieves this goal and he does win recognition for his performance or achievements, he discovers this is not enough. He has to work harder and set even higher goals, and when he reaches those he finds that even these are not enough. The drive to win recognition, acclaim and approval is insatiable, and disappointment and frustration are too painful to bear. He then finds that there is something else that will satisfy his need for approval and recognition, overcome his feelings of powerlessness, relieve his anxiety and depression, make him feel good about himself and give him excitement and pleasure. That "wonderful something" is gambling.

What do we find in the case of female compulsive gamblers? In every instance that has come to our attention, the woman's childhood was marked not only by rejection or indifference, but by trauma. Several were illegitimate and grew up without a father. Others were abandoned and abused by a mother, father or stepfather. In a few cases, there was sexual abuse. In several, the mother or father was a compulsive gambler. In many cases, several of these traumatic conditions were present simultaneously.

The effect, in every case, was devastating. Listening to the women in therapy, or at Gamblers Anonymous meetings or in personal interviews, one hears a disclosure of woe, of battered egos, low self-esteem, feelings of worthlessness. Some readily admit to these feelings. Others try to hide them behind an exterior of toughness and indifference, but they do not succeed in this for long; as they unburden themselves, their inner feelings well up and you hear choked voices and you see tears. In other cases, the feelings had been thrust out of consciousness because they were too painful to endure. In these cases it took weeks, even months, of therapy before these women were able to tap into their submerged feelings and permit themselves to express them.

Feeling unloved, unwanted, disliked and worthless is not either a masculine or a feminine experience. It is a human experience. Little boys feel it as keenly and painfully as little girls do. But what they do about it is different. The little boy is oriented, by upbringing, to masculine solutions— to overcome, overpower, conquer, assert. From infancy on he hears admonitions to "be a man," "don't be a sissy," "fight back," "show them," "don't let them get the better of you." The attitude is assertive, aggressive. He reads the comics, watches TV and sees that the most admired are the successful, the powerful, the important, the heroic, the wealthy, the John Waynes, Clint Eastwoods, Charles Bronsons. These become his heroes and his models, and if he cannot quite match them in their achievements, he can at least try. And if he cannot attain his high goals in reality, he can do so through illusion—the illusions spun by drinking, drugs or gambling.

For girls, the goals and models are different. Girls are not told they need to be strong, important, domineering in order to be recognized and admired. Theirs is a much different objective—to be liked, accepted, wanted, loved, protected. That is what these mistreated, rejected girls most desperately want, and they try, but their self-esteem has been so badly battered that they find it difficult. Some, feeling themselves unworthy, may subject themselves to relationships with unworthy men, uncaring men, even cruel and brutal men—thus reliving the drama of their childhood, this being the only thing they ever knew and the only thing with which they are comfortable. Others, finding it too difficult to achieve love and acceptance as women, or finding this role too fraught with insecurity and danger, reject it and take on masculine work habits and masculine values; in some cases they strive to compete with men and become successful in the men's world. When these solutions fail to work satisfactorily for them or create too many difficulties for them, they take to drinking, drugs or gambling for the "safe" life of illusion, or for relief and escape from a plight that is too much for them to endure.

Take the instance of Angela V., whose story we heard a few pages back. Born illegitimately in a labor camp in Germany, she was brought to this country as a baby and grew up in a shack on a Texas ranch where her mother went to work as a domestic. When she was only 11 or 12, she had to work around the ranch house, too, and at the age of 14 she was raped by a ranch hand. Her mother died when she was 15, and she was placed in one foster home from which she ran away, and then in another where she stayed until she was 18. At 18 she was married.

At first, having a home, a husband, someone she could take care of was enough, but then a natural yearning arose for just a little more. He was her life; she wanted to be part of his life, too. But that was not the way he would have it; it was not the custom among his people. Another woman used to these ways might have accepted this and contented herself with other things. But for Angela, this was another bitter rejection in a lifetime of so many other rejections, and she felt again the pangs of loneliness, of not being wanted or worthwhile. But there was still another possibility. She could fill up her life with a child, a baby whom she could love and who would love her. But that, too, was not to be.

So the years dragged on in gray monotony and Angela kept her days busy with work, and when her health prevented her from working any longer, with housework, shopping, cooking, church.

But hope never died that life would yet bring her some emotional fulfillment, a child's dream kept alive into adulthood. And then "this thing" happened ... "a sign from God," through a dream about her dead mother, to play the number 226, and lo and behold that number won. Then, after that, another and another winning. What real life could not produce, magical thinking and illusion could. Here was unquestionable proof that God had chosen her to win this money and to do good things for other people, with this power God had given her. She could not lose—she had the sense of omnipotence we have spoken about, which all children have and which only some adults retain with any seriousness, among them the compulsive gamblers.

With this power and the good deeds she could now perform, she would no longer need to feel unwanted, worthless, lonely. But that, too, was not to be, because the addiction of compulsive gambling has no regard for the goal of the compulsive gambler—whether it be to validate himself and gain acceptance through the acquisition of material things and a position of power, or to validate herself and gain acceptance through the performance of good deeds. It drags down all its victims, without favor.

Compare Angela's case with that of Mickey T., which follows.

Mickey T.

In broad outline and even in many of the details, the story of Mickey T.'s infatuation with gambling and then the onset and progression of her addiction is like that of numerous male compulsive gamblers, except for the time element. Mickey's first acquaintance with gambling did not occur until she was 20, and her serious involvement with gambling did not start until she was 29.

At the outset, there wasn't much gambling at all. She would go with her mother to play bingo about once a month, buy a lottery ticket every few weeks, go to the track with friends two or three times a year. Clearly, gambling did not mean very much in her life, nothing but "an occasional change and an hour or two of relaxation, and just the faintest notion that I might ever win anything."

This casual, practically indifferent relationship to gambling continued for nine years, with no change at all. Then, for no reason that she knew or understood, Mickey began to go to the track more frequently, first with a group of friends, and then without them when her trips to the track became too frequent and they demurred. From two to three times a year, the frequency of her visits to the track increased to once every two months, once a month, once every two weeks, once a week, then every three or four days. She never gave a second thought to this increase. "I was finding that I enjoyed it a great deal and just wanted to do it more often, the way it is with anything a person suddenly discovers and wants to do a lot more of."

What she liked about it was the excitement; picking the horse and betting and getting "all hopped up, screaming like all the other nuts for your horse to make his. move. There was something else, too," she added, as an afterthought. "I liked just being there at the track. It was a friendly place. I felt protected there, safe from all my worries. They all vanished when I got to the track."

There was nothing spectacular about her wagers. Fifty dollars at the most. Nor was there anything spectacular about her winnings. Sometimes $100, sometimes $200 or $300, hardly ever anything else, "nothing like what you read about in the papers that sometimes happens, $10,000 or $15,000 on a combination bet." So it was not the winning that kept her wanting to go to the track "or any big dreams about castles in Spain, or any other magnificent thing I could do with a whole lot of money. I wasn't really interested in the money. It was nice to have a little more. But I was making a good living and had whatever I wanted by way of an apartment, a car, entertainment and things like that."

It had not yet become an obsession. She felt only the desire to be at the track, but no compelling need that might cause her to push aside other things in her life. Whether it might have continued this way had she not gotten a certain telephone call, there is just no way to tell.

The call was from a friend she had not seen since her high school days. They had been very close and both suffered traumatically when the friends' parents moved East, shortly after the girls' graduation. This friend, Amy, called to say that she was going to Las Vegas on a junket and asked whether Mickey could meet her there and spend the day. Since the town in which they had grown up, and in which Mickey still lived, was only about 150 miles from Las Vegas, Mickey joyfully agreed.

"The reunion was terrific, but it seemed that fate had introduced it just to bring something new into my life—the casinos." Although she lived so short a distance from Las Vegas, the casinos had never piqued her curiosity. But coming into one of the large casinos, with its glitter, entertainment, hustle and bustle, excitement, was like coming into a magic world, "like Alice coming through the looking glass." Most of all, it was the excitement. Following her friend around, she tried her hand at the different games, craps, blackjack, the slot machines, but none of them held her. The roulette table did. "A new spin of the wheel every 20 seconds, with thousands being won and lost, and another spin, and more thousands being won and lost. This was my game." With a little instruction she started playing the rest of the night. That night, the first time out, she won $1,000. But that wasn't what brought her back, she insists. It was the speed and the action and the excitement.

"From that day on, I drove to Las Vegas every chance I got; that was maybe one or two evenings a week and once during the weekend, never so as it would interfere with my work. I have a great pride in work and a great feeling of responsibility." Her regular job was as assistant manager at a health spa where she set up the exercise routines and trained the instructors. Two nights a week she ran a gymnasium for housewives who could not get away during the day. Two other nights a week she gave private tennis lessons. "You could say I kept pretty busy."

While the frequency of her visits to Las Vegas did not accelerate, their intensity and the size of her bets did.

It crept up on me without my being aware of it. My bets went up from $10 to $25, to $50, to $100. I would win some, lose some, but I stayed pretty even. No big wins, but I didn't care. It was the excitement. That, and getting away from my problems. I could have an argument with my boss, or get into a hassle with one of my customers and it would eat on me all day and get me worried and depressed. That would keep up all the way to Las Vegas, but once I got into the casino, that was gone. In just one minute, I felt great, happy, in a hurry to get over to the table and start betting. But on the drive home, the problem would come back again, and if I had lost that night, it was a thousand times worse. Some nights I would drop $2,000, and I'd curse myself and say, "You dumb bastard. You work two and one-half weeks to make $2,000 and you drop it in a couple of hours." I would get so depressed, I wanted to die.

Then the losses started more heavily, but still she was able to keep from dipping into her savings and other cash assets. She'd pay her bills first—that was a firm principle—and gamble with what was left over. The excitement was still there, but not as strong as before. However, that did not stop her from going.

By this time I was hooked. I had to go, whether I enjoyed it or not. After the excitement left, it became a bore and after that I got sick of it, but still I had to go. On the way down I'd think to myself, "Why am I doing this? I'm weary. I feel sick. I'm disgusted. I want to go home and read a book or watch TV or sleep!" But I couldn't turn myself around. It got so I started to hate the whole thing—the dealers, the pit bosses, the other gamblers. But I had to keep on going.

My whole personality changed. My roommate—we had been rooming together for six years—noticed I was edgy, irritable, snappish. I had never been that way. I had always been friendly, easygoing, cooperative. She'd ask me in a kind way, did I have a problem, and I would bark back at her to get off my back.

It was starting to affect my work, too, so you know it was real bad. I'd foul up the schedules, mix up the groups, confuse the instructors, show up late for my night gym and sit on the sidelines instead of working with the women. I was lackadaisical with my tennis students and they dropped me.

The losses continued, and now her earnings were not enough to cover them. The succession that ensued was inevitable. There was $12,000 in savings and that went. There was $10,000 in CDs and that went. There were loans outstanding to banks, finance companies and friends, amounting to $8,000. She would take out a marker for $2,000 at one casino and lose that, then go to another casino and take out another $2,000 marker, trying to win it back, and lose that, too.

That's when I couldn't take it any longer. Even if I wanted to get more money somewhere, I couldn't. There was no place I could get even a dollar. That last night I came home from the casino ready to kill myself if I could find a way. I came in, sat down on the bed and started to cry. My roommate came over and said, "Mickey, you'd better get help." She told me she knew about my gambling. I thought I had been keeping it a secret from her, but she got enough clues without my saying anything. She said she'd called GA and they wanted me to come to a meeting. I went. It wasn't easy going in there with 18 or 20 men and me the only woman. When it came my turn, they asked me the 20 questions, and I made an almost-perfect score. I didn't want to believe I was an addict, but I accepted it. That was two years ago. I'm 37 now. And I have never gone back to gambling since. Four years of gambling hell was enough for me. Will I ever go back to gambling again? I can't swear that I won't. My only sure protection is GA. I know that so long as I keep going to meetings and working with other people who have a gambling problem, I'll never go back to gambling.

That is just one half of Mickey's story, the half having to do with her gambling career. But the rest of her life... what was that like, and does it give us any insights into her gambling? We'll let Mickey tell that part of the story herself.

I was born in Detroit, on the "other side of the tracks" in a rundown slum neighborhood. There were three of us, myself, a brother and a sister. I was born when my mother was 20, my brother when she was 19, and my sister when she was 18. My father walked out on my mother when I was a year old. My mother struggled, trying to raise us and keep us together, but when I was about nine, she just couldn't manage it any longer and gave us up to foster parents. We had to split up; nobody would take the three of us. I got to see my brother and sister maybe once or twice a year, and they had some pretty awful stories to tell—beatings, child molesting, cruelty. I had my share of that, too. Our playground was the streets of the slums, old deserted buildings where winos and drug addicts hung out, empty lots scattered with rubbish, glass, dead cats.

We had gangs, just like in *West Side Story*, not just play gangs, but real tough ones, warring with each other. I was in one gang of about 15 boys and girls, black and white. Everyone of us carried arms. At the age of 13, I was walking around with two switchblades, and for a while there I carried a gun—that's right, a gun, at the age of 13. We got into plenty of scrapes, breaking in and stealing, but we stole only what we needed—food and clothing, never money or anything else we didn't need or couldn't sell for a few dollars to buy food or shoes. We weren't bad kids. We did what we had to do to survive.

When I was 14, my mother showed up out of nowhere. I hadn't seen her in five years. If you haven't been through this yourself, you can't know what it means for a kid to be taken away from her mother and her brother and sister, to have no family, to cry herself to sleep out of loneliness, to be an unwanted kid in a foster home where they mistreat you and beat you and starve you, to have your only meaningful family be a bunch of other kids who have it as tough as you and have to fight to survive, and then have your mother show up one day and say, "Hey, it's going to be all right. It's all over. We're going to be together, all of us, you and I and Joey and Ellen." She said she had married again, a man named Steve, and that he was going to be our stepfather. The thought of living with still another stranger was frightening, and I hated the idea, but I'd have gone to live with Frankenstein or Dracula, if it meant being back again with my mother and sister and brother. We were going to live in a nice house, and I would have a room to myself, and we were going to have decent clothing and plenty of food. No picture I ever had of Heaven could compare with this.

This Steve turned out to be a cruel man, and he was rotten to all of us, but having gone through what we three had gone through, we kids could take anything. Besides, my brother was a strapping kid and Steve didn't want to tangle with him. He zeroed in on me and my sister and gave us a tough time. But then I found out it was going to be worse than that. When we had been living together about a year, he approached me sexually. I was scared to death and would have fought him but he threatened to turn me out if I didn't do what he wanted. The idea of losing my family again and of knocking around as a stranger in foster homes was more horrifying than anything he could do to me. So I thought to myself, whatever you have to do, do it. That kept up for two years, and it really messed me up emotionally. I was going to high school, and they had me singled out as a problem kid. I played hookey, drank, didn't do my work, got into fights with the other kids, used gutter language, messed around with a couple of hoods.

They were about to throw me out in my senior year, when this teacher got hold of me. She had seen my papers and learned about my background. She was the only one who could get to me and get me to do some good work. She could tell I wasn't stupid. I didn't tell her a thing about my problem with my stepfather. I was too proud. But that didn't matter. She worked with me and built up my confidence. She got me to study and to work and coached me and got me into college on a tuition scholarship. She also helped me get a job after school to pay for my room and board. I told my mother I was moving. She wanted to know why. I had never told her about what was happening because I was afraid if I did she would fight with Steve and the family would break up again, and I would do anything to prevent that. I just told her I didn't like Steve and I wanted to get out. I did and never went back.

I majored in economics and business and I worked toward my degree, but that wasn't where my heart was. I became interested in athletics and got on the college tennis team. Most of my friends were people from the school's athletic activities. When I graduated I got a job as instructor in this health spa and then went on to be assistant manager, also doing those other jobs I told you about—teaching tennis and running a gym for housewives.

You can't imagine what that did for my ego—being able to make it through college, then getting these good jobs and making a success of them, and earning about $40,000 a year. All my life, before that, I was nothing, dirt, a kid beaten and molested and starved, a teenager who had to steal to stay alive, a body to be used by a depraved stepfather. Now, here I was a respected person, someone people looked up to and admired.

But still you can't lose your past. It's always there, and if one thing doesn't bring it back, something else does. My mother used to come to visit me, and she told me what a terrible time she was having with this bastard, Steve, her husband. He would abuse her psychologically and physically. It was so bad she started to drink, and I could see she was on the way to becoming an alcoholic. I hated the bastard and wanted to kill him for what he had done to me and what he was doing to my mother.

About four years later, when I was 25, I married. This man, Marty, that I married was a real nice guy, but we just couldn't make it, and we were divorced. I still love him dearly. Most of the problem was sexual. I was so fouled up with guilt feelings about incest that I could never respond to Marty, and that upset him. He was a very sensitive guy, and it caused him to become impotent. We both went to separate psychiatrists, and my psychiatrist worked with me about my guilt feelings about the incest and got me straightened out about that. But the problem between Marty and me had gone too far and we couldn't patch it up, so we agreed the best thing to do was to get a divorce. I was 29 when that happened.

It wasn't a month after the divorce that I got a call from my brother to tell me my mother was in a coma and dying with an embolism in the brain. When I got to the hospital, she was dead. I saw this son of a bitch Steve, and I ran at him screaming; I wanted to kill him. I was about as big as he and a lot stronger, and I really would have killed him if my brother hadn't held me back.

Well, that's the story of my life. The rest of it, about the gambling, I've already told you.

While Mickey was getting her things together to leave after the interview, the interviewer glanced over his notes to check back on what appeared to be a rather significant coincidence in dates. Mickey had said the acceleration in her visits to the track—the first step in the sequence that led to her addiction—occurred when she was 29. Then, much later in the interview, as she was recalling the tragic events of her life, she had said that she was 29 when her mother had died, and that she was 29 when she was divorced.

What about the sequence? Which came first? First the divorce and then her mother's death, and about three months after that, she stepped up visits to the track. The interviewer then asked whether Mickey thought there might be some connection between the trauma and the gambling. Mickey looked puzzled, thought a while, shook her head in wonderment and said, "You know, it really does look like it, doesn't it?"

A COMPARISON

As we compare the early lives of Angela and Mickey we find many striking similarities. One born in a Nazi labor camp, illegitimate, the other abandoned by her father when she was an infant. In both cases, a mother struggling to keep her family together but unable to do so and having to give up the children to foster parents. One was brought up in a miserable shack on a ranch, mistreated by the ranch owners, and made to do the work of an adult. The other was brought up in a slum, a member of a warring gang, having to steal to get enough food and clothing. One raped at the age of 15, the other subjected to incest by a stepfather.

But, after that, the similarity ends. Angela chose one solution, Mickey a different one.

Angela chose what might be called a "feminine" solution. All she wanted was to be loved and wanted, to be part of her husband's life, to have a baby. Had these yearnings been fulfilled, she might never have sought solace and escape in gambling. Even in her addiction, she sought to do the "feminine" thing, to use her money to help others—her sister's struggling family, charities, the church.

Mickey chose what might be called a "masculine" solution. Although her major was in economics and business, she was drawn to the school's athletic program and after her graduation went to work in a health spa, taking on, also, two part-time jobs in athletics—one as a director of a gymnasium program for housewives, the other as tennis instructor. She was married, but her marriage broke up, and after that she lived for several years with a female roommate. She sought to heal her damaged ego, her feelings of worthlessness and powerlessness by taking on a "man-sized" work program and by striving for success in order to win acceptance and approval, very much a traditional masculine goal in our society.

With nothing more to go on than an interview, it is impossible to explain for certain why Mickey chose the "masculine" rather than the "feminine" solution. Yet it is difficult to resist the temptation to speculate. Could it be that she had seen the two most important women in her life—her mother and herself—so debased and abused by men that she felt ambivalent about being a woman? She did, indeed, fall in love with a man and marry him. But then, we would not suggest that when a woman's life experience inclines her toward a "masculine" life role that all her feminine instincts die. There may be a thousand and one variations on this basic theme—the "masculine" or "feminine" orientation in the choice of a life role and its impact on the style and outcome of compulsive gambling.

Neither of these two cases was selected because it represents a certain category of female compulsive gambler. The fact is that we do not yet know enough about female compulsive gamblers to be able to classify them into specific types.

We come now to another case, that of Arlene R., considerably different from the other two, and again we note that we do not yet know whether it is representative of a particular group. We chose it only because of its difference.

Arlene R.

Arlene's recollection of her mother is that of an "aggressive, loud, insensitive person who rode roughshod over everybody" and of her father as a "good-natured, meek, frightened man on whom Mama wiped her feet." There were three other children, but Arlene's recollection of them is scant.

We had so little to do with each other. It was every man for himself in that house and we kids led independent lives, even when we were little, each one sticking to himself. I knew I had to maneuver and plot for anything I wanted. The others did, too.

It was a lonely life. Papa was just a shadow. Mama overwhelmed everything. She had women friends, and she was always out with them, days and evenings, playing poker, gin, canasta, pinochle, going to the track; no time for us, just the minimum. I think she had boyfriends; she was always getting hush-hush telephone calls. A few times I answered the phone and it was a man calling and he'd hang up when I asked who it was.

Every few weeks, the card games would go on in our house—sometimes lasting a whole weekend. They were a noisy, vulgar crowd of men and women who came to play. We children would retreat to our rooms, and my poor father would go to stay with a sister as long as the game went on. There was a lot of money changing hands in those games, sometimes as much as $20,000 during a weekend. I would overhear the conversation even behind my closed bedroom door.

I really grew to detest my mother. Still, I wanted her to love me, to pay attention to me, to be affectionate. But nothing doing. She never as much as kissed me or hugged me. I'm sure she disliked me by the way she looked at me and the sarcastic remarks she made. When I was 11, I became ill with a serious glandular ailment, and they thought I was going to die. I had to stay home, in bed most of the time, for three months. She never even looked worried, never touched me or reassured me. She was too busy with her own interests. She didn't stay home to take care of me, just hired an 18-year-old girl to stay with me. When I was 13, my cousin Sarah—she was 11—came to stay with us. I took Sarah to the playground, and I was pushing her on a swing. She became frightened, let go of the chains, fell and hit her head on the concrete.

She was in a coma for days, and when she came out of it she had a tremor in her hand that she has never gotten over. She was a gifted piano student, and that ruined her life. It wasn't my fault, but my mother blamed it all on me. How would you like to carry that kind of guilt around all your life?

Arlene's father planned for her to have a career as a professional—a lawyer, college professor, doctor—and Arlene consented half-heartedly, but by the beginning of her senior year of high school she "had had enough of books and boredom" and answered an advertisement for a buyer-trainee in a large southern department store. Her father was devastated. Her mother "couldn't have cared less."

By the age of 23, Arlene had become senior buyer for leather goods, moving into a busy circuit of buying trips to Spain, Italy and England, conferences and conventions, with ample opportunities for partying, romance and gambling—all of which she indulged in and enjoyed, on a "playful, not serious level."

"I had no interest, then, in a permanent or even a long-lasting relationship with a man. I was contented with the casual encounters that might last a few weeks or months. They fulfilled my need for excitement and pleasure, and I was not particularly in need of much else."

Gambling, too, was a source of excitement and pleasure, "but it was nothing serious then."

I loved the casinos, the buzz, the charge of adrenalin. I had made many friends in the south of France and in Spain, and whenever I went abroad, they would take me to auto races in France and Monte Carlo and the casinos. But it was all part of a lot of exciting fun. I had no real interest in winning lots of money. It was a bubbly-champagne kind of existence.

One thing would get to me, however. You know the way European men are, macho and patronizing to women. They were that way about my gambling and took pains to instruct me on the techniques and the fine points. I let them play their little act, not letting on that I had had my introduction to gambling lots earlier through the weekend-long card games at my house, and later, in visits to Atlantic City and the track with a group of friends.

They were amazed at the speed with which I learned and at my frequent wins. I would get a real charge out of betting at the same table as these men, seeing them lose while I won. I got a great kick, too, betting against the male dealers at the blackjack table and beating them.

Even to this day, I can't understand why I felt that way. I am certainly not a women's-libber, and I don't hate men. I guess I just had to show how smart or good I was, just to inflate my ego. Winning a lot was proof enough, but I had to go further. I had to show how good I was with men as the competition. Not very feminine, is it?

Arlene's rise continued, and at the age of 30 she had become an associate manager for the entire store, earning upward of $60,000 a year. In the interim, she had lived with one man for a year, another for two years and after that had married and had a child. The two nonmarital arrangements had broken up because Arlene insisted on more independence than either of the men was willing to stand for.

The man she married was himself a rather unemotional person and was willing to enter into a marriage in which both partners put few restrictions on each other. A highly specialized expert in international banking, he was constantly on the move to one foreign country after another; actually, the two were together hardly at all. Most of the time when she was home, he was away, and when he was home, she was away. But neither complained. This is the way they wanted it.

For a year or two Arlene found this an ideal arrangement. A magnificent apartment on Park Avenue. A maid, a housekeeper and a governess to take care of the baby, freedom to pursue her career.

"But then," she added, "it began to pall on me.

There is no question this is what I had sought—independence, a career, competing with men in their own world and making it. But after two or three years of having it all, I began to feel an emptiness. Something was missing. I wasn't so eager to go away on foreign trips. I wasn't so happy about my husband's being away so much, or about his leaving me to myself, even when he was home. Damn it, I was just plain lonely, and I just plain wanted somebody to want me, to care about me, to worry about me, and Henry [her husband] just wasn't built that way.

That's about the time I started to gamble seriously. I had been around the casinos and the gambling houses so long, I knew all the ins and outs and just swung into it, like a pro. With the kind of money I was earning and the assets and property we had bought since our marriage, I could afford to bet heavily right from the start. Of course, I could have started betting on a smaller scale, but it would have been like taking a drink of watered-down scotch when what you really wanted was a double shot of 100-proof whiskey. So I went for the double shot, meaning $500 and $1,000 bets from the start.

Of course, I didn't tell my husband about the gambling. He never had known or asked to know about my where-

abouts before. There was no reason to tell him now. In
fact, there was good reason not to tell him. He would have
divorced me right from the start; he was that type of man.
We're divorced now, but that happened three years after
my heavy gambling started. It took him that long to find
out. It took him only a month after he found out to start
divorce proceedings; he even attempted to take the baby
away from me.

I don't know that I blame him. I think that if I were a
man and my wife plundered her assets the way I did, and
got into the kind of trouble I did, I might want to divorce
her, too. The particulars of what I did? It would take an
hour or two to go into them, and actually, you wouldn't be
hearing anything new.

But I'll sketch it out for you, covering just the major
items. I had, in my own account, about $45,000 in
money-market accounts and about $100,000 in Treasury
issues. I went through those. There was about $25,000 in
jewelry. That went. I had outstanding loans at one point of
$50,000, about half of which I was able to cover, and that
left $25,000 still owing. Of course, I had no problem
getting those loans. I am a businesswoman with my own
lines of credit. I suppose, even today, if I wanted to, I
could go out and borrow $50,000 more with no problem. I
had a beautiful Jaguar, and I sold that and lost the
$25,000 I got for it. I was about to dip into my firm's funds
for $10,000, but my very good friend, the comptroller,
intercepted the papers before I could get the cash, tore
them up, told me, and nobody else, that he had done so,
and saved my skin and my reputation.

My husband found out late in the game, when he came
across the statement from one of my bank loans while I
was away on a trip. When I returned from the trip he
confronted me, and I told him everything. I didn't feel I
needed to debase myself and seek his forgiveness. I was
an independent woman, and if I had fallen on my face,
that was my problem and I would have to face it. I had
hoped he would see it that way and let me work my way
out of it, giving me at least some moral support and
understanding while I struggled with my problem. But

Henry wasn't built that way. As I said, a month after he found out, he started divorce proceedings.

Of course, I was shattered. I didn't want to lose the marriage, and I didn't want to lose him. And of course, I wasn't going to let him take our child from me—and he didn't. But I suppose if you live and work in a man's world, and want equality with men, you can't fall back on the "poor-helpless-woman" role. I'm willing to take my beating and total responsibility for the problem—but it would have been nice if he had stretched out his hand and said: "Count on me. I'll help you." That's neither a masculine nor a feminine gesture. That's just being a good, decent human being who feels the hurt of a suffering spouse—whether it be the husband or the wife.

At the suggestion of the comptroller, who had befriended and protected her at the time of her attempted embezzlement, Arlene went for treatment for her compulsive gambling and became a member of Gamblers Anonymous. Her creditors accepted a restitution arrangement through which Arlene has, to date, repaid about $12,000 of her debts. She still holds her executive post with the department store.

It is interesting to compare Arlene's case with those of Angela and Mickey. Angela and Mickey both grew up in fatherless homes and had mothers who struggled to keep their families together. Both spent much of their childhood in foster homes where they were subjected to abuse. Both were subjected to sexual abuse in their teens. Arlene, by contrast, grew up in a family with a father and mother present throughout. She experienced none of the physical and material trauma that were so much a part of the lives of the other two. But there was trauma there, nevertheless— intense psychological trauma in the form of cruel and cold rejection by a mother whose love Arlene desperately craved but could not get. Angela and Mickey had no fathers, but they did have a mother to whom they could turn for love and with whom they could identify. Arlene did have a father, to whom she might have been able to turn in the anguish of being rejected by her mother. But her father had all he could do to protect himself from the assaultive behavior of his wife. His shoulders were not broad enough to carry Arlene's burdens, too. So Arlene grew up a "loner" who had to fend for herself in a family in which the rule was, Every man for himself.

From these beginnings there emerged a "case-hardened" personality, characterized by independence and assertiveness, capable of competing in a man's world" and making a success of it.

Her self-esteem was as badly battered as those of the other two women. She too had to seek self-validation, acceptance and approval. The strategy she chose was typically that of the male compulsive gambler—to compete, succeed and become important and powerful. Her gambling was similar to that of most male compulsive gamblers, as were her financial excesses when she was losing and trying to recoup. In the end, though, she never did attempt to justify her gambling and the problems she caused, as do so many of the men. She felt her guilt, took the blame for what she had done, followed immediately the suggestion that she go for treatment, become a member of Gamblers Anonymous and work out a program of restitution.

CHAPTER SEVEN

Recognizing and Diagnosing The Compulsive Gambler

IN THIS CHAPTER WE WILL LIST AND DISCUSS A NUMBER OF general indicators of compulsive gambling—indicators by which anyone can detect the presence of the addiction. Then we will list the specific criteria by which a psychiatric diagnosis may be made.

REVIEWING THE SIX TYPES OF GAMBLERS

You will recall the different classes of gamblers: the professional gambler, the antisocial-personality gambler, the casual social gambler, the serious social gambler, the "relief-and-escape" gambler and the compulsive gambler. Let us now review these various types to help you make a preliminary evaluation about whether the individual with whom you may be concerned is a compulsive gambler.

The Professional Gambler

This is a person who makes his living by gambling. It is his profession, and he learns how to do it with great skill. He studies the game or games in which he specializes, devises strategies that will give him the best possible advantage and puts them to work to win. He is not addicted to gambling. He has chosen it because he prefers it to other ways of making a living. If he wants to or has to, he can change to something else. It is not likely he will, because this is what he has been doing most of his adult life, and this is what he likes best; he prefers it to the traditional ways of earning a livelihood chosen by most of society. Although his work will likely bring him in contact with "shady characters," he will not, himself, have much to do with pursuits involving crime.

The Antisocial Personality Gambler

This is a person whose life career is obtaining money by illegal means. One of these means may be gambling. He plays the game with marked cards or loaded dice, or he may specialize in fixing horse races or dog races. He may also engage in legitimate gambling and steal to get money for this purpose.

Because the compulsive gambler may also steal to obtain money for gambling, it is possible to confuse him with the antisocial gambler—the criminal whose illegal activities bring him on the gambling scene.

These criteria will distinguish the two:

The antisocial-personality gambler has never had any ethical concern about harming others or stealing from them, his whole lifestyle has been to operate outside the law, to get money by illegal means.

The compulsive gambler has previously lived by society's rules and departs from ethical and legal behavior only when driven to do so by his compulsion to gamble.

The antisocial-personality gambler is typically a rootless person with no steady work (other than crime), permanent residence or intimate personal relationships.

The compulsive gambler is, in most cases, a family person, with a good work history and deep roots in his community. He becomes alienated from these associations only as a result of his compulsive drive to gamble.

The Casual Social Gambler

The casual social gambler gambles only occasionally

and does so for sociability, entertainment, a little excitement. This is just one of the many things he does for pleasure, and it takes up only a small part of his leisure time. The rest of his leisure time is taken up with a wide range of activities—his family, the movies, reading, golf tennis, ballgames, dining out, parties and so forth. Gambling does not get any special emphasis.

No one need be concerned about a person whose gambling behavior fits this general picture. There is little, if any, likelihood that his gambling is going to become a problem. If gambling is going to become serious, then the indications will show up early and quite clearly in the allotment of an inordinate amount of time, interest and money to gambling—as part of his total lifestyle—and the derivation of an inordinate amount of pleasure and gratification from gambling as compared with the other things he does.

The Serious Social Gambler

The serious social gambler, as the term indicates, is still only a social gambler. He gambles for the same reasons as the casual social gambler: entertainment, sociability, excitement. But, whereas gambling serves the casual social gambler as a minor source of these rewards, for the serious social gambler it is a major source. Winning is more important to him than to the casual social gambler, mainly because he invests a great deal of his ego in this activity. The actual amount he wins, however, and what he can buy with it may or may not be important. Serious social gamblers can get so caught up in their gambling that they may take more time away from their families than their families would like them to. But this is true, also, of some men who play bridge, tennis or golf, who go fishing or who have some other absorbing leisure occupation; there is no special significance to the fact that it is gambling rather than some other pursuit.

Is it possible for a serious social gambler to become a compulsive gambler? Possible, but not very likely. You do not find in the serious social gambler the drive to gamble that you do in the compulsive gambler. The desire and interest are there, but they do not completely eclipse other interests and desires. No matter how important gambling is to the serious social gambler, it is generally second in importance to family and business. There may be a period in the metamorphosis of the compulsive gambler when he resembles the serious social gambler, but that will not last long. "Interest" in gambling will accelerate and become "preoccupation" with gambling. Other interests will be pushed aside and gambling will dominate. If an individual has been a serious social gambler for several years and there has been little change in the extent and intensity of his gambling, one can be fairly certain that he is not going to develop into a compulsive gambler.

The "Relief-and-Escape" Gambler

Gambling provides more than sociability, recreation and a feeling of well-being. Many heavy gamblers report it gives them relief when they are feeling worried, depressed, weary, bored, anxious, resentful, frustrated or angry. They resort to it, too, they say, as a way to escape from dealing with a crisis or a difficult situation they cannot handle. Thus, gambling may be said to offer relief and escape from pressures and problems as well as giving gratification and pleasure. While some heavy gamblers resort to gambling for both the pleasure-giving (euphoriant) effects as well as the tension-relieving and antidepressant (analgesic) effects, there are some who rely on it primarily for the latter. Instead of drinking, as some people do, when they have problems and are anxious or depressed, or when they face a crisis, they gamble. These are the relief-and-escape gamblers and they differ from the serious social gamblers primarily in this respect—they seek the analgesic rather than the euphoriant effects of gambling.

What is the likelihood that a relief-and-escape gambler will become a compulsive gambler? The answer is the same as for the serious social gambler—possible, but not likely. The relief-and-escape gambler is not driven by a craving to gamble. His is a more passive attitude. Gambling is there for him when he needs it, and when he needs it he makes use of it. He may resort to it on a habitual basis, the way some people might take antidepressant or tranquilizing drugs whenever they are feeling uneasy. However, just as some drinkers or users of antidepressant and tranquilizing medication may become habituated to these substances without becoming addicted, so is it possible for relief-and-escape gamblers to become habituated to gambling without becoming addicted. There may be a stage in the metamorphosis of the compulsive gambler when he resembles the relief-and-escape gambler, but many other elements will be present in the portrait that clearly distinguish him as a compulsive gambler: the total preoccupation with gambling, the displacement of all other interests, the condition of being driven, the craving, the insensitivity to the feelings and needs of others, the disregard of the disastrous consequences, the complete loss of control.

The Compulsive Gambler

The compulsive gambler is a sick person, an addict, driven by an overwhelming, uncontrollable impulse to gamble. The compulsive gambler keeps on gambling though this may strip him of everything he owns, cause unimaginable suffering for himself and his family, plunge him into abysmal debt, drive him to lie, cheat and steal, ruin his health, cause his imprisonment, bring him to the brink of suicide.

The casual social gambler can stop gambling when he wants to, so can the serious social gambler and the relief-and-escape gambler. The compulsive gambler cannot stop no matter how hard he tries, even though he may think he can. He has lost control. The impulse to gamble is so insistent, so overpowering, so consuming, that he is unable to resist it and he must continue to gamble.

For the casual social gambler, gambling is just an incidental pastime, one among many others. For the serious social gambler, it is a major source of entertainment and pleasure; there may be other sources, but gambling is one of the most important. For the relief-and-escape gambler, gambling is much more than a pastime; it is an established component of his emotional structure, his conditioned response when confronted by a severely stressful situation or an outright crisis in his life.

For the compulsive gambler, gambling is a source of excitement and recreation. It is also the way he finds relief from stress and crisis. It is also his source of self-validation and self-esteem, of importance and power. It may, at the beginning, occupy only a minor role in his life, but then it becomes more and more important until finally it dominates his life, pushing aside every other interest and concern, undermining his self-respect, his work, his family life and relationships of trust with others, leaving him and desolation in its path.

RECOGNIZING THE COMPULSIVE GAMBLER

Final Stage

Recognizing the compulsive gambler in the final stage of his addiction presents no problem. The manifestitations are unmistakable.

He is rundown, sickly, weary. He eats poorly, sleeps fitfully, has nightmares. He has no concern about his health, his personal hygiene or grooming. He is jumpy, edgy and cannot sit still. He is depressed and given to spells of acute anxiety, thinking he is going to die. He has frequent fits of uncontrollable weeping. He may drink or use tranquilizers to quiet his unbearable nervous agitation.

He alternates between periods of explosive rage and periods of zombie-like automatism. In his rage he smashes things, hurls them about, kicks them. He may assault his wife and children. In his zombie-like phase he may sit or lie about for hours, silent, motionless; or he may walk about muttering to himself, speaking disconnectedly, irrationally. Psychiatrists who have examined patients in this stage of gambling addiction say that except for the history of compulsive gambling and certain other characteristics, they might easily have mistaken them for patients with a diagnosis of schizophrenia.

Late Stage

Recognizing the compulsive gambler in the late, but

not yet final, phase of addiction is not a difficult matter either. At this stage, too, the picture is unmistakable.

He is totally obsessed with gambling and spends every after-work hour (if he still has a job) at the places where he does his gambling. He takes time away from work to gamble, lying to explain his absences. He spends virtually no social time with his wife and children; whatever time he spends at home is given to eating, sleeping, watching sports events on television, telephoning his bookmaker to place bets and get results, dodging telephone calls from creditors and bookmakers.

When he is not on the job or at home or gambling he is running around drawing out savings, cashing in securities, selling or mortgaging property, borrowing from banks and finance companies or relatives and friends. He is away from home frequently without explanation. In his contacts with his family, relatives, friends and business associates, he is short-tempered, arrogant, hostile, impossible to deal with. He is lying not only about his gambling activities, losses and winnings, but about almost everything else. His behavior is frenetic, charged, driven.

Early and Middle Stages

Recognizing the compulsive gambler when his addiction is just taking hold and immediately after, when it is beginning to advance and spread, is not so easy. The obvious excesses are not yet there; the outrages have not yet begun, the character, while showing cracks and defects, is still pretty much intact.

How then are family members, friends and others to know what is happening?

We have selected a number of indicators for this purpose. The time of their appearance will vary from individual to individual; some that show up early in one case may show up later in others, and vice versa. It is not possible to give you a critical number and say: "If you can check off 7 or 10 of these warning signs you've surely got a compulsive gambler." These indicators have not been subjected to research but have been gleaned from clinical experience

and observation of compulsive gamblers and from interviews with relatives. Until their validity and relative weight
are established through research, they should be regarded
only as strongly suggestive rather than as conclusive.

An additional word about these indicators: Most compulsive gamblers are open about their gambling at the
beginning. They see nothing wrong with what they are
doing and see no reason to hide it. Further, they want to be
able to boast about their gambling and winnings. It is only
when their gambling becomes excessive and begins to
interfere with the rest of their lives that they find the need to
start hiding what they are doing, especially when they are
losing and have to resort to unacceptable ways of raising
money, ways they do not want their wives and others to
know about.

Some of the indicators we cite have to do with gambling behavior. Obviously, when the gambling is hidden,
these indicators will not be readily apparent. The rest of the
indicators pertain to changes in the gambler's behavior
brought about by his obsessive gambling. These will be
useful in supplementing whatever meager information the
gambler may be giving out about his actual gambling
involvement.

THE INDICATORS

1. *How much time is spent gambling.* When the
gambling is out in the open, the first thing one needs to look
into is the amount of time the individual spends gambling,
in relation to the rest of his life. Is it more or less than what
others in his social setting are doing? Is it considerably more
than is customary in that setting? One needs to be careful, in
making this evaluation, not to judge according to one's
personal desires and standards but rather by those of the
community. You or I might not want a husband or boyfriend
or son to be gambling as much as he is doing; he might be
gambling too much to suit us. But if his gambling is pretty
much in line with what most others in the community are
doing, it would indicate that so far as this criterion is
concerned, there is no problem. If, on the other hand, the

gambling seems significantly out of line with what is customary, this could indicate a problem.

2. *Increase in gambling time and places*. Let us say he has been gambling normally, on a par with the practice in his particular setting, but then there is a change. He shows more intense interest in horse racing and substantially increases his weeknight and weekend visits to the track. Or, let us say he has been watching one football (or hockey or basketball) game on Saturday or Sunday; now he watches two or three during the weekend and additional games during the week. He may let on that he is betting on the results, or he may not. But it is hardly likely that a sudden surge of interest in the game itself is responsible for his changed behavior. In all likelihood, this would indicate that he has been gambling on the games and that the pace of the gambling is accelerating.

Another thing to look for is a broadening out to new places to do his gambling. Visits to out-of-state tracks or casinos are significant when until now he has been frequenting just one or two local ones. There seems to be a special excitement for compulsive gamblers in going to new gambling haunts. This has in it something of a quest for "new worlds to conquer," new arenas in which to test their power. There is also an element of belief that a change of venue will bring him luck. It is not unlike the fisherman who moves from one spot on the lake to another when luck hasn't been good. He is certain that the "big one" is lurking in the depths at the new location.

3. *Increase in the size of his bets*. This, too—a significant increase in the amount bet on a game or race—can be an indicator of accelerating excitement about gambling and winning, and by that token, of the onset of the compulsive-gambling addiction. Let us say he has been used to betting $5 on a race or football game and now he is betting $20, $30 or $50; or he's been used to betting $50 or $100 a night at blackjack or dice and now he's raised the ceiling for the evening to $300 or $500; or he's been playing poker with a $5 limit and now looks for a game where the limit is higher. Unless there has been a sudden and substantial increase in his income from nongambling sources, which might account for a greater freedom with his money, a sudden and sharp rise in the level of betting should be regarded with suspicion as a possible indication of compulsive gambling.

4. *Working up special occasions for gambling*. Alcoholism counselors say that one of the surest signs of incipient alcoholism is the drinker's practice of searching out or working up social situations in which drinking is going to be a major component. The event itself and the drinking at the event may be entirely innocent. It is the pursuit or creation of such events that is the telltale factor. For example, the drinker may suddenly develop an interest in going to the theater—something he has shunned before—because that means dinner out with a cocktail or two before dinner, wine during dinner, a brandy after dinner and a stopover at a downtown lounge for a sociable drink after the theater. Or, not having had much to do with neighbors before, he suddenly gets the idea to have them over every Sunday for a drink or two, because, "after all, neighbors should be neighborly."

Compulsive gamblers, too, will do this sort of thing. They will be on the lookout for special events at the track in nearby cities or states and suggest that a group drive out and "make a day of it" with partying and celebrating, and of course with ample opportunity for gambling under an acceptable social guise. Then, how could anybody possibly miss the Kentucky Derby, the Preakness, the Belmont Stakes or other racing features; or the World Series, the Super Bowl or games between his alma mater and its traditional rival, with all the attendant hoopla and partying and naturally, the splendid opportunities for gambling. And what about those gambling cruises "to nowhere" or in the Caribbean, the fiesta trips to Mexican gambling towns, the junkets to Las Vegas . . . all legitimate occasions for partying and fun, but also for some heavy gambling in exciting and glamorous settings.

If junkets of this sort have played and continue to play a minor role in his total social life, they need not necessarily be an indication of a problem. There is cause for concern, however, if they become much more frequent than in the past; if the gambler approaches them with a frenetic sense of urgency, insisting that the family or the social group do this rather than anything else, becoming impatient, even enraged, if anyone puts an impediment in the way; or if he pushes aside other pursuits and cancels other significant arrangements that may conflict with the trip or other event he is trying to organize.

5. *The intensity of interest in gambling*. Social gamblers, whether they are casual or serious, do not spend much time talking about gambling, and when they do talk about it, they do so quite casually. The person who is on the way to becoming a compulsive gambler finds it exciting not only to gamble but to talk about it. Between races or games or on the way home he will be full of what's happening and want to go over it in detail, explaining to you, "the amateur," all the fine points and the strategies, showing off his savvy as a "pro." The compulsive gambler is charged up by the race or game or gambling house the way someone else might be when going out to a formal party or some other especially exciting event. If you are with him on the way to the track or game, you can feel his excitement and tension. A snag in traffic or some other delay is likely to evoke a burst of cursing. At the event itself he is like a tightly wound spring held back by a hair-trigger device. The high level of excitement and tension shown by the compulsive gambler may not be much different from that shown by gamblers who are not addicted; the difference lies in the fact that these other gamblers may behave this way on an infrequent visit to the track or casino. The compulsive gambler reacts this way if he's gambling every night.

6. *Boasting*. Social gamblers do not, as a rule, boast much about their winnings. With the compulsive gambler, it is another thing. One of the main reasons he gambles is to achieve a feeling of importance and power, and showing off his winnings is a way he has of doing this. If he should happen to lose, he will, if you are with him, minimize it, make light of it or not want to speak about it at all. He may even try to deny that he has lost and make up a tale about not having bet on that race. If you were not with him at his gambling, he will have little to tell you when he gets home. Boasting about winning and evasiveness about losing are both significant indicators.

7. *Exaggerated display of money and other possessions.*
Nothing could be more normal than an interest in money and the things it can buy. This is the emphasis in our society, and even if it were not, who could find anything wrong with wanting a nice home, nice furniture and decorations, a television set and a stereo system, vacations, nice clothing, dining out, entertaining. It could be a matter for concern, however, if this becomes the predominant interest and overshadows everything else, as does happen with the compulsive gambler. For example: whatever the subject of conversation, he manages to bring it around to the money he has spent on some luxury item, the worth of his possessions, and the like. Of course, many people do this who are not compulsive gamblers, but the one who is will match his talk with an ostentatious display of his money and possessions, flash them around, bring home extravagant and lavish gifts. This would be the case even when he is not winning a great deal; it becomes truly excessive at times when he is winning steadily.

8. *Gambling when there is a crisis.* Different people have different ways of dealing with a crisis. Some face it squarely and realistically. Others run away from it, literally leaving home, a wife, a job, an examination, a school, a business. Others escape not by running away but by dropping out of reality and into fantasy—daydreaming and psychological withdrawal, alcohol, drugs or gambling. The person who takes the gambling route to fantasy we have designated as the relief-and-escape gambler. A person can be a relief-and-escape gambler without necessarily being a compulsive gambler. However, if he is already manifesting some of the other indicators of compulsive gambling and if on top of that he deals with his problems and crises by running someplace where he can gamble, or by a sharp increase in the level of his gambling, one would have reason to suspect this as an indication of compulsive gambling.

This reaction—a sharp burst of gambling—is also likely to occur when there is a change for the better that involves new and burdensome responsibility—a marriage, the birth of a child, a promotion or salary increase, a new job or a new home.

9. Drop-off in other activities and interests. Once a compulsive gambler gets caught up in his gambling, he is "vacuumed" away from everything else. Gambling becomes the most exciting and most important thing in his life, and other things become dull and uninteresting by comparison. Watch for a sharp drop in interest in activities that have been important to him in the past.

We would expect him, for example, to lose interest in tennis or bowling or golf, or in going out to dinner or in having friends over. He may have been quite enthusiastic about family gatherings; now, but he can't be dragged to the relatives' gatherings. He was interested in wines or gourmet food; suddenly, these no longer mean anything to him. Jogging and exercise might have been "a must"; now he regards them with indifference. And, even more significantly, he may have been a most enthusiastic lover, and now he is not sexually responsive at all, or at least not approaching the extent he used to be.

It is possible, of course, that a decrease in interest in things he has enjoyed doing may have nothing to do with compulsive gambling. He may be having trouble on the job, or he may be subject to spells of depression because of physiological changes. However, if the drop-off in other interests is related to compulsive gambling, there should also be other indications of the kind listed here.

10. Frequent absences from home and work. If the gambler has been open about his gambling, he is not likely to try to hide it when his gambling first begins to accelerate and he starts to spend more time away from home. The time when he is likely to start concealing his activities is when his gambling becomes truly excessive and when it starts to cause him problems he doesn't want his family to know about. Depending on the kind of relationship he has with the family, he may just stay away without giving any explanation or feeling that he needs to. If it has been customary for him to account for his whereabouts, then one can expect the customary excuses: some work to finish up at the office; emergency overtime; a special meeting of the lodge or political club; an uncle who has just come to town. These excuses, we admit, are quite ordinary. Compulsive gamblers are often much more creative.

Absences from work to gamble are generally covered by excuses about illnesses and emergencies in the family, visits to the dentist or doctor and the like. The only way the family will know about these absences is when someone from the office or factory calls to ask how John is doing, or whether his wife has recovered from her operation, or whether a child is recovering from his automobile accident injuries, and the like.

Frequent absences without explanation or with shabby explanations are as good an indicator of compulsive gambling as any, and when these begin to occur it is time to look around for the other indicators that will confirm the suspicion.

11. *Excessive use of the telephone.* Gambling through a bookmaker generally means using the telephone. Hence a sudden, unexplained increase in the use of the telephone at home, or an unwillingness to explain telephone calls he is getting, would be cause for suspicion. Supplementary indicators would be his unreasonable annoyance when someone else in the family stays on the phone too long and his need to absent himself at parties, family gatherings, the theater or the movies to "make an important telephone call," the nature of which he refuses to explain.

12. *Withdrawal from his wife and children.* Let us assume that this has been the situation in the family: The husband has been fondly attentive to his wife and the children, has enjoyed spending time with them, doing things together, making sure that they have everything they want commensurate with his earnings. Then changes begin to occur. Not only is he away from home more, but when he does stay home he does not behave toward his wife and children the way he used to.

The wife herself may begin to notice it in the lessening fervor of his embrace; the omission of the goodbye kiss in the morning and the goodnight kiss at bedtime; the excuse that he's tired and worn out when his wife suggests making love; the omission of other little acts of affection—the smile, the pat, the squeeze; his distraction and inattention when his wife tries to tell about something amusing or interesting that happened or to share a bit of gossip or to discuss something that needs to be bought for the house; his irritation and annoyance when his wife insists on getting his attention or complains about his indifference.

The children may not notice it at first, because they are so taken up with their friends, their play, their schoolwork. But then the little ones seem to be pulling on their mother more than they have before for attention, and making greater demands on her time and her involvement with them. They themselves may not know what has been happening, but when the wife observes the situation closely, she discovers that her husband is not hugging the children and picking them up as before, that he is pushing them away when they come to him, that he no longer plays games with them or reads to them and is forgetting about tucking them in at bedtime.

The older ones will be more aware; they may say nothing to their mother voluntarily, but will show their disappointment by spells of silence and withdrawal. When she asks them what's troubling them, they may not be able to put their finger on it right off, but if she pursues the matter she'll find they are upset about their father. He doesn't seem to care about them any longer, they say. He doesn't ask them how they're doing at school or offer to help them with a math problem or history question. He no longer takes them for a walk, a camping trip, to the movies or to get ice cream.

Obviously, something is distracting him, drawing his interest away from his wife and children. In the absence of any other explanation, and in the presence of other indicators of compulsive gambling, this sort of behavior should be regarded as a significant clue to the development of a gambling addiction.

13. *Changes in personality*. A husband's cooling toward wife and children may be but the first step in a protracted change in the quality of their overall relationship. If the wife has been unaware of the change when it was just a matter of reduced interest and demonstration of affection, she will certainly become aware of it when he becomes irritable, picky, impatient, critical, sarcastic, antagonistic. Before, a request from his wife that he pick up something at the cleaners on his way home from work might have been met with ready willingness. Now it is likely to elicit a snappish, "What's the matter? You too busy talking on the phone to your sister?" Before, he might have chided her good-naturedly about curlers in her hair, a run in her stocking, smeared lipstick or lumps in the mashed potatoes. Now it brings a surly, sarcastic comment.

The children, too, find themselves on the receiving end of this emerging hostility. A father who has been genial, supportive and tolerant of their shortcomings, now barks and snarls at them when they ask him for something or get in his way; he calls them stupid, lazy, clumsy when they make a mistake or have a problem in school or with their friends.

The change from warmth to hostility may come long before the losing phase begins. We need to remember that the gambling addiction keeps its victim under pressure, constantly, even when he is winning. When he wins he is driven to bet more and win more; no matter how much he wins, it is never enough. This can have a nerve-frazzling effect and produce fractious, short-tempered, belligerent behavior.

14. *The diversion of family funds*. To get money to feed his gambling habit, the compulsive gambler may commit relatively minor offenses, such as pilfering cash from the family cookie jar, making small secret withdrawals from the joint savings account, borrowing an occasional $25 or $50 from friends and paying it back out of family funds, holding back payment on the rent, utilities or insurance. Or he may be compelled to make much more serious raids on family resources, such as exhausting the family's savings, cashing in insurance policies, redeeming securities and savings bonds or selling his wife's jewelry.

If caught in one of these maneuvers, he will try to lie his way out of it with some specious excuse. When this sort of thing begins to happen, one can be certain that the problem is not just one of simple gambling, but of a gambling addiction.

These, then, are the descriptions of the compulsive gambler and the indicators by which he may be recognized. The next chapter will present the things family and friends can do in those circumstances.

To give a more specific index, below are listed the "Diagnostic Criteria for Pathological Gambling" (synonymous with "compulsive gambling"), authorized by the American Psychiatric Association and reported in their *Diagnostic and Statistical Manual III*, 1982.

THE DIAGNOSTIC CRITERIA FOR PATHOLOGICAL [COMPULSIVE] GAMBLING

Pathological gambling is designated in the APA manual as "a disorder of impulse control," and disorders of impulse control are identified by the following:

1. There is a failure to resist an impulse, drive or temptation to perform some action that could be harmful to the individual or to others. There may or may not be conscious resistance to the impulse. The act may or may not be premeditated or planned.

2. Prior to the act there is an increasing sense of tension.

3. At the time of committing the act, there is an experience of either pleasure, gratification or release. The act is ego-syntonic. (Ed. Note: This means that it is in accord with the immediate conscious wish and aim of the individual. It is not, *at the time,* something he is trying to resist as obnoxious, offensive, wrong. It is something he is wanting to do. Immediately following the act, there may be regret, self-reproach, guilt.)

The "Diagnostic Criteria for Pathological Gambling" are as follows:

A. The individual is chronically and progressively unable to resist the impulse to gamble.
B. Gambling compromises, disrupts or damages family, personal and vocational pursuits *as indicated by at least three of the following:*
   1 arrest for forgery, fraud, embezzlement or income-tax evasion due to attempts to obtain money for gambling;
   2 defaults on debts or other financial responsibilities;
   3 disrupted family or spouse relationship due to gambling;
   4 borrowing money from illegal sources (loan sharks);
   5 inability to account for loss of money or to produce evidence of winning money if this is claimed;
   6 loss of work due to absenteeism in order to pursue gambling activity;
   7 necessity for another person to provide money to relieve a desperate financial situation (a bailout);
C. The gambling is not due to Antisocial Personal Disorder.

In summary, a person may be diagnosed as being a compulsive gambler if his history shows that he has been unable, consistently, to give up gambling even when this has caused harm to himself and his family; if the condition has grown progressively worse; and if the harmful effects to himself and his family include at least three of the seven listed consequences.

To make certain that the individual is a compulsive

gambler rather than an antisocial-personality gambler, these additional factors must be considered:

His history (prior to his preoccupation with gambling) shows steady and intimate relationships with and commitments to family, relatives and friends; involvement with his religious and/or ethnic group, and/or with social, civic, fraternal institutions or organizations; and steady, long-lasting and responsible performance in school, at work or in other occupational endeavors. A general positive picture with respect to these criteria would indicate the individual is a compulsive gambler rather than an antisocial-personality gambler. The history of the latter, would, by contrast, show a record of crime or other antisocial behavior; few, if any connections with religious, ethnic, social or other traditional institutions and organizations; few, if any, intimate personal relationships; few, if any, commitments to a family or other relative; transiency in abode and work.

THE "SOFT SIGNS" OF COMPULSIVE GAMBLING

These diagnostic criteria are what may be called "the hard signs" of compulsive gambling. They are adequate, for professional purposes, to make a diagnosis of compulsive gambling.

There are, in addition, quite a number of behavioral signs that have been found to be associated with compulsive gambling. While they are not in themselves diagnostic factors, the presence of a number of these "soft," or suggestive, signs might add reassurance to the diagnosis. These soft signs have been selected by observing compulsive gamblers and have been verified through research. They have not yet been subjected to rigid scientific testing, but there is reason to expect that when they are, several of them might be moved up to the category of "hard," or definite, diagnostic criteria.

1. He is of superior intelligence, in the 115–120 range (or better).

2. He admits to a high energy level, is proud of it and tends to be scornful of those who show less get-up-and-go.

3. There is a history of excellence in athletics.

4. School performance has been good, except where gambling entered the picture early and disrupted it.

5. There is a history of steady, solid work performance and, in many cases, a preoccupation with work bordering on workaholic dimensions.

6. There has been little or no use of alcohol or drugs while in the act of gambling.

7. While he may say at first that he has no problems sleeping, further exploration shows that his sleeping pattern is abnormal, with episodes of insomnia and nightmares about gambling.

8. He does not have any hobbies.

9. He is not comfortable with conflict and tries to avoid it. He is likely to resort to exaggeration, distortion or lying in order to do so.

10. He does not have any kind things to say about his wife's friends and family; generally, he is very critical of them.

11. When he went on his honeymoon, he took his bride back to a place where gambling was a significant element in the setting.

12. He sets high expectations of performance for himself and for others and is impatient and intolerant with himself and others if they are not reached. He cannot tolerate flaws, imperfections or mistakes,

either in himself or others. He is, in other words, a perfectionist.

13. He has a fond preference for people who gamble and is somewhat disdainful and intolerant of people who do not.

14. He is a risk taker, especially in financial ventures.

15. He likes and admires people who take risks and does not have a high regard for people who do not.

16. He considers himself to be very generous or [surprisingly enough] very stingy, seldom anything in between.

17. He uses the telephone extensively, to the point that it frequently disrupts social or business activities.

18. He gets bored easily in social situations and, although he may feign interest, his disinterest shows through.

19. He is a good organizer but a poor participant. He likes to initiate projects but lacks desire or patience to see them through.

20. Very likely he had no savings account as a child.

21. He does not believe in saving money as a safeguard for the future. He believes in accumulating money in order to spend it.

22. He is a big spender and a big tipper.

23. He has not ever borrowed or stolen money when he has had money in hand with which to bet.

24. Initially his borrowing from lending institutions was

infrequent and for small amounts. This was followed by a steady, progressive increase in frequency and amount.

25. He has cashed in his life insurance policies or he has discontinued them altogether.

26. He has resorted to pawning his own and his wife's jewelry.

27. He is likely to have declared bankruptcy.

28. He carries his money around in cash, even in large amounts; seldom does he use traveler's checks when going on a trip.

29. Winning is an extremely pleasant experience, which hastens his return to gambling. Although the pleasure from winning may diminish as his gambling progresses, his urge to return to gambling is not diminished.

30. Losing is an agonizing experience, which is relieved only with a return to gambling.

31. There is no other experience that is more pleasurable, exciting and relaxing than gambling. Although these feelings diminish over time, the urge to continue gambling is not diminished.

32. The "big win" episodes are clearly remembered and may be recounted, in detail, with relish.

33. The first "big win" was likely to have been counted out in front of the spouse, with a great show of self-congratulation and glee.

34. He has a solid, expert knowledge of the odds, probabilities and other fine points of his preferred form of gambling.

35. When he wins he will pay a good share of his gambling debts, but he will almost always keep enough in reserve for gambling.

36. Seldom, if ever, has he kept a record of his wins or losses.

37. Gambling has displaced his interest in social activities.

38. He has an unusual loyalty to bookmakers, regarding them almost as personal friends and/or "business partners."

39. He has a distrust of the gambling industry.

To reiterate: These "soft," or suggestive, signs are not in themselves diagnostic. They may be useful to reinforce a diagnosis that is in the making, based on the "hard," diagnostic, signs.

THE "20 QUESTIONS" OF GAMBLERS ANONYMOUS

Gamblers Anonymous (GA) has prepared a list of 20 questions it considers useful in identifying the compulsive gambler. Most compulsive gamblers, says GA, will answer affirmatively at least 7 of these 20 questions. Thus, it adds, any individual who answers yes to 7 or more should be concerned about being or becoming a compulsive gambler. (Recent research on the indicators of compulsive gambling tend to show that 7 is too low a figure, that the critical figure should be 12, instead.)

1. Do you lose time from work because of gambling?

2. Is gambling making your home life unhappy?

3. Is gambling affecting your reputation?

4. Have you ever felt remorse after gambling?

5. Do you ever gamble to get money with which to pay debts or to otherwise solve financial difficulties?

6. Does gambling ever cause a decrease in your ambition or efficiency?

7. After losing, do you feel you must return as soon as possible to win back your losses?

8. After you win, do you have a strong urge to return to win more?

9. Do you often gamble until your last dollar is gone?

10. Do you ever borrow to finance your gambling?

11. Have you ever sold any real or personal property to finance gambling?

12. Are you reluctant to use "gambling money" for normal expenditures?

13. Does gambling make you careless of the welfare of your family?

14. Do you ever gamble longer than you have planned?

15. Do you ever gamble to escape worry and trouble?

16. Have you ever committed or considered committing an illegal act to finance gambling?

17. Does gambling cause you to have difficulty in sleeping?

18. Do arguments, disappointments, or frustrations cause you to gamble?

19. Do you have an urge to celebrate any good fortune by a few hours of gambling?

20. Have you ever considered self-destruction as a result of your gambling?

CHAPTER EIGHT

Now That You Know, What Should You Do About It?

LET'S SUPPOSE THAT, BASED ON WHAT YOU HAVE READ IN the previous chapter, you are convinced that a member of your family is a compulsive gambler, or is quickly becoming one. Now you want to know what you can do about the situation.

Because the very large majority of compulsive gamblers are married men, we are going to attempt to answer this question as it would apply to a woman whose husband is a compulsive gambler. However, the principles are universal, and anyone should be able to apply them to the case of any compulsive gambler, regardless of gender or kind of relationship.

The next steps you take will depend on your goal. If you do not want to endure any longer the kind of misery your husband's addiction has brought you, your course is clear; you need to take whatever measures you deem necessary to bring the relationship to an end. For guidance on what to do and how to do it, you might want to go to a family-service agency, a marriage or divorce counselor, or a psychiatrist or other psychotherapist. If, on the other hand, you want to keep the relationship, help your husband quit, work toward the creation of a normal family life unperturbed by gambling and gambling problems, then the rest of these suggestions are for you.

It might interest you to know, in this connection, the results of a recent survey. The subjects of this survey were a large number of members of Gam-Anon, a national organization for the families and friends of compulsive gamblers. Three out of every four of the women questioned said they had threatened to separate from or divorce the gambler. Approximately half of these women eventually carried out the threat. However, practically all of them were able to effect a reconciliation, and at the time of the survey, 94 percent were still married.

The first thing we are going to ask you to do is get a clear fix on the problem. Ordinarily, in the case of a sickness, we concentrate on the patient—the direct victim of the illness. In the case of compulsive gambling, there is another primary victim—the wife.

If you are like all the other wives of compulsive gamblers at this stage of the problem, then you are very likely bewildered, discouraged, frustrated, confused, resentful, angry, frightened, upset. You are probably having bouts of anxiety, self-blame and depression, eating and sleeping poorly, suffering from headaches or stomach problems or other psychosomatic disorders. Therefore, when we are thinking about what needs to be done, we have to be thinking not only about what needs to be done about the gambler but, even before that, what *you* need to do for *you*.

First and foremost, you are going to need to take care of yourself, for your own sake. You need to restore your physical health and emotional equilibrium. You need to free yourself of your frustration, anxiety and depression. You need to regain your confidence and self-respect and rid yourself of feelings of self-blame.

Let us take care of the physical ailments first. If you are not already seeing a physician, go to your family doctor. Let him look you over and treat whatever physical ailments you may have. Some of these may have no relation to the emotional difficulties brought on by the gambling problem; others may.

GET IN TOUCH WITH GAM-ANON

Next, or even while you are taking care of the physical problems, go to your phone book and look up the number of the local Gam-Anon group and call, telling them you think your husband is a compulsive gambler and you need help. In existence since 1960, Gam-Anon has helped hundreds of thousands of spouses of compulsive gamblers live through the ordeal and find a solution to their problems. There are hundreds of Gam-Anon groups around the country, and you will most certainly find one within reasonable traveling distance. If you do not find a listing for Gam-Anon, look up the number for Gamblers Anonymous and tell them you want to get in touch with a Gam-Anon group. They'll help you locate one. If neither of these two organizations is listed locally, you can write or phone the National Council on Compulsive Gambling and ask them to help you locate a Gam-Anon group. Their address is: c/o John Jay College of Criminal Justice, 444 West 56th Street (Room 3207S), New York, N.Y. 10019 (telephone: 212–765–3833).

Gam-Anon is an informal organization, a fellowship. The groups meet regularly at a set location such as a church, synagogue or community house. There are no membership fees or requirements beyond the desire to get help because of a family member's compulsive gambling. Most members have been going there for months, many for years. They keep attending either because they are still dealing with the family member's gambling or because, having already resolved their own problems, they want to give friendship, encouragement and emotional support to others who come needing help.

The moving spirit in Gam-Anon, as in Gamblers Anonymous, is a profound devotion of men and women who have themselves suffered to other men and women going through the same ordeal. The participants customarily have a list of one another's telephone numbers, and they know they can call at any hour of the day or night if they have a problem they can't handle by themselves or if they just need some-one to talk to.

At the meetings, participants may just sit and listen, or they may air their problems and receive the helpful comments of the others. We can best convey to you the benefits of participating in these groups by quoting for you the comments of one woman after she had attended several meetings of the Gam-Anon group in her community. These comments were made at a meeting, addressed to the group.

When my rabbi first suggested that I go, I was very reluctant to do so. I was feeling so isolated, so alone, so separated from the rest of humanity, that I couldn't imagine anyone else could understand about what I was going through, or care. Not only that, I was embarrassed and ashamed. I couldn't imagine getting up in front of some other people and washing my dirty linen in public. I felt ashamed of having such a husband and letting anybody else know about it. I was ashamed of what I had let him do to me and the children. I felt tainted, dirtied. I felt this was something I was going to have to suffer through by myself alone. I had no idea what I could do. Everything was so dismal, so dark and hopeless. I couldn't imagine that anyone could possibly help me. I had no idea that there were other women who had lived through the same thing, who were in the same boat. I thought that it was only me to which this was happening, that I was going through a very unique and unusual experience. I had been locked up in this thing by myself for so long, cut off from my family and my friends, that I thought I was going out of my mind and that I would never be able to climb out of this deep, black hole.

I told Rabbi L. I would think about going and went home and brooded and worried and struggled with it, and then I made up my mind. I knew that my rabbi would not be sending me on some wild-goose chase, that if he was sending me, he himself was convinced that it would be the good thing and the right thing to do. So I called the telephone number that the rabbi gave me, still so nervous and not knowing what to expect. It was Edna B.'s phone, and it was such a friendly and pleasant voice that for a second I felt like crying. In fact I did choke up, and for a few seconds I couldn't say a word. I'm sure you all are used to this sort of thing, because she just waited patiently until I could speak. Then I told her that Rabbi L. had referred me and she said, yes, she knew the rabbi, and then she told me the place and date of the next meeting and asked did I want to come. That was four weeks ago, as some of you know who were present at the meeting, and I have just sat quiet for three meetings and not saying anything, but now I do want to say something, and I want to say it especially for Lois and Marge who are here for the first time and are probably feeling about the way I did when I came the first time.

What I want to say, particularly, is that for about a half hour at my first meeting I was numb and scared, and barely heard what was being said. But then I began to listen, and all of a sudden I realized that here were other women who were married to compulsive gamblers, who had gone through it, who had lived through the same thing as I and that they were there to help each other and to help me. What a wonderful thing it was not to have to feel strange and different and isolated and lonely any longer, to feel that here, in this room, nobody was going to blame or criticize me, or look down on me or pity me. And what a wonderful thing it was to feel the warmth and the friendship, the support and concern of all of you.

I began to realize also that the time would come when I would get up the courage to talk about it. I would be able to tell the group about my own problems and not only get understanding and sympathy but also good advice on what to do about my husband's gambling, the debts, the pressure from the bookmakers, the pressure from the police, the problems my children were having. I'm not ready to start opening up about these things yet. I'm still getting used to this, but I know I will start soon and that when I do, you all will help me.

Your strict rules about anonymity and privacy are very reassuring, and they give me a feeling of safety, I know, for myself, though, that some day I will have the courage and strength to speak openly about my problems, to others on the outside, and that I will no longer be frightened and ashamed to do so.

I really appreciate your being so kind to me and so considerate and concerned; but most of all I want to thank you for just being here, so I can come and be here with you. I will be back for the next meeting next week, and for many more to come.

GET PROFESSIONAL HELP

Our next suggestion has to do with getting professional counseling or psychotherapy. If you have never thought about this before you may be taken aback by this advice. Let's make it clear, then, that our suggestion of counseling or psychotherapy does not mean we think there is "something wrong" with you. It means only that we think you have been under tremendous emotional stress and that as a result you may possibly have developed emotional symptoms or ailments. Suppose we ask you some questions and you judge for yourself whether or not this is so.

Do you find yourself being anxious and worried, not only about the real things about which you certainly have good cause to worry (the debts, your financial condition, separation from relatives and friends, your children's difficulties, the reduction of your life to the bare essentials of survival) but also about unrealistic things? Do you get terribly upset, for example, when one of your children has a cold or a stomachache or falls and scrapes himself? It would be realistic for you to be concerned somewhat, and want to do something to help. However, it would be unrealistic to behave as though the child had a life-threatening illness. Another example: Your father or brother has been paying the rent and the utility bills and has guaranteed to pay them as long as is necessary until you get back on your feet again. It is realistic to have some concern about the fact that someone is having to do this for you and that you cannot do this yourself. It is unrealistic, though, to be in terror that something awful can still happen and that you're going to be put out on the street. It is unrealistic also to be suffering from what is called "free-floating anxiety," that is, being constantly beset by a feeling of dread that "something terrible is going to happen," yet not being able to pinpoint what that "something terrible" might be.

Are you constantly edgy, nervous, jumpy, irritable, restless? If your answer is yes, then it is likely that you are suffering from an anxiety state, one of the most common consequences of prolonged, intense stress.

Now for some questions, related to another condition.

Do you get up feeling very tired? Do you have to struggle to wake up and get out of bed? Is it difficult for you to get started on the regular household chores and the things you need to do for the children, and do you find yourself tiring before you are half through with them? Have you lost interest in getting out, going shopping, seeing friends, fixing some interesting meals, going to church or temple, knitting or reading or playing tennis or watching a favorite television program, or whatever it is you used to enjoy doing?

Do you feel dejected all the time, without letup, to the point where nothing at all can cheer you up or make you smile, not even being with your children, or a favorite friend or relative?

Are you eating without appetite, sleeping poorly, having nightmares, getting up very early, beset with a feeling of anxiety or dread?

Do you feel pretty rotten about yourself as a person—that you've botched up your whole life, that you haven't been much of a homemaker, wife or mother, that you've been a failure at whatever you've undertaken,) that you have never amounted to very much and never will?

Do you feel life is just not worth living any longer, that

everything is just hopeless, that you are helpless to do anything about your situation?

Have you been thinking you might want to end your life?

If you answer yes to several of these questions, then you are very likely suffering from depression, a condition often brought on by prolonged stress.

What about unusual fears? Have you developed a phobia? A phobia is an irrational dread about some situation or object which in itself poses no realistic danger—for example, an irrational dread of elevators, supermarkets, busy intersections, shopping malls, heights, open spaces, water, bridges, expressways, tunnels, meeting rooms, classrooms, theaters, restaurants, dogs, cats, birds, snakes, spiders, etc. Phobias, too—like anxiety states and depression—commonly occur after a person has been subjected to stress and crisis after crisis without letup.

These are the sort of things we are talking about when we say that it is possible you may be undergoing some emotional disturbance as a result of the prolonged, unremitting stress to which you have been subjected—these and physical ailments such as headaches, hypertension, diarrhea, constipation, back muscle spasms and others.

If you are suffering from the kinds of ailments we have described, or any other condition for which there is no ready explanation, then it may very well be that you need professional help from a psychiatrist or some other accredited professional skilled in psychotherapy and counseling. The thing to do, then, is to go to a family-service agency, a mental-health clinic or a community health center, tell them about your problem and ask what kind of help they would suggest. In most cities, the agencies dealing with mental-health problems are listed in the front of the telephone book.

If money is a problem, many family-service agencies, mental-health clinics and community mental-health centers have sliding scales, with fees set according to your ability to pay.

If you have never had counseling or psychotherapy before, the idea of going for that kind of help may frighten you. We cannot go into a detailed explanation of what goes on in psychotherapy and counseling, but we can assure you that there is nothing strange or upsetting about it. What it amounts to, in essence, is that you sit down with the qualified therapist or counselor and talk about what is troubling you. It may be somewhat difficult to get started at first because you may be so tied up in knots that you will find it hard to loosen up and talk; or there may be so many things you want to talk about that you won't know where to begin. But if that is a concern, don't let it worry you. The therapists and counselors are skilled professionals. They know how to put you at ease, to get you to feel relaxed and comfortable and to guide you in discussing the things that are important for you to talk about. What this does at the beginning is give you a chance to "let off steam," but that is only a small part of it. More important than that is putting you in touch with the intense, upsetting emotions that have been agitating you and that you may have managed to push out of your mind. The professionals will help you to tap into these emotions and express them. They will also help you to rebuild your battered self-esteem. Once that is done, they will work with you to get a realistic, confident handle on your problems, and guide you in taking on the practical matters you are going to have to deal with.

Now that we have sketched out an initial program of action for yourself, we will proceed to talk about what you should do with respect to your husband.

DEALING WITH YOUR FEELINGS ABOUT YOUR HUSBAND

The first step in that direction has to do with your own feelings toward your husband. Unless you are different from all the other wives of compulsive gamblers at this point—the point where you are looking for guidance—a list of things you feel about your husband would include many of the following: mistrust, resentment, contempt, frustration, dislike, loathing or even hatred. You very likely see him as dishonest, insincere, irresponsible and immature, and doubt whether he would ever be able to benefit from experience.

In moments of extreme frustration and anger, after he has done some especially insensitive, cruel thing, you wish he could die, or if not that, that some miracle would occur that would sweep him out of your life forever.

You wonder how you could ever have married a man with so rotten a character. You are positive he went to great pains to hide his true character from you when you were first married, and that, eventually, it came out with his gambling. You wonder how it would ever be possible to live with this man again, even if he should reform and stop gambling, how you could possibly efface all the ugliness, meanness and cruelty that you have witnessed, how you could ever reconstruct a positive image of him, how you could ever put any trust in him again after the countless times he has deceived, betrayed and hurt you, how you could possibly ever feel toward him as a loving partner, companion, lover. You may shudder at the thought of his ever putting a hand on you again, let alone making love to you.

If you do not feel this way—the way we have described— it would be unusual, indeed. Yet, having said all this, we would venture a strong surmise that mixed in with all these strongly negative feelings there may be some remnants of positive feeling, possibly sympathy and concern for this miserable creature, perhaps even some affection in the moments when he is not being so obnoxious and you see some semblance of the husband he used to be, perhaps even some stirrings of love. When wives of compulsive gamblers are asked why they stayed with their husbands, one out of every two say it was because of love.

In psychiatry we have a word for this—ambivalence— having opposite and contradictory feelings about a person, feelings of love and of hatred at the same time. It does not mean that a person is crazy if he can both hate and love someone at the same time. It is normal to be able to feel this way; most of us feel it at one time or another. All it means is that the person has stirred in you strong feelings of love, over a period of years, and that these are not necessarily effaced by the things he does to make you hate him. Both these sets of feelings coexist in you, the negative ones coming to the fore when his behavior provokes them, the positive ones reemerging when the behavior subsides.

SEE HIM AS A SICK, NOT AN EVIL PERSON

Regardless of whether you feel ambivalent toward your husband, it is clear that, for whatever reason, you want to get him to stop gambling so that you can reconstruct your lives. How do you do this? Scold, scream at him, try to shame him, threaten to leave him? You have already tried that a hundred times and you have seen how futile that is. Cajole, pamper him, reason with him, try to explain to him how he has been hurting the people he loves, how he has been hurting himself, how wonderful it would be and it could be if he would just realize what he was doing, take himself in hand, stop gambling and make things right again? You have tried this, too, countless times and seen how futile it is.

Why won't these approaches work? Because they are effective only on people who are in control of their senses, people whose minds are working right. These are the approaches that are used traditionally in teaching situations. If you want to teach a child not to do something bad, you scold or punish him. If the child's mind is working normally, he will heed you, he doesn't want to be hurt or punished again, so he will desist from the forbidden act. If you want the child to do something good, you reward him with a cookie, a gold star, a hug and a kiss. He likes that so he will repeat the thing you want him to do.

But try these approaches on a child suffering from a severe emotional disturbance, a psychotic child, a child under the influence of drugs; they will not work. The normal mental and emotional connections that relate behavior to consequences are not operating. The ability to resist impulses and control behavior is weak or missing entirely. The same can be said for the compulsive gambler.

The compulsive gambler cannot respond to reward or punishment because his sensible control is gone. He is driven by impulse. His actions are the products of a mind that is sick. No, we do not mean that he's psychotic or that he belongs in an institution for the mentally ill. We mean only that he is in the grip of an addiction that is making him do destructive and self-destructive things.

If you are going to be able to help him, this is how you have to view him, sincerely, deep in your heart. That doesn't mean that you are going to be able, right away, to put away your anger, disgust and hatred. You will undoubtedly continue to feel these, but you will feel them gradually less if you are able to make yourself step back from the scene, look at it as though you were observing it from the outside, look at your husband as you would look at a stranger—objectively, and without the malice and hatred he has evoked.

What you're faced with, then, is the need to help him bring his addiction under control, to get rid of it. And when he does, you will not only have your "old" husband back, but you will have one who is more mature, one with a better grip on reality, one who is not so insistently driven to prove how smart, important and powerful he is.

He is going to have to go through a rehabilitative process in which he regains control over his impulses, sets limits on his behavior and gets back in touch with reality. He is like a man with an alcohol or drug addiction. He is going to have to kick his habit, and he is going to have to do it "cold turkey." There is no other way. He is not going to be able to do this by himself—any more than a drug addict is able to do it by himself. He is going to need help— systematic, organized help, and it is you who are going to get him to agree to accept that help

What kind of help are we talking about?

Two kinds: Gamblers Anonymous and specific treatment for the compulsive-gambling addiction.

Gamblers Anonymous

First about Gamblers Anonymous, or GA as it is called. This organization is the only national voluntary organization for compulsive gamblers. It is made up entirely of men and women who are compulsive gamblers and who have gained control over their addiction or who are in the process of gaining control over it. The organization has been in existence since 1957 and has tens of thousands of members in about 300 to 400 groups around the country. Membership is not rigidly controlled, as it is in other organizations. All one needs to become a member is a sincere desire to be rid of his or her gambling addiction. Some gamblers may come in, attend two or three or four meetings and drop out. Others stay for weeks, months and years—long after they have gained control over their addiction. It is not at all unusual for members to continue to stay on 5, 10, 15, even 20 years and to have attended meetings regularly, week after week, throughout the entire time. No count is made of the people who become members or how long they stay, but it is safe to say that hundreds of thousands of gamblers have been helped by this organization since its inception.

While the program of Gamblers Anonymous is very much like that of Alcoholics Anonymous and relies also on the well-known "Twelve Steps to Recovery," it has something of a psychiatric orientation. For one thing, it places great emphasis on the fact that at the basis of the gambler's addiction are serious defects in character—inability and unwillingness to accept reality, emotional insecurity, immaturity, deceit, self-indulgence, egotism and selfishness, insensitivity to the needs and feelings of others—and that the only way he can stop gambling and get rid of his addiction is by "bringing about a progressive character change within himself." Also, the meetings in which the members get up to tell about their problems, their progress or their failures, are referred to as "therapy" meetings. However, the organization does not ally itself with any professional agency, faculty or facility, nor do its structure and policy include formal or informal professional guidance.

More About Gamblers Anonymous

People who do not know Gamblers Anonymous well are likely to have a mistaken impression of the organization. They may have heard that it has religious overtones, and this belief may stem from the fact that Gamblers Anonymous has adopted the "Twelve Steps" of Alcoholics Anonymous and that several of these steps make reference to "God *(as we understand Him)*" and to "a Power greater than ourselves." In order to clear up any misunderstanding and to remove any misgivings on this point, we quote these Twelve Steps.

1. We admitted we were powerless over gambling—that our lives had become unmanageable.

2. Came to believe that a Power greater than ourselves could restore us to a normal way of thinking and living.

3. Made a decision to turn our will and our lives over to the care of this Power of our own understanding.

4. Made a searching and fearless moral and financial inventory of ourselves.

5. Admitted to ourselves and another human being the exact nature of our wrongs.

6. Were entirely ready to have these defects of character removed.

7. Humbly asked God (of our understanding) to remove our shortcomings.

8. Made a list of all persons we had harmed, and became willing to make amends to them all.

9. Made direct amends to such people wherever possible, except when to do so would injure them or others.

10. Continued to take personal inventory and when we were wrong promptly admitted it.

11. Sought through prayer and meditation to improve our conscious contact with God as we understood

him, praying only for knowledge of His will for us
and the power to carry that out.

12. Having made an effort to practice these principles in
all our affairs, we tried to carry this message to
other compulsive gamblers.

The few references to God and to "a Power," are, as
you can see, couched in terms that make it possible for the
individual to interpret them in any way he wishes. There is
nothing else in the program and activities of the organization that has any religious connotations. There are no rituals
or prayers.

We are impressed also with the references to "defects
in character" and the need to correct them. This is another
way of describing what psychiatrists try to do to help their
patients. Whereas the psychiatrist uses various professional
strategies, Gamblers Anonymous uses the strategies of mutual support, encouragement and holding the gambler to an
honest, realistic accounting of his attitudes and behavior. If
a gambler, in speaking up (or "giving therapy," as they say)
attempts to gloss over some point, or paint a piece of
reprehensible behavior in a rosy light, or rationalize what he
has been doing, you are likely to hear other members
respond with such comments as "Baloney," or "Stop kidding
yourself; you're not kidding us," or "If you want to keep
on lying to yourself, go ahead. Nobody is going to be hurt
by it but you and your family."

Is Gamblers Anonymous Effective?

We have attended dozens of Gamblers Anonymous
meetings and met with hundreds of members individually.
We say without hesitation that the most important step a
compulsive gambler can take toward recovery is to get into
Gamblers Anonymous and become a steady and active
participant.

We have sat in on meetings and heard men and women
say such things as the following:

My life was a living hell before I came here. Only the Lord

knows where I would be if I had not become a member. I was desperate. I was lying, cheating, stealing. I had committed every kind of crime short of a holdup or murder, and I might have even done that, if I hadn't come here to this room. It was this room that saved me. [Gamblers Anonymous members refer to the meeting place, the people in it and the activities and the program as "the room."] Today I am a respectable human being. I have my family and my business back. I had lost them both, and everything else, including my sense of decency and self-respect. . . . I have been coming to these meetings for four years, and I am going to continue to come as long as I am able.

Last Sunday my wife and I had the joy of seeing our oldest daughter married. She's twenty-five. We were able to give her and her husband a wedding gift of $5,000. Do you know where I was on her Sweet Sixteen birthday? In prison, doing time for embezzlement. I got into Gamblers Anonymous while I was still in prison. There was a group in town, and they arranged with the warden for Gamblers Anonymous meetings on the prison grounds, and I attended. I haven't gambled a single time since then, and that was nearly nine years ago. I don't need gambling. I have real pleasures in life—my wife, my children, my relatives, my home. Sure, I watch football now, but now I enjoy the game. I see the players and the plays, and that's enough of a thrill. I don't need the thrill of gambling any longer. I learned, here in this room, that I didn't need it. Some of the people in this room were here when I got out of prison and attended my first meeting here, and they're still here now. We'll be here for anyone else who comes here the way we did, troubled, suffering, depressed, thinking about committing suicide.

This is only my fifth meeting, but you can't imagine what it has meant to me. As you can see, I'm not very old [The speaker is a twenty-four-year-old man, taking an evening course in business administration.] But I've had this addiction since I was seventeen. I don't mean just doing a little gambling. I mean heavy gambling on almost a daily basis. In fact, I paid my way through three years of college by gambling. My folks sent me the money, but I sent it back to them. I could easily take care of everything with my winnings. I was even in business as a bookmaker, until the college found out and threw me out. Then I got in with some real professional bookies with organized-crime connections, and I'm lucky I'm not in jail or dead today. One of the men I was hooked up with got himself killed; they put out a contract on him because he was siphoning off some of the money. I would have gotten it, too, but one of the other men stood up for me and told them I had nothing to do with it. I was married to my high school sweetheart, but she left me when I was thrown out of college. Since then I've bummed around, slept with all kinds of tramps, prostitutes. I got into drinking and I did some drugs, too. I still haven't got those under control, and I'm going to Alcoholics Anonymous, too, and Narcotics Anonymous. I'm working now, Bob T., here, helped me get it. [Anonymity and privacy are strictly preserved, and participants refer to themselves and each other only by their first name and last initial.] It doesn't pay much, and I'm driving a delivery van, but it sure feels good to be earning my money honestly and not having to worry about where I'm going to get the next $50 to gamble, or to pay the bookie. I've got a free mind and a free conscience, something I haven't had for seven years. I'm going to school at night taking some courses, and maybe they'll admit me to college again when they see I'm trying to straighten out. I haven't bet a dime from the day I first came here, and believe me, it isn't easy. The urge gets hold of me, and I have to struggle not to give in. But coming here to this room is what helps me, and I know it is going to get me off gambling and keep me off gambling, and I sure am a thankful guy.

Specific Treatment for Compulsive Gambling

What about specific treatment for compulsive gambling? Unfortunately, there are, at this writing, probably not more than 20 places in the entire country where a compulsive gambler can go to be treated specifically for that disorder, and of these, five are located in Veterans Administration hospitals and available only to United States service veterans. What about the compulsive gambler who does want to get treatment for his addiction and cannot find it?

The next-best alternative is traditional psychotherapy with a professional in private practice or at a psychiatric clinic, community mental-health center, private psychiatric hospital or the psychiatric service of a general hospital.

While the specialized approach to the treatment of compulsive gambling is still new, having come into existence only as recently as 1971, it is hoped that within the next two or three years, dozens, scores, and possibly even hundreds of specialized treatment programs for compulsive gambling will have come into existence. The essentials of a basic program for the treatment of compulsive gambling are outlined and discussed in Chapter 9.

Now that we have identified the kinds of help the compulsive gambler needs, how are you going to get him to agree to it?

The answer is *direct confrontation*. By "confrontation" we do not mean challenge or threat. We mean raising the problem simply and directly, matter-of-factly, objectively, neither submissively nor aggressively.

Before making the confrontation, you need to prepare yourself with some literature on compulsive gambling, literature you are going to want to put in your husband's hands for him to read. You should be able to get this from Gam-Anon, Gamblers Anonymous or the local branch of the National Council on Compulsive Gambling. The last should be listed in your telephone book under either National Council on Compulsive Gambling or Council on Compulsive Gambling. If there is no local branch in your community, write to the National Council on Compulsive Gambling c/o John Jay College of Criminal Justice, 444 West 56th Street, Room 32075, New York, N.Y. 10019 (telephone: 212-765-3833). Or write to The Christophers, 12 East 48th Street, New York, N.Y. 10017 (telephone: 212–759–4040).

CONFRONT HIM WITH THE ISSUE

The confrontation should be made at home, when only the two of you are present; the best time would be during one of those periods when he is relatively calm and free of immediate pressure. We certainly are not going to attempt to prescribe the exact language you should use, but the approach might go something like this:

"John, we've got a problem and we need to talk about it."

This is likely to bring on the rejoinder ("Not that again!" or "Aren't we ever going to stop?" or "Why can't you leave me in peace?" This is a provocative tack, and it will probably arouse in you an instantaneous reflex reaction to lash back with an angry retort. Anticipate this and be prepared for it. Don't respond to the provocation. Wait till he's finished and say it again. "We've got a bad problem, and we are going to have to do something about it." If he gets angry and storms out, you can do nothing except wait for the next opportunity and then try it again.

When he finally does consent to sit and listen, the thing you *do not* want to say next is "It's your gambling!" or "You've got a bad gambling problem, and you've got to stop" or anything else that deals directly with his gambling or points a finger of accusation. If you go right to the issue of gambling itself, it will only incite him to mobilize defensively, to resist listening to anything you have to say, to lash back at you with a counteraccusation. Instead, begin with the things that are happening as a result of the gambling.

"The bank called again and is threatening to foreclose if we don't pay the mortgage installment."

"I have a bad problem with my teeth, but I haven't any money to go to the dentist."

"It's been a long time since you've taken me anywhere. We hardly talk to each other anymore."

"You're not looking well. You don't eat regularly, and you get hardly any sleep."

"The children miss your taking them out. Joey says he'd love it if you would take him to the ball games the way you used to."

We do not have any unrealistic expectations that with this approach, he is going to break down, become compliant, ask you what he ought to do and then go ahead and do it. No, he most certainly will not. But the chances are that he will refrain from becoming belligerent and may remain silent and wait for you to continue; or he make some noncommital response which will give you the opportunity to carry the conversation further.

If it does develop in that vein, continue to talk about the hardships to which all of you, including himself, have been subjected. Ultimately, the discussion will come around to the gambling itself. And now, there is no longer any way to avoid saying that you think that the problems you have been discussing are a result of his gambling. This will probably produce the explosion you have been trying to avoid. It may not. If it does, let it subside. *Do not respond to it. Do not let yourself be provoked.* When the storm has subsided, tell him you understand what he's going through, that this is something he cannot help. Don't use the word "sick" or "sickness." This will make him see red. Use the words "problem," "difficulty," "trouble." Tell him that although these upsetting things have been happening, you think there is a way out, for all of you, a way to be rid of the trouble, a way he can be free of the terrible pressure he is under, a way to be free of the loan sharks and the police and the finance companies (depending on what your particular experience has been), a way he can have peace of mind and enjoy life again.

Expect that he is going to catch you up on a particular word you use or a particular thing you say and try to prove you wrong. But let this, too, pass. When he has finished saying what he wants to say, go back again to the same theme—you understand; it has been hurtful, but you understand. You want to help, not just for his sake but for the sake of all of you—him, yourself, the children.

If he still insists on disputing you, tell him you've been in touch with Gam-Anon and Gamblers Anonymous or the National Council on Compulsive Gambling and there's some literature you want him to read. He doesn't have to look at it now. He can look at it later.

Telling him you've been in touch with Gam-Anon or Gamblers Anonymous is likely to bring on another explosion with a string of vituperative accusations, but you'll have to let this pass. If possible, leave him alone with the literature saying, for example, you've got to go out to do an errand. Let him be by himself a while, to simmer down and reflect, maybe even to sneak a glance at the literature you have brought him.

This is all you can do at this point. Let a few days go by, and if he doesn't raise the issue, you raise it again. Tell him you've learned about Gamblers Anonymous, and you think it is a good organization and that it might not be a bad idea for him to try attending one meeting. He doesn't have to join or anything like that. If he wants, you can call GA and ask one of the men to get in touch with him. Naturally, if he is agreeable you can go ahead and make that call. If not, let it lie.

Later on, as the opportunity presents itself, you may be able to raise the issue of his getting professional help. This, too, is likely to provoke a storm, and he is likely to tell you that it is you, not he, who needs the help. But you have got to expect this, too, and not be provoked into an angry retaliation.

If you are lucky, he may respond early to the suggestion that he go to GA or that he get professional help. The chances are he will not, right away. That is going to mean that you will just have to keep on raising the issue, over and over again at spaced intervals.

However, that is not all you will be doing. There are some very practical measures you are going to need to take, right away, entirely apart from getting your husband to seek help.

At the point where you tell him you understand his problem, that you know what terrible pressure he is under, that you would try to do what you can to help him, he is going to be surprised. Up to this point you have probably been using criticism, threats, cajoling, imploring—all intensely emotional and directed toward getting him to give up his gambling. Now you are approaching him from another direction, quietly, sympathetically, objectively. You're not asking him to give up gambling. It's an approach he does not recognize, doesn't understand. "What is this?" he asks himself. "She's not beating on me? She's not pleading with me? She's not saying it's all my fault? She says she understands what I'm going through and that she sympathizes with me and is concerned about me."

He won't really understand what you're saying. All he will hear is the softened voice, the sympathetic tone, the personal interest and concern. And he will rise to this like a trout to a fly, but not in the way you expected. He will hear you saying that you've come around to his way of looking at it, that you really understand that what he needs is more money so he can pay off his debts and gamble some more so he can recoup his losses and start winning again. When you talk to him about rebuilding your family life the way it used to be, he won't see evenings at home watching television with you and the children, or going out to dinner and the theater, or having the family over for birthdays and anniversaries the way you used to do. He will see the glamorous junkets to Las Vegas, the gambling trips to the Caribbean, the expensive nightclubs and luxurious automobiles. He will see the glitter and the glamor. That is what he is thirsting for. So when he hears you talking about wanting to help him, he will be thinking you want to help him with more money, or if you are not actually thinking that, he is sure he can work you around to it.

TELL HIM FROM NOW ON HE'S ON HIS OWN

This is the point where you are going to have to let him know, still quietly and objectively, but firmly, that that sort of thing is over as far as you are concerned; you have gone through your savings, helped him take out a mortgage, gotten your father to cosign for a loan in order to get him out of trouble, but now all that is finished. He will never get another dollar from you again for anything that has to do with gambling. You are not going to lift a finger, ever again, to help him get out of any trouble he gets into because of his gambling. When the letters come demanding payment, you're going to turn them over to him to handle. When the telephone calls come, asking to speak to him, you're not going to say he's not there, or pretend not to know where he is. If you know, you'll tell. If the loan sharks come after him, they'll just have to come after him. If the police come after him, you will not cover for him. If he has to go to jail, then he'll just have to go to jail. From now on you're going to protect the family, the home, the children, yourself. He will have to look out for himself, so far as anything that has to do with gambling is concerned. You are willing to try to raise money to help pay for his treatment, but not for anything else.

Again we must caution you on the way you handle this and the tone and attitude you display. This is not a retaliatory action. You are not getting even with him. You are not taking revenge for the hurt he has caused. You are doing something that is vital to a change in the situation.

First, you are imposing limits on his behavior, compelling him, so far as you are concerned, to live within realistic, socially acceptable bounds. This is a psychiatric strategy. It is what psychiatrists do when they treat people who have lost a sense of responsibility to society and to themselves and, as a result, commit antisocial offenses—theft, assault, drunkenness, drug abuse, and so forth. The psychiatrist attempts to impose limits on the individual's unregulated behavior and by the imposition of external restraints, to retrain the patient to impose restraints on himself. True, you are not a psychiatrist, but you are the key player in the situation, and what you do is crucial. No one else is in as good a position as you to guide his behavior. No matter how much he has abused and criticized you, you are still the most important person in his life. He does not want to lose you, and while you are not going to threaten him with leaving him, he will know that this is a possibility and will respond to your initiatives.

STOP BEING A "SUPPLIER" OR "ENABLER"

The second thing you are going to do is cut off the supply of the "drug" that has been feeding his habit—money. Let's face it. You have been one of his major suppliers. You have not only enabled him to plunder your family resources, your children's resources and your own resources, you have been a go-between in getting your relatives and his relatives to help him out, in helping him to get loans, in stalling his creditors. You have helped to keep him solvent, refilling the reservoir of money each time he exhausted it. So when you say—"No more," you are saying in effect, "I refuse to be any longer the one who keeps feeding you the drug that's killing you."

As a corollary to that, you should immediately freeze any assets he might still be able to put his hands on. If there are still any savings left, draw them out and redeposit them in your own name in a bank he does not know, and leave specific instructions that no withdrawals should be permitted to anybody but yourself, in person—circumventing the possibility of his forging your signature on a withdrawal slip. If you have any convertible assets such as stocks and bonds, do what you need to do to get them out of his reach. If there is any jewelry around, put it in a relative's safe-deposit box. Go to the bank or banks you have been dealing with and inform them that if your husband comes in with loan papers bearing your signature, the signature will be a forgery. If you have credit cards destroy them. Or if that is going to be a hardship, leave them with a friend or relative with strict instructions not to let your husband have them on any pretext whatever. If you have charge accounts at department stores, cancel them and destroy the cards. Go to your relatives and his and tell them what you are doing and why, and warn them against letting your husband have money under any circumstances whatever.

It may be very difficult for you to expose your problem to relatives and even strangers, but the time has come when you, too, have to stop hiding and covering up. You've got a sick husband, and there is no reason for you to have to hide it any more than there would be to hide his having cancer. If you expect him to face reality, you are going to have to face it yourself. People get sick, people die, people have extramarital relationships, people become alcoholics, people steal, people become compulsive gamblers. These are some facts about life, and you have to face them and deal with them.

What if your tough stand, your cutting off every available source of funds forces him to forge checks, embezzle, even hold someone up for money to feed his craving? If that is what it does, then that is what has to happen. Is there a better alternative? If you keep on feeding him money or keep on helping him to get it, the time will still come when there are no longer any legitimate resources left; and if he has the capacity to commit some illegal act now, he will commit it later. You will only be postponing it, and nothing that may happen in between is going to avert it—except an intervention. The intervention may as well be taken now, and you ought to be the one to take it. Your action now may forestall much more serious consequences later. Furthermore, with you taking the action, the situation is still in your hands and you may be able to use the cutting off of funds as a means to get him to go to Gamblers Anonymous and to get professional help.

BE ON GUARD—HE'LL PLAY ON YOUR GUILT

Of course, he won't see it your way. He sees himself as a pitiful victim, a poor beaten-down man who is only struggling to get back on his feet, to recover his losses, to make life good again for you and the children. He will interpret what you are doing as treachery and betrayal. He will want to know why you are doing these terrible things to him. He'll call you inhuman, cruel—taking away his money, exposing him to his creditors, to the bookies, to the police, turning his own family against him. He will tell you you are violating marriage's most solemn obligation—the duty of one mate to protect or to shield the other, to be loyal; here you are, not only *not* siding with him when he is in trouble, but actually taking sides with his enemies. He'll say this and he'll believe it. He'll tell you that this is no more than he expected, that you have already proven what an inadequate wife and mate you are. If you weren't, he wouldn't be in all this trouble; now you're only confirming what he knew all along.

He will continue to play on the guilt-and-blame theme as he has before, and if you are not careful you'll find yourself falling into the same trap again, believing his accusations, blaming yourself for what has happened and wondering whether you are pursuing the correct course now, being so tough on him. Beware! Don't fall into the trap.

Don't believe the accusations. Don't try to respond to them or defend yourself. Just tell him you're through swallowing this kind of garbage—that if that's what he wants to believe, well then he can go ahead and believe it. You are not the cause of his problem and never were. What you are doing is right, both for you and for him.

Even if you cannot convince yourself that what you are doing is for his benefit as well as yours, then you need to be content with the fact that at least it is right for you; that it is right for you to extricate yourself from the terrible mess into which he has drawn you and to start breathing free.

STAND UP FOR YOURSELF

What if he should become abusive when you cut off his sources of money? What if he should get into a rage, threaten you, even strike at you? If he is going to do it at this point, he has undoubtedly done it before, even with less provocation, and you have probably cowered before his anger, taken the insults, screaming abuse, even his physical beating. Well, this is the point where you run up your battle flag, stand fast and declare your independence. If this is how he, in his insanity, has treated you, then this is where you have to take your stand and say, "No more!" If he screams, scream back at him. If he threatens, tell him to make good his threats. If he hits you, call the police. This is what abused women are advised to do, and if this is how he treats you, then you are an abused woman and the advice applies to you.

Again, we need to point out, this is not a matter of retaliation or getting revenge. This is a matter of asserting your rights and your needs. *Nobody* has the right to abuse or assault another person, and especially a wife; if this is what has been happening then you need to face the fact that you have been as much a part of the problem as he. In any marital situation, or in any interpersonal situation at all, where one person dominates, degrades, mistreats, suppresses or abuses the other (and it is not always the man who is the aggressor), both parties are responsible for what is happening . . . the one who abuses and the one who takes it and lets him continue to abuse. The one who takes it gives the other a signal that this is okay, that he can do these things and get away with them. By being submissive, the victim gives license to the aggressor.

Relationships can and do change, and they can change when one partner refuses to play the submissive role any longer and insists on having the full freedom, dignity and respect due an equal partner in the relationship. This is a standard strategy in marital therapy. Wives who have been suffering the consequences of a submissive role are taught to assert themselves, to say, "No more!" The effect this has, in the great majority of cases, is to compel the husband to change his style, attitude and behavior, and to become a more compatible and likable human being.

This applies directly to your situation. In asserting yourself and refusing to take abuse any longer, you are forcing a change in the relationship, and you are forcing him to change his behavior. Not only will he stop treating you as an object and as an inferior; he will start to see you in a different light. He will become aware of the fact that he has a great deal to lose if you leave him, and that if you are going to stay with him, he is going to have to change his behavior, *not only with respect to you but also with respect to his gambling*. Do not employ, as part of this new approach, a threat to leave him if he doesn't stop gambling and doesn't reform. You have undoubtedly made this threat before and have not carried it out, and so he is not likely to heed it. These will just be words that will have no effect. The change in your tone and your attitude, the show of firmness, seriousness and strength, the expression of anger and your letting him know that you will meet every one of his attacks with a counterattack will get the message to him much more meaningfully. Up to this point he has been controlling you with his anger and he has made you cower and cringe. Now you need to show him that you have the same kind of strength and power, and that while it is not your intention to make him cower and cringe, it *is* your intention to put a stop to his aggressive, coercive treatment of you.

DON'T BECOME THE AGGRESSOR YOURSELF

However, be careful that in this process you do not

change roles. Here's what we mean. When a person who has been oppressed finally fights back, the other person may back down and become submissive. This may act as incentive for the former victim, now that he has the power, to become the aggressor and to respond in kind. In other words, if, when you stand up for your rights, your husband backs down and becomes humble, you must be on guard not to take advantage of the situation and try to get even for what he has done to you. That's not the point of this exercise. The point is to get him to change his awareness of you and his attitude toward you, and to do something about his gambling. Becoming the aggressor yourself, taking the "one-up" position will not achieve this purpose. It will only stiffen his resistance and spoil any chance of a constructive change in the relationship. The two key words to keep in mind are "reality" and "equality."

Don't think all this is going to be easy—changing your stance, feelings, attitude and behavior. You are dealing not only with patterns of thought, feeling and action that have become firmly entrenched over the years; you are dealing, also we would guess, with lifelong attitudes and feelings about yourself, about what you have a right to expect out of life for yourself, about the way you feel about yourself in general.

If you have cringed before his tirades and verbal abuse before, you will automatically do so again, not because you want to but because you have been trained to react that way. Your reason will say, "Don't flinch. Don't cringe. Stand up for yourself. Fight back!" Your insides will not be listening; they will behave the way they have been conditioned to behave. You will feel fear, depression, anxiety. You will want to run. You will fall into the submissive, abject stance again. You will become tongue-tied. And you will hate yourself for reacting this way. You'll call yourself a coward. You'll continue to blame yourself and say that this is probably what you deserve.

All right, let us accept that this is what is going to happen. (If it doesn't, then you are already well ahead of the game.) So long as you expect it, you'll be in a better position to get a handle on it and control it. You'll know that your programmed emotions are moving you back to where you do not want to be any longer, and that you are not going to let them do this to you; that your mind and your intelligence are going to prevail. When you can just begin to feel that way and believe it, you will have taken the first big step toward making the basic change.

DON'T TRY TO FIGHT THE BATTLE BY YOURSELF

Meanwhile, let's not forget that this is not a battle you have to fight alone. We hope that you will have reached out to Gam-Anon, and, believe us, the women there will support and strengthen you. They've been through the same thing; they know what it takes; they've learned how it can be done, and they will help you to learn that, too. We hope that you will have reached out also for psychotherapy and counseling. There you will get additional confirmation, reassurance, guidance and support.

It may be that this will be another obstacle you are going to have to overcome—the feeling that you have to do this all by yourself; that no one else can really help you; that unless you do it all for and by yourself, it won't last. Feeling that way, you may be reluctant to reach out for help. If you do feel that way, we urge you to fight the urge to remain isolated; you must reach out for help. This is what "mutual support" groups are all about; people with problems reaching out to each other for understanding, acceptance, knowledge, guidance and emotional support.

Another thing you may have to contend with is the "armchair psychology" some people will dish out: that women who marry a compulsive gambler are unconsciously looking for someone who will dominate them, abuse them, punish them; that unconsciously they feel guilty about something or other and the only way they can be relieved of this is to have somebody punish them. We feel about this the way we feel about the theory that compulsive gamblers want to lose because they feel guilty about something and the only way they can be relieved of this guilt is to punish themselves—by losing. To both of these conjectures we say, "Rubbish!"

When people seek each other out in marriage, they are looking for the things most normal human beings want: a caring mate and companion, one who will cherish them and be by their side when there is trouble. This, plus the physical attributes, is what attracts us to each other as mates. The fact that, later on, some of the weaker and less desirable aspects of our personalities and character come out does not change the original proposition. We may regret, later, having entered into the marriage with this particular person because of the way he or she has turned out. But that is *after the fact*. These are things we did not know about, or, if we did see some hints or suggestions, we chose to brush them aside, ignore them, rationalize them because we wanted that man or woman so urgently; because we were in love with him or her. In fact, it is the powerful memory of the good times and the good features of the mate and the marriage, and the hope that they may return, that keeps so many troubled marriages going. That, in fact, may be what is keeping your own marriage going—the hope that it can be the way it used to be or even better, free of any involvement with gambling.

What we are saying is this: Have faith in the good things in your relationship, don't be misled by pseudo-psychological theorizing that you are a masochist who married a sadist because you wanted to be punished, that it is a sick relationship at its foundation and therefore needs to be dissolved.

Possibly, you feel so angry at your husband and so upset about the things he has done that you cannot summon up a single good feeling about your marriage or imagine how you could possibly ever feel any less hostile and resentful toward him than you do at this moment. However, we assure you that if you both find help—through Gam-Anon, Gamblers Anonymous, counseling and psychotherapy treatment—your anger and resentment will go, and you will be able to find and work with the positive things in him and in the relationship. Recovery, and rehabilitation to a much healthier level, is possible in the very great majority of marriages that have suffered the disaster of compulsive gambling.

START TO BUILD A NEW LIFE FOR YOURSELF

Start to build a new life for yourself, centered around you. By that we don't mean that you should separate from your husband or divorce him. We do mean that you should begin to create a meaningful life for *yourself*, within the marriage, if at all possible.

Take a look at what your married life has been since the gambling began. From that point on your personal life has revolved around his gambling. When he was winning, you were living a life of pleasure based on his gambling . . . buying the things and enjoying the luxuries his winnings brought you; going to the resorts, parties and special events where he could gamble. When he was losing, your life was dominated by the troubles heaped upon your head—the creditors, loan sharks, bookies, police, courts, indebtedness to your family, deprivations. One by one all of the pleasures you enjoyed were stripped from your life—pleasant social activities, nice dinner parties and theaters, visiting with family and friends, interest in your appearance and in clothing, interest in your job if you happened to be working, playing bridge, tennis, backgammon or mah-jongg, gardening or little theater or the Girl Scouts, reading—whatever your favorite leisure-time activity happened to be.

He and his gambling and the problem they brought you became the focus of your existence. Struggling to deal with them, to keep yourself and your children alive and your family in one piece, absorbed every bit of your time and energy. Without knowing it or wanting it you were sucked into the whirlpool and became an abettor to his gambling. Your every breath, thought, feeling had to do with him, his gambling, the problems and survival.

What about the way out?

It is not going to be enough to get help, to try to get him to stop gambling, to remove yourself as his accomplice and supplier. It is going to be necessary for you to start to shape a life for yourself, consisting of *the things you want to do, and with relationships that you enjoy.*

Stop, sit back and think. What are some of the things you have always wanted to do, but didn't or couldn't, either because it required too much effort at the time, or because you felt you needed to give yourself entirely to your marriage, your husband and your children?

Did you give up your job after you were married? Have you thought about going back to work? If so, then this is the time to do so. You may be worried about having lost your job skills. You may be worried that you are not as young as you were and so might not be able to meet the competition. You may be worried that there are no openings. All right. You are worried. You don't have much confidence in yourself right now. But what have you got to lose? And think of what you have to gain—a restored feeling of confidence, competence, independence, freedom, self-respect, a feeling that you are *somebody,* doing something *you* want to do, in a situation where you are wanted, accepted, needed and *paid*.

Suppose you have never worked, but right now it sounds like a good idea. What are the kinds of things you would like to do and believe you might be good at? There are many places where you can get training. Look at the advertisements in your newspaper. Visit your nearest community college and find out what kinds of courses they offer. Talk with your relatives and friends. Inquire.

It doesn't have to be work, if that is not what you want. There are clubs you can join, church or synagogue activities you can get involved in, volunteer work you can do. Check with your local high school about their nighttime adult courses. There you may be able to take a course in anything from ceramics, painting, carpentry and needlepoint to computer programming, finance and investment, working as a travel agent, Hebrew, Chinese, French, aerobic dancing, ballet—whatever, and all at a very reasonable cost.

If you've been wanting to go to the museum, the zoo, a dog show, a flea market or antique show, the movies, ice-skating, hiking—go. Call up a friend and do it together.

The important thing is that you *start to do something,*

something that will give you a new focus of involvement other than your husband and his gambling, and will let you get away from the house, if possible, at least for part of the day.

What about the children? Do what you would do in an emergency—and you can rank this as being an emergency—call on your sisters, aunts, parents, cousins, neighbors, friends. Ask them to help out. Explain that this isn't just a flighty idea, that this is, right now, a vital step in your life.

If you've stopped visiting your parents or other relatives, start making the visits again. Get back into the warmth and protective embrace of people who care about you.

If you have let your friendships drop, renew them. Take the initiative and make the telephone call. It may be somewhat embarrassing, uncomfortable. All right, so be it. But that will be over in a minute or two and you will be back on the track again. People understand. They're sympathetic. They care. The important thing is to reestablish relationships with others, as many as you can, and to establish new friendships as well. When you join a club or take a course or go to work, make it a point to open yourself up to new relationships with people—relationships that will relieve your solitude, enrich your life, put some lightness and joy into it.

GET IN TOUCH WITH THE YOU INSIDE YOU

All these moves we are proposing are intended to do more than just get you involved, busy, away from the gambling worries. We hope they get you in touch with something inside yourself that has been saying to you, "I am an individual, a separate person, with my own spirit and mind and hopes and aspirations. I am not just somebody's wife or homemaker or mother. I can be all those things— wife, homemaker and mother—but I am also me, and being me is important. I don't have to stop being one thing in order to make room for the other. They can both be part of my life. Right now, the "me" part has to get priority because it has been neglected so long. It needs special attention and concentration. The other can move off the center of the stage, for just a little while, until the new part gets established. Then, when that's done, both can take the center of the stage together."

Psychiatrists call this "individuation" and "self-realization." But don't confuse this with a "I'm-for-me-and-to-heck-with-you" attitude. That is not what we mean. We think that is as destructive and unhealthy as "I'm-for-you-and-to-heck-with-me" attitude. Our approach very definitely does keep other people in mind. We believe a person can be a much better companion, spouse, lover, parent, friend when he has fulfilled a piece of himself, becoming some of the things he feels he is or wants to be, doing and enjoying some of the things he wants to do, feeling satisfied and gratified, rather than empty, deprived and disgruntled.

The fulfilled person can give of himself freely and generously. The unfulfilled person not only cannot give, but is likely to impose on spouse and children with excessive demands for attention and affection and beat up on them because of his unhappiness and dissatisfaction with life.

Building a new life, in which you yourself occupy a place of major importance, needs no further justification. You are entitled to it as a human being. Nevertheless, it has many additional advantages so far as the gambling problem is concerned.

1. You will be much less available to be sucked into your husband's problems. This will not only be good for you, but it will force him to take on responsibility for himself.

2. You will be less reliant on him for your own emotional needs, and therefore less likely to feel you need to comply with his demands.

3. Your continued survival will no longer be tied to your husband's fate. You will not go down with him if he sinks. If he can tackle his addiction and

struggle his way out of it, with your help, wonderful. Then you have a new chance at a good life together. If he cannot master his gambling problem, you will already have laid the foundation for starting a new life without him—a life for yourself and your children.

4. Separating yourself from him in this fashion will force him to struggle harder and to draw on his own internal resources, with a much better chance to lick his addiction.

5. Separating yourself from him will take a burden off his back and give him a better chance for survival. No longer feeling tied down to him and dragged down by him, you will not need to go at him with blame and accusation. You will have thrown back the responsibility to him entirely and will no longer need to feel involved, except to help him as you can. While he may miss your direct involvement, he will also benefit from being free of your recrimination and blame.

This last of the steps we're proposing will no doubt be the most difficult. It will mean cutting deep emotional ties that have bound you together for years. While these ties have been noxious ones, ties that have enslaved you, they are nevertheless there, and anyone who thinks that deep emotional ties are easy to break because they have caused both parties pain is badly mistaken.

Consider the married couples who hate each other, do destructive things to each other, yet remain bound to each other in misery and "quiet desperation" for the rest of their lives. They do not do this because they want to or because they enjoy the misery. They simply lack the emotional strength to tear themselves away from each other. This is called dependency—unhealthy dependency—the intense emotional need of one person for another, though they may be driving one another to self-destruction.

We refer to this only as an illustration. We are not

counseling separation or divorce. However, the act of differentiating yourself and developing as a separate individual with your own identity may feel to you as though you are getting a separation or divorce. It is not the physical break that is painful; it is the emotional break. Moving away from a mate, emotionally, in order to establish your own identity may cause you to become depressed. It may cause you to feel disloyal. It may cause you to feel that you are abandoning someone who has relied on you for strength. And, paradoxically, you may feel that you yourself are being abandoned, even though you are the one striking out for independence.

If you are tied to your husband by this sort of emotional dependency, then we do not think you are going to be able to handle the emotional separation by yourself; we believe you are going to need help, and you can get that help from Gam-Anon and from counseling or psychotherapy.

If you are worried that when your husband sees you separating yourself from him, it may make him feel despondent and insecure and that this may drive him back into gambling (if he has temporarily stopped) or deeper into gambling (if he hasn't), you need to remember that he, too, may be getting help—from Gamblers Anonymous and from psychiatric treatment. Under any circumstances, only he can make the decision to stop or to go back into gambling. All you can do is help his recovery by taking the necessary steps—the ones we have suggested—or hinder it by failure to act.

CHAPTER NINE

The Treatment of Compulsive Gambling

Author's note: In this chapter we are going to tell you how compulsive gambling is treated and where. But we also want to tell the dramatic story of how the very first treatment program got started just 14 years ago, entirely by trial and error, with no precedent or experience on which to draw. Since this is the personal story of Dr. Custer, what follows will be his own account.

The story starts in April 1971. I was then director of the alcoholism-treatment program at the Veterans Administration Hospital in Brecksville, Ohio.

One morning, a man called me on the telephone, saying he was from Gamblers Anonymous, and that he would like to set up an appointment for himself and a group of other GA members. They had a serious problem concerning some of their members they wanted to discuss with me and they thought I might be able to help them. I had heard about Gamblers Anonymous a few times in my contacts with Alcoholics Anonymous, and while I knew little about the ailment of compulsive gambling, I knew these would be sincere people, like their AA counterparts, and I readily agreed to see them. They came the following day and proceeded to tell me about their problem. They said they had some truly desperate members and they themselves did not know how to help them. One had attempted suicide. Another was threatening to commit suicide. Another was threatening to embezzle funds from his firm to get money with which to gamble. They said they could deal with the usual situation of a compulsive gambler who was struggling with the problems of staying off gambling, of indebtedness, family disruption, unemployment, and so forth. These they knew how to handle. They had had good success over the years and had helped hundreds of men and women to break with gambling and reconstruct their lives. But these others— the suicidal ones and the ones on the verge of committing a crime—they didn't know what to do with. They said if we, at the hospital, could work out a program to "screw their heads on right again," Gamblers Anonymous would be able to handle the rest. They wanted to know, at the same time, whether we could start an institutional program there at the hospital for the treatment of compulsive gamblers, similar to the one we had for alcoholics.

Although I had done some thinking about the subject of compulsive gambling and had heard it discussed once or twice at psychiatric meetings, I had never had occasion to treat a patient with this disorder and would not have known where to begin if someone with that ailment came in and asked for help. I knew only about the psychoanalytic approach, which held that compulsive gamblers are masochists and need to undergo psychoanalytic treatment to relieve their guilt and their supposed need to be punished. I did not hold with this view. To me, compulsive gambling appeared to be a disorder of impulse control, and I believed that any treatment that was devised would have to approach it from that position. But we had nothing to go on. We would have to start from the very beginning, which meant observing the compulsive gamblers and trying to get a line on the people and the ailment. So I arranged to go to several Gamblers Anonymous and Gam-Anon meetings. I knew, in advance, that Gamblers Anonymous was patterned after Alcoholics

Anonymous, and I knew about AA and its program intimately because of my work with alcoholics. On that basis, I was prepared for the similarities. But what struck me after just a meeting or two was not just the similarity in the programs but the similarity between the people—the compulsive gamblers and the alcoholics—and between the two disorders—compulsive gambling and alcoholism. This, frankly, came as a great surprise, because I could not see how there could possibly be any relationship between an addiction to a drug and a behavioral problem like compulsive gambling. Nevertheless, the similarities were there. I saw desperate people, in great pain, suffering, helpless and hopeless, and, from a psychiatric standpoint, these were people we would regard as emergencies. As we listened to the accounts of the new members, as well as those of some of the old ones, a picture began to emerge that was remarkably similar to the picture of the progressive development of alcoholism: starting with apparently harmless symptomatic behavior and progressing slowly but inexorably along an increasingly destructive path until the victim has destroyed his family, lost his possessions and truly hit bottom—physically exhausted and sick, psychologically shattered, desperate to the point of suicide. When it came to alcoholism I knew we were dealing with an addiction—the victim's inability to control his drinking, having to drink until he was destroyed. Here I saw the same thing—loss of control over gambling, with the victim having to gamble until the habit destroyed him. Could it be that we were dealing with an addiction in the case of compulsive gambling, too?

Then I compared the people themselves—the alcoholics with the compulsive gamblers—and saw some startling similarities: people with low self-esteen driven to compensate for feelings of inadequacy; poor impulse control; low tolerance for frustration and delay; the need for immediate gratification; the need to escape into a world of illusion; the need for a euphoriant to give them a high and make them feel better about themselves; also the need for an analgesic to relieve the pain of their low self-esteem, their anxiety and their depression. The compulsive gamblers were using gambling the way alcoholics used alcohol—to escape from reality, especially when they were under severe tension or when they faced some responsibilities or crises they could not handle. Alcohol served all these purposes for the alcoholic. Gambling served all these purposes for the compulsive gambler.

Now I could begin to understand why Gamblers Anonymous had been able to take the program of Alcoholics Anonymous and with very few alterations make it work for compulsive gamblers.

That brought me to the next logical step: If the basic AA program could work for gamblers, why would not the treatment program we used at the hospital for alcoholics also work to treat compulsive gamblers?

Starting with that as our tentative premise, we were on our way.

INITIAL TREATMENT THE SAME AS FOR ALCOHOLICS

My associate Alida Glen, Ph.D., and I designed a treatment program patterned after the one we were using to treat alcoholics.

The compulsive gamblers were given individual counseling relating mainly to the control of the gambling urge and on practical problems such as marital strife, their debts, the family's financial needs. In addition to that, there was group therapy, where the gamblers got together and, led by a professional psychiatrist, psychologist, social worker or nurse, discussed with each other the way they had gotten into gambling, the problems it had caused them, their feelings of hopelessness, what they thought was wrong with them, their personality defects. In other words, while counseling dealt with the facts, group therapy dealt with their feelings, giving them a chance to ventilate, and to get some insight into themselves and their compulsion. In addition, there were lectures on the nature of the gambling addiction, so they could get an objective view of themselves and their problem. They also went through relaxation training as a way to deal with their pent-up tensions, pressures and agitation.

Finally, and of equal importance with anything else we were doing, was their attendance at Gamblers Anonymous meetings.

We insisted on total abstinence, as we do with alcoholics, but we did permit them to play competitive games—checkers, pool, cards—but without betting. We also allowed them to watch sports events on television, but also without betting. While this did not do for them what gambling would have done by way of relieving their agitation and tension, it did help to a degree. We explained to them that if we were to permit them to continue gambling for the purpose of relieving their pain, it would take away their only real motivation to get better, thus defeating the purpose of the treatment program.

We were struck by the fact that their state of agitation, nervousness, restlessness, anxiety, depression and paranoid sensitivity resembled very much the withdrawal syndrome when alcoholics stop drinking, and which can only be relieved by taking another drink. In the case of gamblers the "drink" was indulging in some gambling, even if only for nickles and dimes.

The first week or so was pure trial and error; we just worked and waited to see what would happen. We had only a vague idea about what we were dealing with and how it ought to be handled. But then when we got together in our staff conferences—the counselors, psychologists, psychiatrists, social workers and nurses—we found ourselves zeroing in on something. As these patients began to tell us in detail about what they had done in the course of their compulsive gambling, we realized that they all had in common several negative traits of personality and behavior.

DISTINCTIVE TRAITS BECAME APPARENT

These people were dishonest. They lied, cheated, deceived in order to get money to gamble. They were abysmally insensitive to other people's needs and feelings, borrowing without any intention to repay, stripping their nearest and dearest kin of their money and possessions. We did not know, at that point, whether these traits were there before the gambling problem began or whether they developed as a result of the addiction. We subsequently learned that it was the latter, that these had been honest, responsible, considerate people before they had become addicted.

They were also provocative and manipulative. These traits, too, were products of the addiction, and they continued to show up in the course of their treatment. They tried to manipulate the staff the way they had manipulated others before. But with the staff the object was not to get money. They tried to manipulate the staff to get special privileges for themselves, to get out of the treatment regimen, to avoid having to stick with the rules and regulations. They were also stubborn and obstinate about having their way and not accepting someone else's opinion or interpretation. They gave the impression they thought they were the only ones who knew the right thing to do. They had not been too eager about getting into treatment to start with, but after having agreed to do so, they wanted to do things their way. They resisted treatment procedures, rejected psychological interpretations of their behavior and refused to see themselves as sick people, as addicts. And with all that they insisted on a quick cure. They were generally intolerant of people who were not like themselves, who disagreed with them about anything, or who saw things in a different light than they.

Having worked with alcoholics, and having come across some of the very same traits in them, we realized that the negative, intolerant, resistive, stubborn, manipulative behavior was an integral part of the problem. Gambling had become their whole life, their only reason for existence, and now it was their only source of relief from their psychic distress. They saw us trying to take this away from them. They were addicts and we were trying to take away their "drug." Naturally, they would resist and would connive to obstruct treatment. We knew this, and we had to do our best not to become impatient, angry and disgusted and tell them to go get help somewhere else. We had to keep trying to remember that these were sick people, addicts, who couldn't help what they were doing. If you became angry and rebuked them, it would only confirm for them their miserable opinion about themselves. They were all incredibly sensitive to rejection, and they would see a rebuke as a rejection. The way they had dealt with rejection before was to gamble. If we were to reject them, it would reinforce their urge to gamble and defeat our treatment purpose.

At this stage, the compulsive gambler is very hard to take, to like or even to sympathize with; unless the treatment team or the individual therapist, as it may be, understands this, is prepared for it and knows how to deal with it, there is not very much chance of success. The treatment regimen is very important, but even more important than that is the person doing the treating—his or her insight, sensitivity, empathy and tolerance.

We also identified several other maladaptive traits— traits that appeared to be basic to these people's personality and which were more likely to have been part of the cause of their gambling rather than products or consequences.

These were impatient people. They could not tolerate setting up a long-range plan and going at it piece by piece or step by step. They had to have immediate solutions, immediate success. If it didn't work right away, to heck with it.

They were poor at dealing with and solving reality problems. At this point, the problems had to do with giving up gambling, paying their debts, getting back with their families, dealing with legal actions pending against them, getting back to some sort of work so they could support their families. We realized, after some study, that this had been a basic flaw even before they got into gambling and probably one of the reasons why they did get into gambling. The way they had of dealing with a life problem they could not handle, or with some life crisis, was avoidance. They would either run away from it—literally—or evade it by plunging into gambling.

They were poor planners and decision makers. It was difficult for them to tackle a specific problem, work with the therapist in mapping out a plan, deciding which of several alternatives would be the better one to take.

They ducked responsibiiity. They would rather somebody else make a decision for them rather than make their own decision and be responsible for it. They also did not like to burden themselves again with being responsible for their debts, their wives, their children. They tried every way to wiggle out of these duties.

DECISION TO CONCENTRATE ON MALADAPTIVE BEHAVIOR

The staff met in one strategy session after another, trying to identify the basic treatment issue and how to deal with them. Out of these came a clear, firm conclusion and decision. Certainly, we were going to continue to deal with the gambling, per se, trying to motivate the patient to give up the gambling, to get his gambling under control. But right along with that we had to deal with the personality and behavior problems—the dishonesty, impatience, intolerance and manipulation, inability to plan and make decisions, avoidance of responsibility, insensitivity to the feelings and needs of others, poor problem-solving ability. We knew that even though we might, temporarily, be successful in getting the patient to stop gambling, he would slip right back into it if we didn't help him correct these maladaptive personality and behavior traits. How could he possibly tackle the monstrous problems that would be facing him if we had not helped him to change his ways and adopt a much more realistic, constructive and productive approach? He would only crash again. He would bring on himself new rebukes and punishment from the people he hurt, offended and alienated. His failures and the new blast of rejection would drive him right back into gambling.

We decided that the most effective way to take on this rather formidable task, and to effect some basic changes in the remaining time we had left, would be to concentrate most of our efforts on group therapy. Group therapy permitted open confrontation—not necessarily by the therapist conducting the session but by the patients themselves. We knew from our own experience, from long-established practice, that this sort of reaction does occur in group therapy: the open confrontation of group members ·by each other, their being "tough" with each other and themselves, not permitting anyone to dodge the issues or avoid responsibility.

In group therapy, people relate to each other the way they have been relating to other people in real life. If they happen to have been evasive, abusive, deceptive, manipulative, irresponsible in real life, that is the way they will behave toward each other in the group-therapy session. It is life being acted out in microcosm. But the difference between what happens in real life and in group therapy is that in real life you may be able to run away and evade the consequences of your behavior. In group therapy you cannot. The others—the victims of your abuse, insult, manipulation—will snap right back at you and call you on your behavior, even though they, themselves, may have been guilty of the very same offense. Each person is compelled to sit there and face the group's reaction, which may be a very tough one, the kind he never had to contend with before.

This forces the individual to see himself the way others see him, to come face to face with his faults and maladaptive behavior, and to correct them. Why correct them? Because few people—least of all compulsive gamblers—can stand disapproval and rejection by the group. In order to win acceptance and social approval, they are going to try to correct their ways.

Changes can take place very quickly in group therapy. Lifelong ways of feeling, thinking and behaving can be changed in just a few sessions, and this is what we counted on in our daily group-therapy encounters. While, technically, we had just four weeks altogether, including the time lost in exploration, we had a notion that many of the gamblers would want to stay on longer than that, and many of them did, some as long as eight weeks. This gave them and us a chance to work longer on correcting their maladaptive behavior patterns. It also gave the staff a chance to study them further and learn more about the compulsive gambler, knowledge out of which we could begin to construct a theoretical approach to the causes, development and appropriate treatment of this disorder.

Another method we devised to retrain the gamblers into adopting a responsible, constructive, cooperative lifestyle was to ask them to set up their own self-government. That way, they would again have to deal with each other, and since each of them was already aware of the devious devices they used, they would not permit the others to get away with them.

Simultaneously, we tried to tackle a number of other problems the gambler had to face. To put these problems in visual form, we devised an acrostic, the initial letters spelling out the word GAMBLING. G—Gambling; A—Alienation; M—marital problems; B—behavior problems; L—legal problems; I—indebtedness; N—needs, mainly money with which to support the family; G—goallessness. Our aim was to take up these problems with each patient and help him work out short-term, intermediate-term and long-term plans for dealing with each of them.

Restitution, mentioned here for the first time, was one of the most important. We felt—and in this we had gotten some very valuable guidance from Gamblers Anonymous—that the process of making restitution bound the gambler to a realistic, tough problem that would keep him tied to reality, discipline him from wandering off into gambling again and give him the feeling of satisfaction and self-liking that comes from achieving something worthwhile—in the case of the gambler, making good on a moral debt, a debt to people he had injured. The restitution might not be more than $25 or $50 a week, depending on what he was able to earn when he got back into the mainstream again, and it might take anywhere up to 10 years to complete it, but it was regarded as a fundamental element in the process of emotional, moral and social rehabilitation. This, as you may have recognized, derives from two of GA's Twelve Steps: "Made a list of all persons we had harmed, and became willing to make amends to them all," and "Made direct amends to such persons wherever possible, except when to do so would injure them or others."

Once the agreement had been reached, in therapy, to make restitution, the practical business of working out the method and the amount was turned over to Gamblers Anonymous, since it would be a long-term proposition and they could handle it much better than we. Gamblers Anonymous members who have gotten their gambling problem under control and are back working again, make it a part of their long-range debt and obligation to each other to find work or business opportunities for those going through their rehabilitation. Many GA members are businessmen, industrialists and professionals with considerable influence and have helped many thousands of their fellow members to find work again, regardless of the crimes they may have committed to obtain money for their gambling.

Compulsive gamblers who have "hit bottom" and are given an opportunity to work again do not seem to mind it when the job they get is a menial one, inferior in status and remuneration to the one they held before. They are, as we have pointed out several times, energetic, hard-working people; giving them something concrete to do that will earn them some money is one of the best things that can be done to help them. They will accept the job, whatever it is, and work hard to make a success of it. Naturally, they hope to improve their status after a while, but this does not hinder their giving a full dollar's worth on whatever job they are able to get.

At this point they are feeling tense, frustrated, edgy. They desperately need and want something to do, some way of relieving the tension. Some of that we handled by giving them a vigorous exercise schedule. But they want something more, something into which they can direct their creative and productive energy, and that's what working does for them. Also, they are feeling lonely, hopeless, worthless. Work restores to them a sense of being needed, of being useful, of being accepted, of optimism and hope for the future.

Even in their first weeks at the hospital, when they were still in the depths of their discouragement and despair, many of the patients asked us to try to get work for them either in the hospital or in the community. The money they earned, they would put in reserve for later.

BASIC TREATMENT GOALS AND PROGRAM FORMULATED

By the end of the third week or so, we had a pretty clear idea of what our treatment goals should be for the remainder of our work with these first patients, and for the groups of patients who would come later.

1. Enable the patient to stop gambling.

2. Strengthen his self-esteem and confidence so he would no longer need gambling as a way of avoiding life's real problems or as a world of illusion into which he could escape.

3. Help him develop sources of gratification, pleasure, self-fulfillment to replace the void left by the removal of gambling.

4. Help him accept the need to make restitution and engage in a realistic plan to do this.

5. Arrange for follow-up outpatient treatment, as needed, in the months and years after his discharge from the four-week hospital program.

We realized early that even with the best therapy, the gambling addict would find it very difficult, perhaps impossible, to achieve recovery all alone. The family, we realized, plays, an immensely important part. With this in mind, we tried to get the wives of the gamblers involved in a joint therapy program. We arranged for the wife of each married patient to come in and attend a private therapy session together with the husband.

This proved to be a disaster. The wives were so full of rage and hostility, they could not do anything except vent their violent emotions on the gambler husband. This was something they had been aching to do, and here was their chance, in a protected setting where, they felt, they had the freedom and sanction to do this. That was the last thing we wanted. The gambler husband was depressed and defeated enough without having his wife attack him. He reacted by defending himself, and the therapy sessions turned into battles royal.

We dropped that idea quickly and worked out an

alternate strategy. While the gambler was still in the hospital for his four-week treatment program, one of our therapists would see the wife separately, in private therapy sessions, at the hospital. These sessions went on for three months, once a week. This provided an opportunity for the wife to work out her rage and bitter hostility and to begin to see her husband as a sick person who had taken a positive step toward getting rid of his addiction and becoming a different sort of person. The therapist also worked with her in getting rid of her guilt and in starting to shape a new life centered around herself.

Simultaneously, during this three-month period, the husband would come in—after his discharge from the four-week hospital program—for individual therapy sessions, once a week, to continue his progress along the lines laid down during his group-therapy sessions in the hospital. By the end of the three-month period, or when we felt that both spouses were well enough along the way in their recovery to be able to meet with each other in a joint therapy session without the danger of a renewed explosion, we would have them come in together for weekly sessions. In those sessions the therapist would work with them on communicating with each other in an open, honest, nonthreatening fashion, being neither submissive nor oppressive, both being able to assert their desires and needs without fear of angry retaliation.

In these sessions we would also get them to work on some of their most urgent practical problems. One that always came up was who was going to handle the money. The husband would resist giving up control of the family funds. This was a blow at his pride. However, it was generally worked out that he would relinquish control for several months and after that they could work out joint control, if they wished.

We would have them come for these joint weekly sessions for several months. When it looked as though they would be able to handle their emotional and practical problems without the aid of a therapist, we revised the schedule to once every two weeks, then once a month, then once every two months; after that it was left on an open-ended basis. They did not need to come in on any schedule, but were free to call and ask for a session whenever they were facing a crisis, especially if there was a chance the husband might relapse into gambling.

This is the program we worked out at Brecksville in 1971. It has remained the prototype for the four other Veterans Administration Hospital programs established since then, and it is also the model for programs established outside the VA. To summarize, the basic elements are these:

1. group therapy for the gambler, followed by

2. individual therapy for the gambler, simultaneous with

3. individual therapy for the wife, followed by

4. joint therapy for the wife and husband, plus

5. relaxation therapy and activity therapy, as needed, and

6. Gamblers Anonymous for the gambler; Gam-Anon for the wife.

Where the gambler is not married and is living with his family, we would work with members of the family, and the joint therapy referred to in the case of the married gambler would instead be family therapy, with the gambler and the family members attending the sessions together.

REDUCING THE GAMBLER'S TENSION: AN ESSENTIAL STRATEGY

While this outline covers most aspects of the program, there is one element that I have not yet touched on. It has more to do with sensing and dealing with the fundamental vulnerability of the compulsive gambler, rather than with treatment method and structure.

I got my first inkling of its importance in listening to one of my first patients at Brecksville. He was telling me about a plane trip to Las Vegas to gamble. Here, in essence, is what he said:

> The whole three or four hours out, I couldn't sit back and relax. I saw one man with a briefcase full of papers and a slide rule and a small calculator. He was deeply engrossed in what he was doing, unconscious of what was going on around him. The stewardess even had to poke him to let him know she had his lunch. He ate it, then went right back to his work. But he was enjoying it. You could see it in his face. He was calm. He was at ease. He was busy at work but he was relaxed. He wasn't edgy and jumpy. Me, I couldn't sit still the entire time. I had to light a cigarette every 15 minutes, go to the john every half hour. I was thinking about what my strategies and bets at Las Vegas should be, how much I might possibly lose, how much I had to win. I wished I could sit there and work, relaxed the way he was. Other people were sitting talking to each other. Others were snoozing, all relaxed, except me. I see families having a cookout, and everybody looks so happy and relaxed, having a good time. But when we have a cookout at home, because the wife and the kids ask for it, I'm like a cat on a hot tin roof. I can't stay in one spot. I pace around and give everybody the jitters. I'm thinking about my next bet or about the race results, or I'm sneaking away and listening to the football game on the radio. I realize what I'm missing. I've wanted all that. I wish I could have it.

As this man spoke I could actually feel his tension; it was like a boiler getting ready to explode. With this clue, I looked for the same thing in the others and it was there. They were all under great internal pressure and tension.

Then, as they revealed more about themselves, I began to see a very crucial connection between their tension and their gambling. These are basically tense people to start with. Once they start gambling, even before it becomes addictive, the internal pressure level builds up. Then along comes a stressful life situation. The boss chews him out because he messed up a project. He gets into a quarrel with his wife. One of his children gets into trouble. His mother has a heart attack. The crisis sends his internal pressure and tension to an even higher level, and he is just about ready to explode. He has to relieve this pressure somehow. So he runs someplace to gamble. Somebody else might go out and get drunk, or get into a fight. His way of letting off steam, of reducing his tension, is to gamble.

One of our basic goals in therapy was to help reduce the pressure level so that the next time he got into any kind of a difficult encounter or crisis, the pressure level might go up, but it would still be far below the "blow-off" point that would drive him into gambling.

Our method of doing this was, first, to get him to talk about his problems and work off some of the tension. Meanwhile, we would be trying to get him to see the connection between his tension and his gambling. His awareness of the relationship gets him to look for other ways to handle the tension, when it starts coming, other than to think about gambling. We might suggest to him that he throw himself into some repair work around the house, get out and jog, get into a swimming-and-exercise program at a health club—anything he can jump into when he hits a snag and the tension builds up.

We detected, also, that in particularly every one of these conflict situations—whether it was at home, on the job, with friends—the underlying element was being or feeling rejected. That was their response to criticism of any kind. They took it not as criticism of what they were doing, but as a devastating criticism and rejection of themselves. Their subjective reaction to this was to feel defenseless, under attack, vulnerable, frightened, anxious and angry—emotions that shot up their tension and sent them running to find relief in gambling.

The more we were able to get them to reveal these sensitivities and upsetting feelings, and to understand why they arose, the more we were able to bring down the overall tension level, reducing the likelihood that they were going to have to relieve unbearable tension by gambling.

During the course of therapy, one of the best signs we had that the patient was beginning to recover was that he was behaving in a more relaxed fashion; that was a sign that his tension was going down and staying down. You could see the physical signs—sitting easily and comfortably in his chair, not bunched up or tensed up; hands relaxed in the lap, not clenched or twisting; facial muscles relaxed, eyes brighter, smiling and laughing as he spoke or listened. He tells you that he is sleeping better, eating with better appetite.

Aside from these signs of physical relaxation, there are even more significant signs of emotional relaxation. He has a more relaxed attitude about himself and about life. He no longer reacts to every little problem as a life-threatening, world-shaking crisis, every little critical comment as a devastating assault on his pride, masculinity, worth. There is a clearly reduced sensitivity to rejection. He doesn't feel as threatened and insecure. He can laugh at himself and some of the things he used to do. He doesn't get as upset when he has a quarrel with his wife or a problem on the job. He takes these less seriously, more objectively, with more realistic perspective. In fact, the conflict-full encounters and problems become fewer and fewer. His demands on himself and on others become more moderate, more in keeping with reality.

As you see an increase in these signs, you know that the threat of his going back to gambling is diminishing, that he is thinking less and less about it and is better able to deal with the urge if it should arise.

ADDITIONAL SIGNS OF RECOVERY

There are a number of additional signs that indicate recovery is taking place.

1. The gambler admits he has a gambling problem, a sickness; that his problem is not the need for money to gamble and recover his debts, that it is this sickness that has been causing all the trouble, and he wants to be rid of it.

2. He begins to have some understanding of his maladaptive emotional traits and behavior and how they are perpetuating his gambling problem.

3. He begins to resume work quickly, looks for help in getting a job, and when a job is located, goes to work.

4. He develops a complete, detailed, long-term budget and a specific plan for restitution of debts.

5. He becomes an active member of Gamblers Anonymous and is eager to help others with the same problem.

6. He shows a sincere concern for his family and their needs, and demonstrates it by concrete deeds.

7. He has increased ability to isolate specific problems, work out a plan to deal with them, and take action to solve them.

8. There are fewer crises and problems in his life.

9. The decisions he makes are sound ones.

10. He begins to develop a sense of pride in himself, in what he is doing and where he is going.

11. There is an improvement in his relationship with his wife, children and other members of the family; he spends more time with them.

12. He accepts himself, realistically, with his weaknesses and strengths, without exaggerating or dwelling too much on either.

13. The subject of gambling comes up less and less frequently; his interest in gambling dwindles.

I want to caution that the cessation of gambling does not, in itself, necessarily mean the gambler is recovering. It is possible for compulsive gamblers to stop for weeks, even months, without having really brought the problem under control. Unless the other behavioral, emotional, attitudinal and practical evidences of fundamental changes in his personality and character are there, the cessation of gambling will be only temporary, and with the next crisis he will plunge back into it again.

SIGNS OF FAILURE TO PROGRESS

There are several ways you can surely tell that progress is *not* taking place.

The gambler will continue to insist that he does not really have a problem, doesn't need help, but, since his wife (or his parents) think there is something wrong with him, he is willing to go along with their desires and "take a crack at it." After he attends a meeting or two of Gamblers Anonymous, he will come away sneering at "those poor boobs" and poke fun at the Gamblers Anonymous meeting procedures. Even if he did need help, he says, you wouldn't "catch him dead" at one of those GA meetings.

His involvement in the treatment program will be desultory and routine, and he will not manifest the anxiety that the initial therapeutic confrontation generally arouses. He may pretend to be going along with the treatment, but it will not be difficult to detect his insincerity. He'll make no effort to go back to work and will balk at working out plans to straighten out his problems. If he does go back to work, he'll be slipshod about budgeting and procrastinate about restitution.

Some patients swing over in the other direction. They throw themselves into the treatment program enthusiastically, assure you of their dedication, exclaim aloud that this is "the most fantastic program anyone has ever devised," and they're just aching to get out and tell the whole world about it. This, too, is a self-deceiving, escapist device to avoid coming to grips with the real and difficult work ahead. It is the same old dream that something magical is going to happen and make everything come out right without any effort. However, this is not as difficult a problem for the therapist as is total indifference, cynicism and lack of motivation. If the therapist works slowly and patiently with the over-enthusiastic patient, he or she can generally get him to settle down and proceed to deal with the issues realistically.

WAYS TO TELL THAT THE WIFE IS RECOVERING

The therapist treating the wife will also have ways to tell whether she is making progress. If she continues to be hostile, vengeful, implacable, accusatory toward her gambler husband even after weeks of therapy, she is not making much progress. She has to be able to relinquish this adversary position and truly see him as a sick person—not necessarily like him any better or want to forgive him right off, just accept that he has an illness and that the things he did are symptoms of the illness—before there can be much progress. Before proceeding to the next step in the therapy process, this issue has to be worked on, patiently, until there is a change in attitude and feeling.

Another indicator of the wife's progress is her relinquishment of guilt. There are two types of guilt she is dealing with. One is the guilt about what she believes she has done to bring about her husband's downfall, that is, not being an adequate woman and wife. The other is the guilt about her role as "enabler." In the course of therapy she will have gotten insight into the harm she did by helping her husband to get money to pay his debts, bailing him out, protecting him from the retribution of creditors and bookmakers, letting things drag on without seeking help. While these insights ultimately have a constructive influence, their effect, at first, is to produce strong feelings of self-blame. She will agonize about what she has failed to do and "whip" herself for not having acted correctly.

Until both these types of guilt are resolved—until she stops blaming and punishing herself—her own recovery cannot progress. When she begins to see the past objectively and realize that she was as much a victim as her husband was, and that she did what she did only because she thought it was best, that is another strong indication that she is on the road to recovery.

Some wives, as a way of handling their guilt feelings,

start to mother the gambler, do things he should be doing for himself, plan for him, make decisions for him. This creates a new problem for the compulsive gambler and hinders his recovery. The wife must realize that what her husband needs most at this point is to be on his own in order to plan and direct his own rehabilitation, and that what she needs most is to detach herself from his problems.

Detachment will mean cutting off all sources of money, refusing to take his abuse any longer, refusing to bail him out or make amends for his offenses, refusing to shield him any longer, ceasing to worry whether he will return to gambling, and taking no measures to interfere with him if he does . . . separating herself in her mind and in her heart from the entire mess so that it is no longer her problem, only his.

A sure sign that this is beginning to happen—aside from her disengagement from his gambling problems and his efforts to deal with them—is movement toward finding satisfying relationships and occupations for herself, as discussed in Chapter 8. These are the first true indications of progress. At first she may take these steps in a mechanical, dutiful way, without much enthusiasm, but the time will come when she will be full of excitement about something she's done or some new friend she has made, and that will be a sign that a true and vital change is taking place in her feelings and emotions, and that she is not likely to be dragged down again, should there be a hitch in her husband's recovery.

PRINCIPLES IN THE TREATMENT OF COMPULSIVE GAMBLERS

Since 1971 I have been directly involved in the establishment of a number of treatment programs for compulsive gamblers, and I have personally treated a large number of these patients. In the course of this experience several treatment principles have emerged:

1. *Compulsive gambling is a serious and dangerous disorder.* Because the disorder is not yet well

known, many people's reaction, on hearing about a case of compulsive gambling, may be that it has only to do with gambling and does not have any more serious consequences. The fact is that it is a life-threatening illness. Eighteen percent of compulsive gamblers in treatment have made suicide attempts—100 times the national average. How many compulsive gamblers have actually committed suicide is not known, since this factor is obscured when inquiries are conducted into the cause of a suicide. The exceedingly high rate of attempted suicide would indicate that the success rate, too, is many times the national average.

This disorder has many other serious consequences. One out of every 10 patients in treatment for compulsive gambling has been in jail. The very great majority have suffered devastating damage to their physical and psychological health, and severe losses with respect to family, business, finances and material possessions.

2. *Many compulsive gamblers need professional help.* Specific treatment for compulsive gambling is the most desirable. That failing, psychotherapy incorporating the basic elements and goals outlined earlier would be the next best alternative. Psychiatric treatment for specific clinical diagnoses other than compulsive gambling is seldom necessary.

3. *The therapist's availability may be critical.* Compulsive gambling is an impulsive disorder, and in such disorders, the impulse to act mounts quickly and may become overpowering when the individual is under stress. Therefore, it is essential in cases of outpatient treatment that the therapist be available when a patient feels he is in danger of yielding to the impulse to gamble. The therapist might learn quickly, over the telephone, what is causing the patient's stress and suggest something to do to resolve the problem, or at least to reduce

the tension. If that cannot be achieved, then the patient should be seen on an emergency basis. If the gambler is told he cannot be seen within the next few hours, and that he will have to wait for his regular weekly therapy session or for an interim session two or three days later, he will interpret it as a rejection. The perceived rejection will make his tension shoot up and will perhaps drive him to find relief in gambling.

4. *A back-up network is essential.* Since the therapist cannot be available at all times, it is essential that, in emergencies, there be someone else the patient can call who can help "talk him down" and reduce his tension. This is one important reason (among many) why the compulsive gambler should be urged to attend GA meetings and become a part of the group. The group circulates a list of its members, and many of them are available to be called day or night. The therapist should also encourage the patient's friends, clergyman, attorney or employer to be available whenever possible.

5. *The therapist's attitude and approach are critical.* When the compulsive gambler comes for treatment he is frightened, depressed, mistrustful, shaken. He will react negatively to a cold, judgmental approach. The therapist needs to be patient, understanding, accepting, supportive and warm, while still being able to confront the gambler with the issues, problems and goals.

The patient may initially react to therapy by backing off and sulking. This may very well be an indication that he is angry but is reluctant to express his anger for fear of being reprimanded and punished. Every effort should be made to encourage the patient to speak openly about his feelings and to express his anger if that is the way he feels. This is something he needs to do as a basic part of his recovery. If he is discouraged from doing this in therapy, fearing retaliation from the therapist, he will never learn to be able to do it outside the therapeutic situation.

6. *Special attention and precautions are advised when withdrawal symptoms occur.* Most compulsive gamblers will have withdrawal symptoms for a week or longer after they discontinue gambling. The symptoms will include extreme restlessness, agitation, insomnia, discomfort, depression, anxiety, anger—altogether an extremely painful state. It is to be expected that the patient will feel in desperate need of relief, which he may seek in gambling. Unless the patient is watched carefully and measures are taken to bring down his tension and to help him endure the symptoms of withdrawal until they subside he is likely to go back to gambling.

7. *Once they genuinely accept treatment, compulsive gamblers are motivated, receptive and responsive.* They learn quickly, and put to use what they learn. Even though they may be insistent (at first) on their old way of seeing things, they are quite willing to listen to and accept other approaches to problem-solving. An active role is indicated here for the therapist, suggesting several alternatives and helping the patient to choose.

8. *The compulsive gambler seldom needs psychotherapeutic medications.* Frequently there may be a need for mild sleep medication because of sleep starvation. Although tension and depression are frequently present, a regimen of tranquilizers and antidepressants is rarely necessary. A routine of regular meals, exercise and sleep is, in most cases, adequate.

9. *The treatment goals need to be specific* and they should be shared with the compulsive gambler. These have been dealt with specifically earlier in this chapter.

10. *The patient needs to be informed that he is taking a difficult course* but that the discomfort and pain will diminish and that good results will come.

11. *Getting to the roots of a patient's gambling problem is not important,* although he may insist on finding out. It is more important to uncover what stimulates the individual to gamble at present and to minimize these stimuli, and also to strengthen the personality so that gambling will no longer be needed for self-validation, relief and escape.

12. *The family is of critical importance in treatment.* Information from the family is very valuable in appraising the problem, since the gambler himself may lack insight or may, as has become his habit, attempt to deceive the therapist. Once the diagnosis is clear and a treatment plan formulated, the family should be informed. The family is generally weary, irritated and pessimistic about the chances of recovery. Nevertheless, they should be kept informed on the treatment process as it develops.

    The family should not be given responsibility for keeping the patient in treatment. Their involvement should be limited to refusing to supply more money for gambling or repayment of debts, or in any other way abetting the continuation of gambling.

    The family is as much in need of help as the gambler, and should be referred to Gam-Anon or to Gam-Ateen (the organization for teenage children of compulsive gamblers), and for psychotherapy or counseling.

13. *A thorough evaluation is essential before a treatment plan is developed.* Differential diagnosis should be made to identify such conditions as manic-depressive illness, schizophrenia, brain tumor, sociopathic personality and other disorders that may mimic or coexist with compulsive gambling.

14. *Some seeking treatment want only immediate relief, not long-term help*. Acceding to this desire will eliminate the only motivation the gambler has for getting better—his emotional pain.

15. *Complete honesty about debts and a plan for restitution are indispensable*. It may be extremely difficult for the compulsive gambler to be 100-percent honest about his debts. There may be some debts that he is especially ashamed about and that are too painful for him to mention. He figures that since he has revealed all the others, it is all right to keep these two or three debts a secret. However, he is wrong. These undisclosed debts will continue to gnaw away at him, and he may still have it in mind that he will be able to pay back just these debts by his customary method—gambling. Therefore, the patient should be impressed with the importance of revealing *all* his debts and that all debts be included in a plan of restitution.

16. *Gamblers Anonymous and Gam-Anon are essential parts of the recovery program*. The importance of these two organizations, in respect to the compulsive gambler and his family, has already been mentioned many times in this book, but the point cannot be overemphasized. These groups are true experts in helping the compulsive gambler and his or her family. Their availability, skill and devotion are invaluable in the recovery process. Professionals involved in the treatment of compulsive gamblers, or planning to undertake treating them, are advised to attend meetings of these groups, and become acquainted with their principles and practices.

THE STATUS OF TREATMENT SERVICES TODAY

Following is a full accounting of the treatment services in operation today that deal specifically with compulsive gambling.

Five are in Veterans Administration hospitals located in these cities: Brecksville, Ohio; Brooklyn, New York; Miami, Florida; Lyons, New Jersey; and Loma Linda, California. All are fully developed programs functioning at a high level of organization.

There are also two state-operated programs in New York, one in Staten Island, New York City, and another in Rochester. Both exist within the program structure of community mental-health centers. There is also a state-operated program, in Bridgeport, Connecticut, operating within a community mental-health center, and another at the Philadelphia Psychiatric Institute.

At this writing, there is only one private (nongovernmental) treatment program for compulsive gambling and that is located in South Oaks Hospital, Long Island, New York.

In 1984, a new treatment program for compulsive gambling was opened in a facility called Taylor Manor, located at the University of Maryland in Ellicot City. It is operated by the National Foundation for the Study and Treatment of Pathological Gambling, a voluntary nonprofit organization whose intention is to establish a network of residential and outpatient treatment centers for compulsive gamblers. These centers will conduct research and train professional personnel to staff additional treatment programs elsewhere.

Several states have bills pending to use money from lottery and other gambling revenues for the creation and operation of treatment services for compulsive gamblers, and it may well be that in the next year or two there will be an increase in treatment services for compulsive gamblers in many parts of the country. Since these are not likely to get much public exposure at the beginning, some are apt to be in operation for months before those who need them are aware of their existence.

Compulsive gamblers seeking treatment, or family members trying to locate help should not automatically assume that there are no treatment programs in their state or community. They should make inquiries at community mental-health centers, mental-health clinics, mental-health associations, family-service agencies, private psychiatric hospitals, public psychiatric hospitals, state and local mental-health departments, state gambling commissions and the National Council on Compulsive Gambling to find out if such services do exist in their state or community, and if so, where they are located.

INDEX

By the year 2000, 2 out of 3 Americans could be illiterate.

It's true.

Today, 75 million adults… about one American in three, can't read adequately. And by the year 2000, U.S. News & World Report envisions an America with a literacy rate of only 30%.

Before that America comes to be, you can stop it… by joining the fight against illiteracy today.

Call the Coalition for Literacy at toll-free **1-800-228-8813** and volunteer.

Volunteer Against Illiteracy. The only degree you need is a degree of caring.

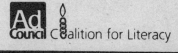

Ad Council Coalition for Literacy

Warner Books is proud to be an active supporter of the Coalition for Literacy.

158